STARTING YOUR INTERNATIONAL SCHOOL

A Handbook for Sustainable Start-up Success

by André Double, Chris Nash
and Gráinne O' Reilly

The Choir Press

Copyright © 2024 André Double, Chris Nash and Gráinne O'Reilly
www.leadingyourinternationalschool.com

All rights reserved. No part of this publication may be reproduced, distributed, or transmitted in any form or by any means, including photocopying, recording, or other electronic or mechanical methods, without the prior written permission of the author, except in the case of brief quotations embodied in critical reviews and certain other non-commercial uses permitted by copyright law. For permission requests email: leadingyourinternationalschool@gmail.com

The right of André Double, Chris Nash and Gráinne O'Reilly to be identified as the authors of this work has been asserted by THEM in accordance with the Copyright, Designs and Patents Act 1988

First published in the United Kingdom in 2024 by
The Choir Press

Paperback ISBN: 978-1-78963-449-5
eBook ISBN:

Cover Image: Dulwich College, Singapore

Note: Every due care and attention has been taken in the process of editing and printing. Neither the authors nor the publishers of the book hold any responsibility for any mistake that may have inadvertently crept in.

Acknowledgments

A book like this is built upon the warmth, generosity and support of others. During the past year, I have had the pleasure of meeting and interviewing international school leaders and their stakeholders from around the world. Each discussion in its unique way helped develop the contents of this book. The following people helped to make this book happen. I am forever grateful.

Grainne O'Reilly for being such a powerful fountain of knowledge about founding international schools and an incredible support mechanism for my ideas and where they are headed.

Chris Nash for being such a good friend, advocate and ongoing mentor.

The LYIS team including Jane Gay, Grace Hu (for her incredible devotion to all aspects of sustainability in the book), Conan Magruder, German Rincon, Sandy Bansal, Nimesh Kumar and Amy Zhang.

To Jason Cox at TIC Recruitment for letting me stay in New Zealand and sharing some never-to-forget experiences.

Barry Cooper for your continued support as the host of the LYIS Podcast.

John Todd and Jo Evans for your support and appearances in our Start-up webinars

Warren Cook at TAHR Services for your knowledge and support on all matters HR

Greg Parry – Global Services in Education (GSE)

Paul Ellmes – Global InSync Education

Acknowledgements

Thank you to all of the following for their time, thoughts and ideas they have shared:

Chris Seal
Iram Myford
Matt Seddon
David Gregory
David Ingram
Ariane-Baer-Harper
Alejtin Berisha
Al Kingsley
Anne Dickenson
Malcolm Phillips
Conan Magruder
Beth Jones
Matt Chomicz
Satyadeep Srivastava
John Tighearnan
Jonathan Gastel
Yvonne Fan
Paul Ellmes
Nalini Cook
Oliver Kramer
Sabah Rashid
Ma Keyu
Julian Jeffrey
Martin Harris
Nancy Lloest Squicciarini
Nigel Davis

Liz Free
Brett Girven
Nick Magnus
Adam Neufield
Nicola Kirby
Rizky Tielman
Chris Nicholls
Rob Ford
Catherine Mary Cooke
Peter Heddelin
James Brightman
Timothy Glare
Nicholas Belcher
Marco Damhuis
Joshua Barr
Gareth Roberts
Estelle Hughes
Eamonn Mullally
Conrad Hughes
Cheraine Escott
Bob Findlay
Benjamin Derrick
Alex Reynolds
Angeline Aow
Fiona Carter
Richard Stokes

Contents

Foreword		vii
How To Get The Most Out of This Book		xiii
Part 1	Organisational Foundation	1
Part 2	Develop Your Infrastructure	96
Part 3	Human Resources	132
Part 4	Build Your Educational Programme	180
Part 5	Marketing, Communications and Admissions: Building a Community	224
Summary		246
Glossary		248

Foreword

Starting Your International School

Start-up. Everyone who has done it says it is a truly unique experience. Most of you who are reading this book are either about to embark upon a start-up, are in a start-up or are involved in the process of start-up.

I remember a very wise man (at that time, my boss and since, my long-term mentor) telling me that a start-up was something that would either overwhelm and defeat me or something to which I would become addicted - like a drug. He was right about the latter - I did become addicted and after many start-ups across countries and continents I can say that the thrill and the highs (I think that's where the drug analogy came in!) are unlike any other school headship or leadership experiences.

Many of you may be very experienced, skilled and talented Principals who have developed a reputation for getting the job done - and done well. Such people are ripe for the challenge of a start-up and over the years I have appointed many such talents to their first start-up principalship.

To each of these colleagues, I have warned that the experience will take them far outside their comfort zone, that they will discover things about themselves that they never knew (in some cases, never wanted to know!) and that they will develop skills that they had no idea they needed.

In every start-up, it is not what one knows, or even that which one is aware one does not know that catches one out; it is what one doesn't know one doesn't know. Embrace those unknown unknowns with both humility and determination. They will develop you professionally and personally in ways never imagined and, if nothing else, will give you stories with which to regale others for a lifetime.

Look after yourself- you need good health to survive and flourish in a start-up environment, especially as a Principal. Everyone will look to you - for leadership and vision. For guidance, strength, support and for decision-making in all areas in both successful and challenging times. You will feel as if you are working 24/7 for at least the first year or so and you will see little of your family and friends. You will, however, need them more than ever as you must have a support system to keep you strong, both mentally and physically.

There will be days filled with what seem like insurmountable problems at all levels. There will be days when you wonder if the school will ever open on time or if your staff will ever receive their visas. You will have deliveries that afford you every book and paper you ordered, but not a single pencil, pen or writing implement. I opened one school without a single chair. On the first day, we asked everyone to bring their own chair with them - it was not exactly the opening day message I had hoped for, but those children, their parents and the staff, never forgot it!

Good luck on your journey - I only wish that this brilliant book had been around when I started on my journey many moons ago. It is going to be unique, invigorating, frustrating, inspiring, exhausting, inspirational and the most exciting professional experience of your life!

Gráinne O' Reilly
November 2023, Foshan, China

The Changing International School Landscape

I am an educational corporate expert with twelve years of International School experience in various directorship-level positions in Singapore. During this time, I've seen the International School landscape change dramatically and you – the next generation of aspiring and current school leaders –must embrace this change, too.

The landscape of International Education has experienced a monumental shift in the past five years. This shift has been brought about by the emergence of a cluster of large School Groups that own a significant portion of the 2500 international schools of size globally. While we previously had 'groups of schools' we now have the emergence of large 'School Groups'. These School Groups have corporate structures, systems and shareholder expectations previously unfamiliar to the education sector and definitely unfamiliar to most educational leadership.

According to ISC research completed in January 2022, there has been significant growth in the International School sector with the number of students attending International Schools increasing from 3.7 million to 5.7 million and revenue increasing 96% from US $27.5 billion to a staggering US $53.5 billion in ten years. (Data Source: ISC Research January 2022: Copyright ISC Research).

Schools Groups are competing to build their market share and have made large investments when buying and building new schools and with this investment comes expectations of the school leaders to perform.

The type of leader School Groups are looking to attract to senior leadership roles are those with a strong corporate understanding. The commonly known educational leadership positions of 'Principal' or 'Head of School' have morphed into the new title of an Educational Chief Executive Officer (ECEO). The two are very different and the latter requires a much wider set of knowledge, skills and understandings. International Schools in Schools Groups are fundamentally businesses and there is a requirement to be run like a business and perform like one, too.

To meet these challenges school leaders should be humble and identify they require upskilling in the landscape of educational corporate leadership. This book will help equip them with the knowledge, skills and understanding required to be successful in this new educational landscape.

Sir Steve Hansen, past Allblacks coach, said when speaking of leadership 'leaders need to understand the business or game they are in' and this book will help you as an educational leader to know the business of corporate education and grow into an effective and successful ECEO.[1]

Matt Hall
June 2023, Singapore

---

[1] 'How to build a Winning Team with Sir Steve Hansen', *Lead on Purpose with James Laughlin Podcast*, 6 January 2023. https://podtail.com/en/podcast/lead-on-purpose-with-james-laughlin/how-to-build-a-winning-team-with-sir-steve-hansen/ .

Longevity – The Secret of My Success

'It was the best of times, it was the worst of times, it was the age of wisdom, it was the age of foolishness'.
Charles Dickens, *A Tale of Two Cities*

I've been an International Headteacher for ten years, all of this time in the same school in Beijing. When I arrived in Beijing in 2013, I had ten years of experience as a headteacher in the UK, I had a master's degree in Education Management and the UK's National Professional Qualification for Headship (NPQH). Even so, looking back, I was woefully prepared for the contextual challenges of international school leadership I would soon face. What I needed was a book like this. It is also clear that the record of international schools contains as many failures as successes. When a school goes wrong there are significant consequences for all involved, not least the young people.

At the same time, you must be ready for challenges on a scale you have never encountered before, challenges that can easily become career-destroying and perhaps even worse, soul-destroying, as you realise that the school you lead is actually going in the opposite direction of every educational principle you live your life by and there's nothing you can do to stop it. I'd worked all my life in London schools with large numbers of bilingual students and the joys and challenges of very high levels of ethnic diversity. I'd even led the start-up of a specialised vocational school from scratch. If I could meet myself stepping off the plane in Beijing now, I would say to myself, in the immortal words of 'Game of Thrones', *'Chris Nash, you know nothing!'*. Yet here I am ten years later leading a successful, sustainable and stable school, built from nothing. So, how did I get there?

The best advice I can give is: be resilient, accept mistakes will be made and learn from them. I believe that alongside the cohorts of successful students, some of them now starting their own careers, alongside the teachers I've developed to international standards and alongside the communities I've contributed to, there have come deep rewards of personal and professional growth. This book is about the critical stages of school development and their chronology and what can easily trip you up as a new international school leader if you miss out or implement them in the wrong order. It is also about the values, virtues, skills and behaviours you will need to model and instil in others if you are going to lead a successful international school start-up. At the moment there are well-developed markets for international education in North America, Western Europe, the Middle East and some parts of Asia, but inevitably this picture will change as the world economy changes. You don't know where your future career might take you, but the advice and support we share in this book might inspire you to make the journey.

Who is this book for?
This book is for those involved in the cross-cultural challenges of planning, starting, leading and managing an international school. In particular, it is for three types of reader:

1. **Newly appointed leaders/ CEOs** of an international start-up school. The book is full of practical advice and lessons learned that will help you manage the learning curve of adjusting to your new context quickly and effectively.
2. **Anyone making the transition to Executive Headship and CEO role** and likely to be involved in the start-up of an international school in the future and facing the changing corporate world of our international schools.
3. **Investors/commercial groups** who find themselves opening a school.

There is a growing community of experienced school leaders who are getting it right and creating academically successful, socially vibrant, sustainable schools with deep roots in their communities and that make significant contributions to the country they find themselves in – many of whom, you will read about in here. We want to connect you to the best thinking and practices of this international community of school leaders.

Chris Nash
November, 2023 Beijing

How To Get The Most Out of This Book

In order to gain the most from what you read and how your read it, it is important for you the reader to understand two things:

1. Although we have presented here the main ingredients behind starting an international school – the recipe can and does often change. Your school Mission may already be firmly established; your governance model may consist of one individual – the owner; or you may have no choice than to accept a partner based on their financial offer for your school.
2. The ingredients within this book can be prepared at similar and varying stages. You will continue to develop your curriculum at the same time as you endlessly market; you will need to physically construct your campus at the same time as you hire the staff that will fill it.

Enjoy!

PART ONE

ORGANISATIONAL FOUNDATION

PART ONE - ORGANISATIONAL FOUNDATION

Develop Your Educational Vision And Model — 3
- Identify Your Purpose — 4
- Sustainability — 7
- Get The Right Market Research — 12
- Identify Your Target Market — 20
- Profit or Not-For Profit? — 22
- Build Your Educational Vision — 25
- Identify Your Competitive Advantage — 28
- Choose The Right Location — 30

The Right Business Model — 34
- Choose The Right Partner(s) — 34
- Negotiating The Right Business Deal — 37
- Compliance — 41

Governance And Leadership — 44
- The Right Governance Model — 44
- Get The Right Leadership Team — 49
- Agree on How You Will Make Decisions — 56
- Identify Where You Need Help — 59

Budgets And Timelines — 62
- Set Your Budget — 62
- Set Your Timeline — 69
- Set Your Salary Scales — 71
- Set Your Fee Structure — 74
- Breakeven Analysis — 78

School Structure — 80
- Agree on Your School Structures — 80
- How Will Staff Be Organised? — 81
- Develop A Quality Framework — 82
- Adopt A Communication Strategy — 84

The Master Plan — 91

Develop Your Educational Vision and Model

In this section, we examine what you need to do to set the foundation of your school. Here you will learn how to:

- Develop the Mission and Vision for your school that drive your subsequent strategy and influence how you make decisions and create your operational systems. The best approach to this is to work backward from an understanding of what you want your students to achieve.
- Define your international context, target market, and the compliance issues you will face, and locate the right research for your start-up.
- Make effective decisions that support your school's growth and development.
- Keep sustainability at the forefront of your new school and its long-term strategy.[1]

You will also learn about:

- The importance of compliance and being compliant and how the CEO is held to account on all compliance issues.
- International school start-up strategies from research that include professional practice and business contexts, including how to make effective decisions that support the long-term operational viability of your school.
- Research on a variety of organisational foundation issues, through school and non-school contexts and the powerful professional voices of principals and start-up specialists who have experienced school start-ups, or who are currently working in them now.

---

[1] This chapter contributes to the following UN Sustainable Development Goals

IDENTIFY YOUR PURPOSE

The first step in developing your mission and vision for your school is to identify your purpose.

Challenge

International schools have the potential to deliver outstanding student outcomes. However, this can be compromised by competing purposes originating from different stakeholders.

Solution

An investment in international education has to be for the greater good – a sustainable future for us all. Identify what you want your students to achieve when they leave and how that can benefit future generations and help create a sustainable future for all.

The purpose of a new start-up school is not as straightforward as you think. Arriving in China as the Founding Principal of a start-up school in Beijing, Chris Nash notes,

> I assumed the purpose of the owners of the school was one-dimensional – students achieving maximum grades and graduating to elite universities. Ironically, my determination to achieve academic excellence ran into resistance from the owners and other stakeholders who held the holistic views of the humanist purposes of education I had always aspired to, but which had been beaten out of me by the increasingly mechanistic, narrow focus on examination scores in the UK. Once this barrier was overcome, one of the joys of my international leadership has been the freedom to evolve the 'purposes' of the school to match the needs of students, families, our community, the nation and the international context. Now, this means strategising how we can develop a stronger environmental purpose for the school by developing global sustainable citizenship.

Jonathan Gastel, Cogdel Chengdu Academic and High School Principal, suggests starting with a 'graduate profile'. This may help in articulating to parents and high school students more clearly about the knowledge, skills, abilities, and other characteristics (KSAOs) students are likely to need in an evolving job market space.

Key Aspects To Help You Find Your Purpose

- Know, understand, and be able to see your vision, without exceptions or limitations.
- Understand what is negotiable within that vision and what is not – on both pragmatic and physical levels.
- Develop and actively practise servant leadership and support for the whole community.

What Research Tells Us

The current global population of 7.6 billion is likely to reach 8.6 billion in 2025 and 9.8 billion by 2030. From 2017 to 2050, India, Nigeria, the Democratic Republic of the Congo, Pakistan, Ethiopia, the United Republic of Tanzania, the United States of America, Uganda and Indonesia are expected to account for nearly half of any future increase.[2] Add to this forecasts of increased global warming; already, the last 8 years – 2015 to 2023 – are likely to be the warmest since records began.[3] Both of which tell us the purpose of your school and the education children receive are likely to rapidly evolve – and that you have a wider overall purpose and responsibility.

Some of the top 10 skills expected to be required in 2025 will be:

- problem-solving
- self-management
- working with people
- technology use and development.[4]

Presumably, AI will also be a required skill set. McKinsey's Global Energy Perspective 2022 suggests that 'by 2026, global renewable-electricity capacity will rise more than 80 per cent from 2020 levels (to more than 5,022 gigawatts)'.[5] As global societies age, the challenges that this represents will be immense. Bernard Marr, a *Forbes* contributor, says that the two biggest challenges that will shape the future of education are 'what we teach' and the 'way we teach it'.[6] One growing approach in the way we teach is the International Baccalaureate (IB). From 2018 to 2022, there has been an increase of 34.2% in the number of IB programmes offered across

---

[2] World population projected to reach 9.8 billion in 2050, and 11.2 billion in 2100 – says UN.
[3] Info from the World Meteorological Organization 2022.
[4] :Top 10 skills of tomorrow. WeForum.
[5] Global Energy Perspective 2022. McKinsey and Company.
[6] The two biggest trends in education. Bernard Marr. Forbes.

the world.[7] Behind the IB programme is a purpose-centred philosophy filled with values and service to others.

We also need to accept that international schools are not always a direct consequence of the educational aims that we may have come to accept in our careers. The consultancy firm Cairneagle suggests, 'About half of companies operating British schools worldwide were originally property developers, some of whom were incorporating campuses into a wider project'.[8] International Schools are big business and a lot of people are now waking up to the fact they can potentially be a significant long-term investment return.

What Do You Want Your Students To Achieve?

The knowledge, skills, abilities and other characteristics (KSAOs) you might want your students to acquire and develop in their time in your school are vast. The more you want your students to achieve, the more it may cost in terms of infrastructure and staffing. For example, you may want them to be, have, or develop, in addition to core academic knowledge:

- Principled and caring attitudes, as emphasised in the IB
- English Language Skills
- Sustainable Development awareness
- Problem-Solving skills
- Commitment to global peace
- The 6 C's: character education, citizenship, collaboration, communication, creativity, and critical thinking[9]
- Democratic and open-minded
- Confident, responsible, reflective, innovative, and engaged, as per the Cambridge Curriculum[10]
- Agents of social change and justice
- Human Rights awareness
- Self-awareness, awareness of others
- Effective relationships
- Emotional/Physical wellbeing
- Physical health
- Awareness of business and enterprise

---

[7] IB Facts and Figures. The International Baccalaureate.
[8] International schools shift to new markets after China boom stalls. Financial Times.
[9] M. Fullan and G. Scott (2014). Education PLUS: The world will be led by people you can count on, including you. Collaborative Impact SPC: Seattle, WA, USA.
[10] Cambridge Curriculum.

These are just a few of the skills and qualities you might want to have as graduation criteria.

Key Note
During the countless iterations and editing of this book, one question we were continually drawn back to was: 'Does a school's purpose come before, or after the market research that underpins it?' There are two schools of thought.

- The *first*, altruistic in nature, suggests that your purpose is always indefatigable: it is the 'why' of what you are attempting to do.
- The *second* suggests that, to have as strong a purpose as possible, you need to closely understand who it is that you are going to represent and build your school culture around.

Thus, you need a nuanced approach that measures people's needs and how you intend to respond to them to generate the most effective purpose you can. There is no right or wrong way. However, we do suggest that you carefully consider both options, before determining which approach might work best in your context.

Sustainability

Changing The Paradigm of The Sustainable School

As Larry Fink, Chairman and CEO of Blackrock, said in his annual 2022 letter to CEOs, 'Every company and every industry will be transformed by the transition to a net zero world. The question is, will you lead, or will you be led?'[11] As Fink has previously suggested, as principal and CEO of your international school, a key question for you to ask yourself is – How will your leadership and management of your school benefit each stakeholder, teachers and the wider staff body, school suppliers and the wider community in which you are based and serve? Leading an international school in economic and environmental isolation is a sure-start road to failure. When the chairman of a company whose global asset investment portfolio runs into trillions of dollars of deposits poses such a question, it is time to stand up and take note.

---

[11] Annual (2022) Letter to Blackrock CEOs - Larry Fink.

'When I work with NGOs and Corporations, and even schools and education groups, one of the most frequent questions I get asked is: "What is sustainability", Grace Hu, Global Head of Sustainability – Leading Your International School, says. 'Who I explain the meaning to and how, depends on the audience'.

What Do We Mean By 'Sustainable School'?
Sustainable companies are ones that 'sustain competitive advantage for the long term by integrating a contribution to society into their business models'. Moreover, 'These companies show strong performance in the following areas: financial, environmental, social and governance'.[12]** When we achieve the United Nations 17 Sustainable Development Goals (SDGs), then we can say we are sustainable. 'The first five goals (which are focused on people) are fundamental to solve the global challenges that we are currently facing', adds Grace.

Why Become A Sustainable School?
As principal and CEO, you have the responsibility of developing a school culture that helps to prepare our next generation of students for the future challenges we face as a global society. Increasingly, the world as we know it is not just waking up to the changes we need to make to our everyday lives and society – it is demanding it. If you take the time to embed policies and practices that place people and their purpose at the heart of your school's overall mission and philosophy, it is highly likely that in the aforementioned areas, you will:

1. Make significant financial savings in the long term.
2. Contribute to the enhancement (not degradation) of your school's local environment and the overall environment.
3. Improve social mobility and cohesion in doing so.

To achieve these, you will need to develop a sound governance model that places people and the planet at the heart of your school curriculum, its culture and wider community.

---

[12] Miller Perkins, K. (2019), p.9. Leadership and Purpose: How to Create a Sustainable Culture (1st ed.). Routledge. https://doi.org/10.4324/9780429265952.

CASE STUDY:

The Education in Motion's (EiM) Schools Carbon Road Map Project

Education in Motion, who own Dulwich International School, one of the biggest International school brands in mainland China, started to make their annual ESG (Environmental, Social, and Governance) reports public from 22 April 2022 to contribute to their commitment to Sustainability, Global Citizenship and overall group value. Highlighted in the report is the start of a Carbon Roadmap programme in 2019 in all their schools globally. The Carbon Roadmap programme contains three steps: 1) Carbon MRV (measurement, reporting, verification); 2) Carbon Reduction; and 3) Carbon Offset. So far, the expectation is that Dehong Xi'an, and all other schools under the EiM family of brands, will have finished at least one round of carbon mapping, based on the annual footprint from both operation and people behaviours. With all those, EiM is working on its carbon target and designing a detailed carbon strategy, which can contribute not only towards global climate action but also to help inspire the next generation of students with responsibility for the future and help to link their behaviours to the overall bigger global picture.

As a non-listed educational institution, currently, EiM is not subject to mandatory disclosure of ESG or carbon emissions in any country. But there are already many international schools that have started this work because as educators, we shoulder great educational responsibilities. To some extent, our behaviour and attitude determine the future direction of the students and families who choose us.

CASE STUDY

Artemis Education's 'The Promise'

At the Artemis group of schools, educators need to connect to sustainability. One way they do this is in their promise. As the group's CEO states: 'We believe that education for the next generation includes a responsibility to leave our children a better planet. As educators, we must equip our students for life in the 21st century with an understanding of the impact that we as individuals, collectively as communities and broadly as society have on our planet. As an organisation, we must continuously strive to neutralise our impact on the environment, embed sustainable practices and learning in our schools and integrate them into the communities in which we operate. As parents and educators, we are standing up and making a promise to deliver a better planet to our children, their families and the communities in which we live: "The Artemis Promise"'.

The Promise has its own page on their website: Promise - Artemis (artemis-education.com). Principal Martin Harris says, 'We will embed this in everything that we do: from recycled pasta used for straws, recycled material used for the majority of the uniform, including buttons on our uniform and sourced locally (wherever possible) so that it isn't flown halfway around the world. There is no plastic in school, and school minibuses will be electric'.

What Gets In the Way of Sustainability?

- Existing frameworks and paradigms of education maintain the separateness of knowledge from its context and deprioritise the competencies that will help us build a more abundant world.
- The increasingly competitive economic model, particularly in international education, that pits schools against each other.
- The training of teachers deprioritises the knowledge, dispositions and pedagogical approaches that help us educate for a more abundant world.
- A lack of interest or understanding by the Board or Proprietors who may not be willing to invest in sustainable projects due to attitudes around financial relevance.

Professional Advice On Sustainability
Brett Girven, Principal of Arbor School in Dubai, shares his thoughts on the current and future approaches of our international schools toward sustainability.

The first question to ask yourself is always – "Are you happy with the status quo?" Sustainability is about maintaining the current status quo. We could maintain our current status more or less indefinitely, without actually improving anything. In ecological terms, any organism that is not growing is effectively dying. Do you want to be part of a system that is growing quantitatively or qualitatively? If so, then set your sights north of neutral. Is wellbeing enough or do we want people to *flourish* in their lives and to influence others with their energy and positivity? Do you want an environment that maintains the current status or would you prefer one which is abundant? Here at the Arbor School, we have recalibrated our initial thoughts on sustainability so that we are always aiming north of neutral. With that in mind, we design with the intent to achieve those loftier goals. What models of systems do we have that are proven to work?

A healthy ecosystem is diverse, it's resilient, it has emergent properties... meaning that the whole is more than the sum of its parts. Each part of the ecosystem collaborates (directly or indirectly) for the health of the whole. Rather than reinventing the wheel, we are teaching our children fundamental principles of ecosystems and empowered with that knowledge, we aim to create sustainable human futures. We try to avoid the pitfalls of sustainability being a 'bolt-on' aspect of the curriculum.

In the five years since opening, the Arbor school has grown to approximately 1300 students and is a through-school grounded in the national curriculum. As Brett tells me, 'It is about the how'. Whilst parents initially might have joined for price and proximity, the general feeling is that families join The Arbor School because of who they are – not where they are... an encouraging thought for those schools looking to develop a competitive edge, with sustainability at the core.

To Embed Sustainability in Your Start-up

- Model sustainable practices in all your operations.
- The default position of your school should be inclusive and diverse if you want it to be resilient and adaptive.
- Collaborate, connect, and make mutually affirming decisions with partners.
- Develop your school as an ongoing 'case study' of good practice for others to learn from and mould their ideas around.

- Adapt, contextualise, and scale your curriculum and its teaching to the audience and their worldview.
- Avoid the teaching of 'learned helplessness' – we want our children to experience both success and failure in solving problems if we want them to believe that they can positively influence the future they are going to inherit.

Get The Right Market Research

Challenge
Market research and being 'data-informed' are key drivers of both business and founding international schools that go on to be successful. Too much of the wrong data outside of your context can negatively influence your overall strategy.

Solution
It is fundamental to carry out your own research to support that from other organisations. Talk to school heads, owners and board members, and visit other schools. Learn from their successes and mistakes, fast!

Your Research Base
ISC Research is dedicated and committed to supporting the broader international schools community by providing data, trends and intelligence. Since 1994, they have guided schools with their growth plans, informed investors on new school development, helped universities to engage with international schools, and advised education suppliers that are supporting the market.

Research carried out in 2020 by ISC Research into past global crises, including the 2008 global financial crash and the 2014 oil and gas crisis, demonstrated that the international schools market recovered surprisingly quickly from serious setbacks. Their latest data shows 445 new international schools opened globally between July 2021 and June 2023. This shows how resilient the international schools market remains post-COVID-19 pandemic. 65% of these schools are based in Asia.

'ISC is aware of another 300 future international schools due to open by 2027'. Its global research team are directly in touch with international school leaders. The countries where they are aware of most new school development occurring and in the planning process (as of June 2023) include:

- *India*: Many international schools are entering the Indian market and existing schools are expanding their campuses.
- *Japan*: Demand from host national families remains relatively low but the country is attracting more expatriates including families from China who are moving to access international education from an early age.
- *Vietnam*: There are several plans underway for international school campus expansions as well as new international schools entering the market.
- *Cambodia*: This is a newly emerging market and one that is experiencing more interest in international school development, particularly in Phnom Penh.
- *Singapore*: The expatriate market continues to grow in Singapore, particularly with the development of the country as the financial hub of Asia.
- *The UAE*: The UAE continues to see urban development, particularly in the suburbs of Dubai and Abu Dhabi.

To find out more about ISC Research, visit their website at https://iscresearch.com/for-schools/

Additional research resources include:

- Global Services in Education (GSE), at https://www.gsineducation.com/. With more than 20 years of experience setting up and managing international schools worldwide, GSE is the market leader in the area of market research, feasibility studies and financial modelling for international schools.
- Cairneagle, at https://www.cairneagle.com/
- EY-Parthenon, https://www.ey.com/en_us/strategy/about-ey-parthenon
- Research Journals, such as
  - International Educational Research (IER)
  - Journal of Research in International Education
  - International Journal of Educational Research
  - International Schools Journal
  - Journal of International and Comparative Education
  - Compare: A Journal of Comparative and International Education
- Partner schools

- Websites, including:
  - School Management Plus; Educational Digest International (EDDi): https://eddi.substack.com/
  - RIPE: https://www.ecolint-institute.ch/publications
- Your own 'in-house' research, including surveys, interviews, school visits and consultancy calls, e.g., with Leading Your International School.
- LinkedIn surveys.
- Individually appointed consultants, including Leading Your International School.
- Leading university lecturers and voices in international education, including Denry Machin, Tristan Bunnell, Mary Hayden, Chris James, Jeff Thompson, Paul Tarc, Aparna Mishra Tarc, Conrad Hughes, James Cambridge, Alexander Gardner-McTaggart, Ian Hill Hyejin, and Kim Lucy Bailey.
- Online blogs, e.g., the LYIS Principal's Bog/, newsletters and articles.
- Education Bureaus in the relevant country, such as the DfE in the UK and KDHA in Dubai.
- Accreditation organisations – COBIS, IBO, ISI, PENTA, Australian Boarding Schools Association (ABSA)
- Books, e.g., *Leading Your International School*.[13]
- The IBO, which shares studies on their programmes: https://www.ibo.org/research/.
- Case Studies (Schools in The Middle East). For instance, international school data from the KDHA in Dubai which suggests several lessons emerge for prospective international school leaders.[14] Here we summarise four key recommendations based upon such research.

Pedagogy – Not Curriculum – Has To Come First.

The international school you apply to lead could have a wide range of curriculum approaches. British and American-style curricula are the most typical, but there is considerable diversity around what type of international school you could potentially lead. In the future, it is likely, as in China now, that local national curricula will play increasingly important roles alongside international curriculum models. While there are distinct advantages to having prior experience with a particular curriculum, we

---

[13] André Double and Warren S. Cook, Leading Your International School (16Leaves, 2023). https://www.leadingyourinternationalschool.com/.
[14] Dubai's Private Schools Open Data the Knowledge and Human Development Authority (KHDA) – January, 2023.

would argue that it's more important for an aspiring international school leader to understand the back engine of effective teaching and learning which can be adapted to any particular curriculum model. Highly effective pedagogical approaches and student-centred learning will be the key to success whatever the curriculum framework your start-up school adopts.

Agility Is Key
As a future international school leader, you need to be able to demonstrate agile thinking and the ability to apply your principles and qualities as an educator to a variety of school types. It's not just the diversity of the curriculum. Look too at the vast range of school sizes, from small community schools to mega campuses: underlying principles are key. Regardless of school size, your future employers are looking for the same things. Do you have the people skills to be able to build high-performing teams across staff with diverse backgrounds in education? Do you have the communication and empathy skills to be able to build active and loyal parental engagement with customers who may have a range of social, political, and cultural interests in private education? Can you form effective relationships with owners who will have a range of reasons for involvement in the education business? And can you help them build a compelling narrative about education, especially if education is not their primary business?

All-Through Education
Schools that follow an 'all through' model of education from kindergarten to high school may be at a distinct financial advantage. There are clear business advantages to this model. It allows owners to monopolise a local market, reducing the scope for competitors to siphon away customers at each transition from one level of education to another. It also offers opportunities to create brand loyalty. The implications for future international leaders are twofold. First, wherever possible, gain knowledge across the various age groups. Chris Nash – with ten years' experience as an international school leader – notes, 'Although I was high school trained, I dedicated some time to teaching in the primary sector so I had insight into effective primary pedagogy. Furthermore, as a High School head, I was able to include the experience of working in an Education Action Zone cluster of neighbourhood schools. Therefore, I enhanced my international K-12 setting skills in working effectively with Primary and Middle school leaders and was knowledgeable for example, about strategies to improve literacy levels from infancy to university application'.

Expect Some Form of Inspection System in Your New International Setting

Whatever the local or national frameworks for school inspection are, get to know them in detail as quickly as possible. Nothing will deter your new employers from seeing out your contract quicker than a failed inspection and the consequent reputational damage. The best way to prepare for external inspection is to establish your own rigorous internal self-evaluation. This should cover the sorts of things the inspection team will be looking for, but there's an excellent adage: 'Measure what you value'. Identify the unique or essential features of your educational vision and use self-evaluation to gather evidence that these things aren't just fancy words in a brochure and that you are making measurable improvements to the students and the community. These days it's very tempting to attract customers with the label of 'sustainability' but the real impact comes from being able to demonstrate improvements in campus design, student thinking or curriculum provision. Rigorous and reliable self-evaluations can be shared with external inspection teams and might just get you through a temporary downward blip in performance if the self-evaluation shows strong improvement trends.

When gathering your data, carefully consider:

- How an over-reliance on organisations that may not be as committed as you in achieving your goals might affect the quality of the data.
- The reliability of data that is collected and collated from third-party sources.
- A belief that data is the only answer. It isn't.

Professional Advice On Market Research

Paul Ellmes of InSync Global Education says, 'You need to do an extensive study of the city you are going to be in, identifying people who may be able to support you. Whilst engaging a consultancy might seem the obvious thing to do (and I have heard of schools in Dubai spending up to US$100,000 on this), the real value for money is in the feet on the ground you have'. It makes sense therefore to make sure the consultancy you plan to work with can offer that possibility.

When the former Police Commissioner of New York Bill Bratton wanted to decide on the use of new and updated smaller squad cars, he chose to assess their practicality by riding them in full Police regalia around the city. It didn't take long to realise that they were not the right purchase for the job. Spending a short amount of time in and around your proposed new campus may tell you a different story. Does your market research data talk to the coffee shop owner about their clientele? Will it take you on a car journey to and from your proposed campus at different times of the day that parents might experience? And will it serve you the kind of food that your students will be eating from the locally trained staff you will need to hire? Effective modern market research is as ethnographic as it can be. It follows the lives, the successes and the snags of your potential market and allows the people who may be your customer base a voice. It is vital, therefore, that members of your founding team visit the location at an advance time and that the school principal visits it months (if not a full year or more) before they take up their post.

Key Questions Your Research Needs To Answer
Compliance – Legal & Financial Oversight & Accountability

- Does the company that is building/already owns the premises have the legal right to open a school?
- What evidence and background research are being provided to the construction company/landlords and where is it from?
- How will you achieve compliance at every stage of your development? Do you and your business partners know and understand the local, state, and national laws relating to International Schools, Private Education, and Bi-Lingual Schools and the license requirements for each?
- Are there local or state-level issues that may negatively affect an opening (E.g., historically contaminated water/land pollution)?
- What are the fee models at all other schools, both International and domestic local private schools?
- What is the financial power of the local area and its segments?

Strategy & Infrastructure

- Is there a verified need for an International School – what evidence supports this?
- Is there a clear need for a K-12 educational model, or are others more economically viable?
- Is a full international school necessary, or would an innovative approach to bilingual education be a more realistic and economically viable option?
- What is the family demographic of the area (families with children of school age)? Are they actively encouraged by the government?

- What gaps in the market are there that your school could potentially fill?
- If your model is constructed around an international customer base – is there an international business/community already present?
- Are international demographics emerging in the allocation of visas?
- Are international communities present and, if so, where?
- Is the proposed school location appropriate: Is the area safe / Has it suffered political unrest, kidnappings, or hostage taking?
- Will a school be accessible by transport and how busy are the school routes?

Culture, Communication & Stakeholders

- What cultural sensitivities have you / are you likely to uncover and how will they be addressed?
- What communication tools are used locally by successful schools? Are blogs, TikTok, Facebook, WeChat, TV channels, radio/podcasts, local magazines, or newspapers popular with potentially targeted members of the community?
- Will the local government support (or even prioritise) your application for an International School? How do you know – what evidence is there for this?
- Are large-scale long-term construction/infrastructure/consultancy projects planned that have been awarded to international companies?

Red Flags From Your Data

If, during any of your preliminary research you come across any of the following red flags, stop and revisit your purpose. They may pose a serious threat to your future ability to operate and you will need to research further in more comprehensive detail and, where necessary, professional expertise sought.

Issue	Key Questions
Several schools have previously started and failed in your proposed area	Learn the WHY, fast!
The license appears beyond reach	Is a license obtainable within the timeframe you plan if you remain compliant?
The school has limited outdoor space	How are you planning to organise whole-school events? What value do you place on children's physical & mental wellbeing?
Visa issuance for visits and research has proved painstaking	How will this be affected with multiple teachers and staff from around the world?
Contracts and the people who have sought them are easily influenced and open to bribery	Is your governance policy and its procedures suitably robust and is there sufficient buy in from all key stakeholders about ethical governance?
Attracting staff to your location is likely to be extremely difficult.	How can you compete financially against similar schools in better locations?
Inaccessible links	Have infrastructure promises been made and not delivered upon?
Local services and facilities are in poor condition and in need of huge investment	Who will be investing in the local area, how and on what timescale? Have local authorities made promises that seem unrealistic?
Is there a specific skills shortage in Human Resources or Finance management?	Who will support the development and training of your HR department?
Are contracts expected to be honoured by 'word of mouth' agreements?	Will the owner/board accept 'word of mouth'?
Demographic research is hard to carry out or inconsistent with others' findings.	Is your market research company one with a historical reputation of delivering success?
Your partner has failed to develop an overall strategic plan to back up their proposal.	Are their priorities clear or is the plan being made up as it goes along?
Budgets are undefined, or loosely referred to.	How will this transpire during the subsequent phases of school development?

IDENTIFY YOUR TARGET MARKET

Challenge

The very viability of your school may depend upon the skill of yourself and the marketing team in identifying the sorts of parents most likely to buy education from your school, and then attracting and retaining such parents in the face of competition. It is all too easy to fall into assumptions about the 'new middle classes' and the sorts of career profiles and aspirations they have.

Solution

Put yourself through a steep learning curve to develop expertise in the demographics of the city and society you are working in, keeping an open mind. You need a high-quality local team who have been thoroughly trained to be 'on message' throughout the whole recruitment process – from the initial inquiry to the after-care follow-up once the student is enrolled.

Research tells us that students attending international schools in the Middle East are 'mostly students whose first language is English. Most of these students are the children of professional expatriates and affluent local families'.[15] International schools in the US provide homes to students of families employed by international or government organisations, often situated in larger cities. Parents, as such, often want their children to receive a European-style education.[16] Chris Spring, a school Principal in Nigeria, says of investing in education in Nigeria, 'If you get it right, you could potentially make a lot of money. Nigerian parents want the best for their children. They want top-quality education at a sensible price'. As a bilingual principal in India, Samuel notes:

"You should bear in mind that parents are increasingly demanding that international education be combined with the teaching of local traditions and values. This is not mere narrow nationalism. If your students in the future are to play a leading role in the domestic society and economy, they need deep-rooted knowledge of local history, cultures and language. A curriculum that harmonises the best of international with the best of local education, may be a persuasive marketing mix".

---

[15] Sprint Education.
[16] The Beginner's Guide to International Schools Marketing. Sprint Education.

What Affects Your Potential Target Market?

- The integrity of your marketing strategy. Over-promising/under-delivering. Parents will need demonstrable evidence to support your marketing claims.
- The quality and experience of your marketing team.
- Resources – ongoing marketing campaigns are expensive and time-consuming.
- Shifting demographics, for instance, a shrinking expat population (e.g., Hong Kong) or declining birth rates and populations, make long-term projection and stability difficult.
- Unreliable or inaccurate data from a local government census.
- Geopolitical situations that affect the issue of visas.

Professional Advice To Those Starting A School:

Understanding the target market and what motivates people to choose international private education continues to be an area of deep professional learning for Chris, mixed with fascination and frustration. Marketing experts identify three strands to working with target markets: *demographics, geographics,* and *psychographic* segmentation. The last, Chris notes, is the most fruitful, and allows you to engage at depth with the social psychology and cultural identity of the parent group. Devote time to listening to potential parents (challenging if you're relying on a translator) and you will begin to understand commonalities in their hopes for the future, anxieties about their child, and the present situation they find themselves in. With active listening and culturally sensitive reflection, you begin to anticipate the mindset of the niche market. Tailor your message to match the needs of your audience. 'Our school in Beijing draws a proportion of its intake from the province of Shanxi, which is distant from the capital and has a distinct culture and even dialect. I have found that an insight into the province and two or three typical dialect phrases go a long way to gaining the trust of many of this parent group', adds Chris.

You will need to become an expert in the various marketing channels that are most effective with your target market. Initially, I could not understand why my company didn't pay more attention to its 'web presence', which was my key marketing tool in England. I then came to understand that *'Weixin'* (WeChat), the highly popular social media channel in China, was far more than a platform for staying in touch with friends and was the most effective way to engage and inform potential customers. I am impressed by the way my company operates a parental education channel which is seen as offering a public good to all in society but also acts as a subtle marketing mechanism, very in tune with Chinese cultural values and reaching a much wider audience than a website. An effective media presence needs similar levels of insight into the social communication infrastructure in your context.

To Help Identify Your Target Market

- Profile who your students will be and where they are going to come from.
- Spend as much time in the country/on the ground in your prospective location(s) as possible and, wherever possible, meet with local representatives.
- Sell your education philosophy and vision to the local community and build a reciprocal platform on which those who share the same values can join you.
- Visit international schools around the world and learn how they attract students.
- Look at your competitor schools and analyse their student intake.
- Get good at analytics of your social media and other web presences.

PROFIT OR NOT-FOR PROFIT?

For-Profit

A for-profit international school may be owned by a sole owner/investor/family, group of investors/Educational Group, or a private company – both educational and non-educational. Once operational costs are met, monies generated from the overall school operations are used for non-educational purposes. As a founding principal, a very important (and early) question you need to ask yourself is, can you accept and work under such a model? Key to the early initial success of an international school for-profit model may be the reputation of the school's owner and any subsidiary business that appears in the background of your school, or underneath its banner. Your school's educational credibility and accountability are vitally important. As a result, you will need to secure an overall pathway towards accreditation or external verification that can establish and support your school's reputation in the local community and with your key stakeholders. It is possible that your overall performance as principal/CEO will be measured by your ability to meet key opening and enrolment targets themselves accompanied by large financial incentives and bonuses.

Not-For-Profit

On the surface, a not-for-profit school serves its community and, in doing so, endeavours to safeguard its overall mission. Surplus funds are invested directly back into the school, to support its key objectives, improve teaching quality and the wider facilities, and – ultimately – raise outcomes. There is, however, a certain amount of naivety when it comes to the hiring of principals for not-for-profit roles. You will absolutely be expected to return a profit and indeed many of your school practices and operations may simultaneously run on 'profit' lines.

CASE STUDY: THE INTERNATIONAL SCHOOL OF RHEINTAL, SWITZERLAND

The International School of Rheintal is a *not-for-profit* school in rural Switzerland whose historical context can be traced back to one local company that employs expatriates. When the school first began twenty years ago, 'There was a competition in the valley across all the different towns to see who would get the International school', notes Liz Free, The School's CEO and Director. 'So, one school volunteered a field, somebody else volunteered an old people's home, all kinds of different things', adding, 'There was funding from the company, the local government, and local and regional support to set up the school'. The school went on to stabilise at around 120 students, but as I learned from Liz, 'A school that runs all three IB programmes with 120 students is not likely to be financially sustainable', and it required support from the local partner. A decision was taken in collaboration with the school's founding partners to design and build a new 30-million-dollar campus, which Liz now oversees. As Liz states, 'The school is now working towards becoming operationally self-sustaining'. One of the most important pieces of advice that Liz gives to founding heads and their schools is that 'The early start-up phase of a school is around building capacity within your organisation', and in doing so, it's key to build institutional knowledge and operational practices, making sure that these are knitted into the fabric of your school. You may therefore want to consider how you can find a model of leadership that suits your own current or future context.

Questions To Discuss With Owners Over The 'For Profit' Model

- Will a 'for-profit' model of education limit the overall opportunities and experiences of the students?
- Will it affect your overall quality of education and the commitment/bespoke level of education and service that the students will receive?
- Is the long-term financial model built on an incremental increase in profits, and what happens if lean spells, such as those during Covid, occur?
- Will staff, parents, and wider stakeholders be able to accept the overall mission of the school if profits are to be re-directed into lesser ethically acceptable practices?

Professional Advice On Profit vs. Not-For-Profit

What do *'profit'* and *'not-for-profit'* mean in your country legally? There are many different definitions of what these mean – do not assume that you know what that means in the country in which your school will be. You may not even have a choice if your country doesn't allow 'for-profit' schools to operate. If this is the case, you will have to change your business model to reflect this. The owner/company/proprietor will still expect the school to be profitable, so how are those profits going to be shown? One answer may be through management or royalty fees. A not-for-profit organisation/school in the USA comes under 501c3 – this will need to be set up and will take a long time. It is nowhere near as simple as setting up a company, as 501c3 organisations can receive donations and the donor receives considerable tax relief. Most US private schools are 501c3 as they are driven by fees and donations. There is still (although slightly less, now) suspicion in The USA regarding for-profit schools and their motives.

It's also important to consider the perception of profit vs. not-for-profit in your school's country. Be sure to understand the definition plus the perception. In the first 3-5 years this will be a constantly repeated question by prospective parents and a firm, clear understanding and answer is necessary. If one is in a not-for-profit school what does that mean for the business model and budgeting? If one has never been in a not-for-profit school, not only can budgeting be precarious, particularly for the first 3 years as the school shows itself to be successful/sustainable, but also long term. Staffing must reflect not only the usual Director of Admissions and Marketing staff but also – crucially – fundraising staff. The governance of the school will also be different. On most for-profit Boards, the Principal will be a full voting member (not on the actual Board of the company ownership, but the school itself). On not-for-profit Boards, the Principal may often *not* have a vote – this affects the overall leadership, management and running of a school. Remember: politics can be even more powerful than money! Especially amongst those who have money to spend/donate. Every large (and even small!) donation comes with some sort of strings attached – be aware of this!

Ultimately as Dr James Brightman, Principal International Community School of Addis Ababa tells us you may need to ask yourself: 'Is the mission of the school aligned with the core values of the owner/ownership group?' Ask yourself: What if your school and its group are owned by organisations that have links to unsustainable practices, including deforestation and palm oil plantations? How will you respond to parents, students and the wider community who may challenge you? Remember: 'A school's registered status does not automatically equate to the value-driven behaviour or the operational culture you might expect', an anonymous teacher quoted on the TES magazine website.[17]

Build Your Educational Vision

Challenge
Many international schools do not specifically refer to their vision. Some have elaborate core values and guiding statements that are ambiguous and difficult to measure.

Solution
Develop a powerful vision that goes well beyond its intended purpose and unites all those who serve it – long after the people who designed it have left the building.

What Research Tells Us
Leithwood et al.'s 'Seven Strong Claims About School Leadership' suggests that, 'Almost all leaders draw upon the same repertoire of practices' and that 'Vision Building' was a key aspect of this claim.[18] The Wallace Foundation defines one of the five primary roles of the school principal as 'Shaping a vision of academic success for all students'.[19] A study of 27 principals from elementary to high schools in Alberta, Canada, showed that those classified as 'high performing' 'were all led by principals who

---

[17] The TES Magazine 27th November 2020. To profit or not-for-profit, that is the question.
[18] Leithwood, K., Harris, A., & Hopkins, D. (2008). Seven strong claims about successful school leadership. *School leadership and management*, 28(1), 27-42.
[19] The School Principal As Leader: Guiding Schools to Better Teaching and Learning: The Wallace Foundation.

clearly articulated vision, mission, and goals'.[20] Key to such performance was the principal's beliefs about what success looked like.

The average length of a vision statement is around 35 words or two sentences.[21] As we see from the International School of Paris's vision below – less can be more.

UWC	At UWC, we inspire young people to put their talents and energy into social change, no matter which future path they choose. We select promising, passionate students from all over the world, and give them the knowledge, skills and confidence to make a difference.
British School – Muscat	A world class British education where everyone is valued, respected and inspired to learn.
Qatar Academy – Doha	Empowering students to achieve high levels of academic growth and personal wellbeing and to be responsible citizens who are locally rooted and globally connected.
International School of Uganda	We seek to foster lifelong learners who are agents of their learning and wellbeing; who seek a deeper understanding of, and connection to, themselves, others in the school, Uganda, and global communities; and act upon personal passions and strengths to contribute to the pursuit of a more sustainable, equitable, inclusive, and just world.
The International School of Paris	Educating for Complexity

Figure 1.1. Five Schools And Their Visions

When Vision-Building, You'll Need To Overcome:

- Resistance to change and conflicting interests.
- Failure to communicate that change and/or coach people through it.
- Leadership transience, as leaders may come and go during the initial start-up phase of your school.
- Lack of awareness of how to measure the implementation of your vision.

---

[20] Mombourquette, C. (2017). The Role of Vision in Effective School Leadership. *International Studies in Educational Administration (Commonwealth Council for Educational Administration & Management* (CCEAM), 45(1).

[21] Characteristics of a Good Vision Statement: Paper 07/11 University of Hawaii 'i.

Professional Advice On How To Embed Your Vision
Vision building has long since been recognised as a successful means of drawing staff together in the name of the organisation and uniting everyone with a shared focus. Tesla's vision – 'To accelerate the world's transition to sustainable energy' – serves a far-reaching wider purpose than simply transporting its customers from A to B in the most sustainable manner. Leaders model great visions when placing value on all teaching and learning interactions and those in the wider learning community. Give teaching and non-teaching staff relevant training on what your mission and vision are and how to embed and develop these.

Regularly review the curriculum for learning opportunities to embed specific values and develop a broad base of activities that can support your school vision. Use your vision to facilitate wider stakeholder engagement and develop successful collaborations that can work together for mutual benefit and sustainable outcomes. Use HR to conduct 'culture conversations' to gauge and measure the cohesiveness of staff and the collective buy-in of your vision.[22] If you are going to set an organisational vision, set the biggest, hairiest, most audacious goal you can – or 'BHAG'[23] as Jim Collins calls it – but in doing so, make sure it has integrity. Instagram's vision to 'Capture and share the world's moments' is beautifully simple and manages to say everything it needs to say in six words.

Successful School Visions Make A Good P.O.D.C.A.S.T:

- **P**urposeful. Have learning at their core and contribute to a sustainable future.
- **O**wnership. They mean as much to the school guard as they do to the teachers.
- **D**istinctive. They aren't the same as the school down the road.
- **C**hallenging. They set goals that require your people to achieve their potential.
- **A**pplicable. They relate to your people and your cultural context. They permeate everything you do in supporting your core purpose.
- **S**uccinct. Staff and stakeholders can recite them, with ease.
- **T**angible. Easy to understand by those who pursue them. They can be broken down into KPIs, managed and measured.

---

[22] Double, A and Cook, W. (2023). *Leading Your International School. 16 Leaves, India.*
[23] Collins, J. C., Porras, J., & Collins, J. (2005). *Built to last: Successful habits of visionary companies. Random House.*

Identify Your Competitive Advantage

Challenge
There are approximately 12,220 English-medium international schools in the world, with a combined enrolment of around 6.3 million students.[24] Many are remarkably similar.

Solution
Your context holds the key to your advantage.

What Research Tells Us
Research tells us that 72% of respondents to an Ipsos survey for the World Economic Forum predict that higher education will continue to move further towards an online learning model.[25] Commonly cited advantages for joining international schools include an internationally recognised curriculum, global understanding, and academic excellence.[26] The Amerikanska Gymnasiet in Sweden attempts to make sure that its students are 'ready for the world' with both 'knowledge and skills', notes its CEO and Co-Founder Peter Heddelin. "The knowledge that we attempt to impart means that our students are ready to study at university and have learned how to navigate the world. Our skills are affected by our values, the most important of which is personal leadership: to speak for yourself, handle yourself, and develop in ways that are personable and related to the world at large. 'Our school is set to make graduates "ready for the world"', says Peter.[27]

What Others Say
Prioritising and mould-breaking innovation may require a cultural shift within your school, Dr Marc Mesich, Principal of The International School of Penang (UPLANDS), suggests. 'Adaptability and emotional intelligence are important traits that international school leaders should develop', he conveyed, adding, 'Heuristic intelligence is essential for effective leadership ... it is about having situational awareness for interpreting data and being able to quickly make decisions that are relevant'. School leaders, it would appear, listen, interpret, and communicate effectively to gain a competitive edge. 'Unfortunately, the reality is that competitive advantage comes through results. Parents care

---
[24] Data from the International Schools Consultancy (ISC).
[25] World Economic Forum – Is this what higher education will look like in 5 years?.
[26] Benefits of international Schools - World-Schools.
[27] www.amerikanskagymnasiet.se

and focus on results', he says.
Failing to gain a competitive advantage can often be traced back to:

- Lack of contextual awareness of your school – a new curriculum requires significant investment in resources and training.
- When your cultural context and its geopolitical landscape shift unfavourably away from the model of private education.
- Disassociation with the international education market – research is not updated and advantages become barriers if mindsets cannot be drawn away from it.
- Leadership that is detached from a wide number of stakeholders, fails to engage, and believes success can be isomorphic from one international school to another.

Professional Advice On Competitive Advantage
If your school happens to be linked to a successful overseas partner school/group or organisation, then it is important that you leverage that link to its potential to enhance your competitive advantage and the overall quality of education being delivered. If your school is linked to a big group, then you should be leaning on that group for demographic information and the systems its uses; its pedigree and prestige; outcomes and exam results; and established services –including marketing, ordering, HR, uniforms, and food – that can develop your procedures, improve efficiency and offer an overall better-quality product or service. It is thus crucial to get this in writing when signing your partnership agreement.

In a competitive market, international schools can and do differentiate themselves in an increasing number of ways. These include personalised curriculum and their unique programmes; student support, well-being, and holistic care; and the excellence of teaching and student outcomes and innovation. Help your school create a unique identity that sets it apart from other schools, one that appeals to families/students who are searching for a school that also prioritises cultural understanding. Offer bespoke professional development opportunities to your teachers to differentiate yourself and add to your competitive advantage. Investing in the professional growth and development of your staff is likely to improve both teaching quality and attract and retain talented educators, who again may go on to form part of your overall competitive edge.

'The best schools around the world', notes former Founding Principal, Malcolm Phillips, 'Are for holistic education – developing the whole person'. He adds, 'Be careful that your marketing team doesn't over promise and leave you in a position where parents are holding you to account for services you simply cannot offer'.

Ways To Develop Your Competitive Advantage

- *Develop your culture.* Observe and refine it. Give staff freedom of choice over work practices and students a greater say in how your school is run. Trust in others.
- *Design a unique curriculum.* Develop a curriculum that reflects your school's values and mission. Focus on project-based learning or experiential education or incorporate local culture into everyday learning and teaching.
- *Offer innovative programmes.* Use your current staff body and the local talent pool to offer supplementary services that add value to your school.
- *Emphasise your community.* Invest in your local area, its people, and services. Generate a community environment that people are both proud of and want to be part of.
- *Prioritise sustainability and innovation.* Focus strategic meetings at all levels on addressing problems and developing sustainable solutions to reduce your school's carbon footprint.
- *Drive wellbeing.* Do not forget that your biggest competitive advantage is likely to be in the academic *and* holistic wellbeing of your staff and students.
- *Tailor your expectations* to what you can deliver.

CHOOSE THE RIGHT LOCATION

Challenge
Many international schools and their owners favour glamorous locations, over practical and sustainable settings. A great location might not necessarily turn out to be the right choice – especially with increases in rent and a declining infrastructure.

Solution
As well as focusing more on what goes on inside the building as much as we do where it takes place, look for areas of potential growth and development.

What Research Tells Us
Choosing the wrong location can lead to several problems, including poor accessibility and low-quality transport infrastructure that can hamper logistics and generate unexpected costs; power outages and fluctuations

that can force you to scale back your operations; CO_2-intensive energy sources that can undermine your CSR performance; an unreliable telecommunications network that makes it harder to communicate externally with partners – and internally with headquarters and other entities within your company.[28]

CASE STUDY: DULWICH COLLEGE PUXI, WHY WE CHOSE OUR LOCATION

When Dulwich College Shanghai Puxi opened on the outskirts of the city, very few people would have thought the school would be able to sustain itself, given its location and the apparent lack of amenities. Several years later China's economic model of growth sees the school well placed to benefit from the establishment of a high-tech AI zone and the development of an environmental recreational zone with spacious green communities. These areas appeal to internationally-minded families who value outdoor play, nature, and healthy living. The school's unique location enabled it to become the centre of this community and complemented the development of the area. When considering the location of a campus, it is worth considering what the area will be like in 5 years, 10 years and 20 years. People will travel to a good school', the School's Principal, David Ingram tells me.

Challenges To Finding The Right Location:

- This is a politically sensitive issue in your international context, with new builds needing the authorisation and support of local authorities.
- Acquiring the required amount of land may be prohibitively expensive in the sorts of cities that have the largest customer base.
- Growing mature markets for private international education. The so-called 'first-tier' cities in China (Beijing, Shenzhen, Shanghai) now have significantly more places than demand, leading to difficult financial decisions.

---

[28] Nord Invest, France - What are the risks of choosing the wrong business location?.

Professional Advice On Finding the Right Location

Many governments and their local authorities are actively attracting international schools as a means of securing favourable investment and supporting their overall growth strategies in their cities and towns. They want to draw in fee-paying students from around the world and teachers who earn above-average salaries, which help support the local economy. It is vital you establish and maintain a key link to the local government and its potential fund of investment before, during, and after your site is acquired.

You *must* understand that international private education is *market-led*, rather than determined by the needs of local communities. Just as producers may change a product over time to increase its attractiveness to different consumer groups, you may find that the school owners change the location of your school to meet their interpretations of market conditions. In my ten-year tenure as the head of a private international school in China says Chris, 'I've managed three changes of location as the owners sought the best competitive advantage in the hotly contested Beijing market. Each of these locations had varying advantages and challenges. The first was closest to the city's Central Business District (CBD) – attractive for international teachers and a short taxi journey away. Attracting and retaining staff was not a problem. However, the area attracted more and more competitor schools until eventually, the school was at risk of losing students. We then chose a polar opposite location, on the very fringes of the city. Rent costs dropped considerably and we were able to market the school as being in an attractive and healthy semi-rural environment. Transport links into the city were poor, though. For someone like me, committed to a lifestyle as close to that of our host country as possible, this was a wonderful location. Attracting and retaining international teachers to share this lifestyle was all but impossible. The third and current location, says Chris is a compromise between these two extremes. Far enough from the CBD for land prices and rents to enable the school to thrive, but 5 minutes from a metro line so that staff and students alike are connected to the city. This has enabled us to recruit much better qualified and experienced teachers'.

The lesson? You need resilience and adaptability as a Founding international school principal/CEO. I have resisted getting over-attached to any particular location or lifestyle. As a school leader, the core of your life is the stability of your students and staff to ensure a good learning culture. If changes of location maintain or enhance this aspect of your life you should be able to adapt and enjoy changes of housing and scenery.

To Secure The Best Location for Your School

- *Generate a Location criteria checklist.* Make a thoroughly detailed analysis of what your staff and students are going to need from the site, e.g., accessibility, and outdoor space. Location criteria must include local mandated or statutory elements such as space requirements or licensing restrictions depending on the age of students or use of the facility.
- *Longlist* your preferred locations.
- *Shortlist* your locations. Spend as much time viewing them (at different times of the year, particularly during rush hours to assess viability for bussing/drop off/pick up.
- *Compare and analyse each site against the other.* When you have a shortlist, develop a formal set of specifications.
- Share search selection criteria with key stakeholders / local partners you are opening your school with.
- *Communicate your proposed timeline.* Ensure local partners are aware of the process, which includes, shortlisting, sight selection, and rental/purchase agreements.

Consider the benefits of locating the school in an area with relatively fewer direct competitors weighed against the challenges of recruiting students and staff. Remember, 'Finding a building often involves not only the challenges of real-estate finance but also politics and luck. Invariably, it will require a lot of your time.'[29]

---

[29] Lake, R., Winger, A., & Petty, J. (2002), p.60 The New Schools Handbook: Strategic Advice for Successful School Start-Up in Partnership with School District Officials, Staff and Community Members.

The Right Business Model

CHOOSE THE RIGHT PARTNER(S)

Challenge
Finding the right partner(s) so that your school and its values are aligned can be strenuous. Like half of all marriages, they often end in a costly divorce.

Solution
Ensure that your new partner is assessed and stress-tested for their integrity.

What Research Tells Us
According to Wasserman (2013), the decision of when to add cofounders to your school start-up team may be based on the *Human, Social,* and *Financial Capital* that others can bring. 'Human capital includes the explicit knowledge derived from formal education and the tacit skills derived from prior experience. It is a rare founder who already has all the skills and knowledge needed to build a new organisation from nothing'.[30] Finding the right partner, therefore, is crucial. As an international principal recently told me, 'Many partners do not have experience working in education and know absolutely nothing about education per se. Everyone thinks they know about education, especially if they went to an international school, then they think they are an expert'.

Wellington College International actively promotes its search for potential partners on its website, and in doing so 'continues to expand and explore the potential to broaden our education impact… [whose] key to success in this is not only to find the right location, though this is critical, but to find the right partner. WCI is looking for partners who share our values and ethos, and who share our vision for holistic education and excellence in all areas where great examination results are just the start'.[31]

---

[30] Wasserman, N. (2013), p.59. È. Princeton University Press.
[31] Wellington College International - Partnership Opportunities.

Partners to Avoid

- *Shirkers.* Those who fail to provide you with the necessary relevant information.
- *Con artists.* Anyone providing the wrong, deceptive, or erroneous information, such as a lack of liquidity or upcoming financial outlays.
- *Control freaks.* Individuals who can affect or control the management or administration of another school or educational institution that may conflict with your own, either directly or indirectly.
- *Romeos.* A potential partner who holds several shares/interests in other schools or acquires them during the process of starting your school.
- *Career criminals.* Anyone prohibited by law from holding such a role they claim to hold; criminal convictions not spent, or who has received one in financial regulation, or business regulations and is currently under investigation for such matters.
- *Racketeers.* Any individual or group of companies who are prohibited from conducting business in any country.

Professional Advice On Business Partners

From an ethical and pragmatic perspective says Chris, 'work out who you can do business with. Almost certainly, as a newly appointed international Principal/CEO, you can expect to be the subject of some curiosity from board members and, if my experience in China is anything to go by, be ready for heavy rounds of socialising to build up trust. Learn as much as you can beforehand about the cultural norms and expectations of such events'.

A commercially competitive market means that you may be involved in the endless search for business survival or market advantage through attracting new investment partners to the company or the school – this has been my experience. At first, I resented the intrusion on my leadership time in school, especially since the majority of time was spent speaking to people from outside of the educational sphere. It wasn't helped by my inability to communicate meaningfully in the host language. On one occasion a school owner turned up unexpectedly and I had five minutes to make sure the school day could run smoothly before being whisked on a three-hour journey to a gruelling round of meetings! Expect the unexpected and build up your resilience.

There is, however, another way of looking at it: being involved in the process of seeking out partners can prove to be a rich source of information about the context in which your school operates – an opportunity to sharpen the focus of your messages for students and parents as you read the currents blowing through the education world. Taking part in business meetings, conducted entirely in the host language, is a crash course in improving your ability to communicate your ideas in that host language and present yourself in culturally acceptable ways. Relish that challenge. This will improve your relationship with the school owners, who will come to respect you and ask for your opinions of the prospective partners. Only the hard work of learning to read all of the signals in a meeting – verbal and non-verbal – develops your 'gut instinct' for choosing the right partners.

It's also an opportunity for you to articulate and discuss your school values. Asking, 'Is this the right investor for our school?', leads your owners back to values-led decision-making and means that you can focus their understanding on what you are trying to achieve through the school. When sharing your vision for the school with potential investors, engrain your vision into the thinking and vocabulary of the school owners. As I remind myself, the winners of getting this right are the teachers and students who stand to benefit from improvements in resources and facilities.

A Successful Approach To Choosing The Right Partner
Arlo Kipfer, former Consultant – School Establishment & Legal for the International Schools Consultancy (ISC), suggests to 'Identify the right local partner: invest a significant amount of time and do your due diligence on any potential red flags, such as too rapid growth, design flaws in existing schools, or a lack of voice in decision-making'.[32] Approaches to reducing the risk of corruption and to increase transparency in your new school should also include:

- Having a strategy in place, agreed upon and shared between stakeholders.
- Ensuring your school and its governance understand its oversight role.
- Funding and its disbursements are planned, transparent and include the publishing of payment schedules in the local press, local communities, and school websites.
- Quality baseline data/information (with detailed initial costs) used to evaluate ongoing estimates.

---

[32] Harris Sliwoski - So You Want to Start an International School? Legal Structure and Local Partner

- Standardised contracts for each hired company with stringent record keeping.
- Ongoing site supervision from suitably qualified professionals, with clear reporting lines, and responsibility for monitoring and verifying personnel and materials used.
- Adequate training and support for people on the start-up team to optimise their performance against your objectives.
- A 'whistleblowing' policy that allows for the reporting of suspected corruption, without fear of reprisal and retaliation.

Negotiating The Right Business Deal

Challenge
Schools often enter into contractual agreements with partnering schools and/or investors only to learn to their horror of underlying obligations or a lack of decision-making and brand autonomy that can hamper recruitment and operation.

Solution
Choose the right deal structure that places the school and its long-term sustainable future at its core.

What Research Tells Us
International schools have historically used a variety of business models when opening a new international school overseas. Here, ISC Research, in its 2020 White Paper, lays out options that are available to schools looking to develop an overseas presence.

Model	The School	Strengths/ Limitations
Direct investment	Provides funds to build a new school, distribution, to establish/further its presence in the host country.	High risk / high reward Increased competition may force the least productive local companies out of business.
Brand/license	Provides an existing brand name/image and a fee is negotiated for its use.	Risk to reputational damage.
Management/ franchise combination; ('manchise')	Increases brand visibility with royalties tied in. Preserves management/overall school control.	Lower risk, management schemes & requirements provided. Quality of staff hard to monitor.
A joint venture, also known as a co-operative agreement.	Partners with an investor who is usually based in the new school's country. Generally, assumes responsibility for education management. A certain level of control over the school brand, school ethos, and the teaching and learning. The investor forms the property company, provides capital, then manages the land and building development.	Shared resources/gain new expertise or insights. JVs are not permanent arrangements/ not taking long-term risks. An exit plan which may affect a school's reputation. Companies can sell their shares of a JV (if applicable).
A service agreement or management contract	Provides the management of teaching and learning, \ supplies features of the curriculum. Introduces brand elements: house system, extra-curricular activities, aspects of brand ethos, higher education pathway guidance, and staff development to new/established school. The school's brand name is discreet and typically not used within the name of the partner international school. Currently, one of the only development models possible for foreign independent school brands wishing to benefit from the huge demand for premium brand learning by Chinese families in China.	Saves time & resources/provides expertise. The risk is low and the brand name is not jeopardised, while the return can still be very favourable for the founding school. Loss of control / risk of reputational damage/conflict of interest.

Figure 1.2. Business models for opening international schools.[33]

[33] Adapted from ISC Research White Paper, 2020.

The Legal Structure of Your Deal

It is paramount that you have a legal structure/framework for your deal that protects the sustainable interests of the students, staff, and the local population that the school serves. The first consideration is the deal structure. Whether it is a franchise, shareholder agreement, sponsorship, or structured retreat, take the time to make sure the arrangement suits the school, its students, and the local context. If you plan to withdraw all international aspects of the school by a certain time and the school does not have sufficient leadership capacity, your brand may be seriously damaged. The second aspect is Intellectual Property. It is standard practice for leaders and teachers to bring former ideas, thinking around policies and strategic ideas to their new schools. Many leaders and staff are not consciously made aware that curriculum resources, lesson plans, and professional development materials are the property of the school where they have been developed. Ensure staff understand this when they join – not when they leave. To avoid confusion as a new Founding Principal, you may want to forewarn your new employer that the child protection and safeguarding training you will bring is the same one you have delivered for the previous twenty years.

Remember: Schools not only own their own brand's proprietorial and intellectual property, but also yours, whilst working for them.

Barriers To Negotiating The Right Deal:

- *Lack of focus.* You may focus your negotiation with one local partner, only to be distracted by compliance issues you may struggle to meet.
- *Emotional instability.* Negotiations can be protracted, tiresome, and in some cases, incredibly boring. You'll need to stay the course.
- *Misaligned vision and values.* If your vision and the values of what successful international education looks like aren't a good match – walk away.

How To Negotiate Successfully

Step 1: Research

Successful negotiations happen due to the exchange of added value. A perfect 'win-win' negotiation rarely takes place. The key to preparation is acquiring sufficient information on what adds value and thinking in the shoes of your counterpart. Knowing what gives value to your counterpart is critical. Many things you could offer may be worthless to them. Remember:

- Analyse and research your counterpart and consider the fact they may not express what they truly want as a strategy to confuse you during the negotiation.
- Understanding the cost to your counterpart of fulfilling your demands is another crucial but often overlooked part of your research. Ensure you know your counterpart well enough and know the limits to their abilities.
- Research local policies and ensure that the deals you negotiate are compliant. Sometimes your counterpart may suggest and give you something non-compliant during the negotiation in exchange for your resources.

Step 2: Preparation
Successful negotiations often bring massive value to the organisation, but preparation can be time-consuming, so allow plenty of time and use it well. Once you have researched the values, put your findings on paper, weigh them against each other, and use the following formula to see if it is worth it for your counterpart.

Benefits that you offer − Cost to satisfy your demands = Negotiation value for your counterpart

If you fail to reach a positive negotiation value for your counterpart, you may need to find more things to offer or be prepared to give up on some of the things you demand.

- Write a negotiation plan and prepare to give up some of your wants to fulfil the most important ones.
- Prepare decoys for your negotiation. Decoys are things that offer little value to you and could cost your counterpart greatly to fulfil. Giving up on decoys is an easy strategy to show your counterpart your commitment to making things work without compromising on important things you want.
- Prepare for some of the hardest questions you are likely to face. Discuss them, write them down, and role-play them with each other.

Step 3: Negotiating
Negotiating is often more emotional than rational, but the one who lets their emotions win loses the deal. On the day(s) of the negotiation, ensure you stay rational and stick to your plans. Negotiations can be tiresome and it can be tempting to derail when your counterpart offers you new things. It rarely benefits you. Use empirical evidence with sound judgement and industry experience, not one over the other, while assessing your

counterpart's deals. Remember, your counterpart could also use decoys to make you feel like they are giving up a lot to satisfy you. Experienced negotiators often sway you away from the deal you want. Stick to your plan and prevent yourself from being dominated by your counterpart and getting the worst end of the negotiation.

Bear in mind that, most of the time, initial negotiations do not amount to anything. Successful negotiations could happen after rounds of failed negotiation attempts. Giving both parties a short 'cooling off period' is far better than realising you've made a mistake further down the line. Finally, analyse the reasons for the failed negotiation and ensure you further research during these cooling-off periods to win the next one.

Compliance

Challenge

Compliance issues are far and wide and extremely significant for international schools. Failing to professionally assess your compliance risks can leave you open to litigation, and encourages staff to actively complete cases of recrimination against you.

Solution

You must develop a deep understanding of the compliance and regulations that the school and its compliant context are required to follow within a jurisdiction.

What Research Tells Us

There is a very useful document published by the Committee of Private Education (CPE) in Singapore. This document gives detailed guidance on the standards required for setting up and developing a successful school. Although it is focused on Singapore the same principles can be applied elsewhere. The CPE was set up to protect customers for private, international education and ensure that Singapore schools have strong enough organisational structures and systems to be successful for at least the four-year cycle of their review (and hopefully beyond).

Factors That Increase Your Risk Of Non-Compliance

- Lack of local legal knowledge, frameworks, and procedures.
- The knowledge, skills, and abilities of the Founding Management Team are weak.
- As Principal/CEO you fail to assess your own ability in the area of compliance.
- A lack of knowledge, skills, abilities, and other characteristics (KSAOs) on your founding team represents a lack of intellectually divergent thinking.
- Failing to engage the right legal and Human Resources counsel.
- Lacking evident documentation and record keeping in the founding process is indefensible and will not withstand any possible legal challenges it may encounter.

Professional Advice On How To Remain Compliant – Matt Hall, Director of Learners' Acquisitions, Nexus International School, Singapore

Before you set foot in any building or have your first conversation or interview with potential recruits, you must begin to develop your understanding of the compliance issues of the educational context you will be working in. The way a school sets up its approach to compliance has to be based on the structures and systems put in place to enable compliance to have shared ownership by all members of the school community, but ultimately as Principal/CEO, the buck stops with you. Visually share the processes, vision, and policies using cloud-based systems that are visible and updated continuously. Set up the process first – the systems for making and reviewing policies and having policies (visible) as your Standard Operating Procedures (SOPs). By having cloud-based systems, people can always put their finger on the most up-to-date policy; you can track the changes and history of that document – incredibly important in a court of law – should you later have to rely on such a document. If you have a policy bank, it is easy to review and access. This is incredibly important in a school.

It is critical that you understand the jurisdiction from within which the school is operating. One has to realise that there are large corporate consequences for not understanding (in-depth) the laws and regulations for how a school is to operate within a jurisdiction. Investors provide a large amount of equity into a school project and it is the Principal's responsibility as the CEO to ensure they are followed. The jump that we now have to make and understand is that private education is in a corporate landscape. As Principal/CEO, you must understand as that you have legal responsibilities and can be held accountable for those. Saying 'I did not know' or 'I was unsure' is simply not acceptable in a court of law. The power of humans is in our shared wisdom, so use it wherever you can to support you and your school in your current and future compliance issues.

Key Note

The UAE Private schools' policy and guidance manual has a policy on 'Official Photos and the UAE Flag and National Anthem'.[34] It sets out whose photograph should appear prominently, where, and in what order. Consequences for not following the correct procedures are in the worst cases likely to be severe.

To Remain Compliant

- Before you create the rules/policies, set up the structures and systems (SOPs) first. They will outline the processes and systems and the review process for them.
- Always seek the experience of a professional expert who has a deep understanding of the compliance and regulation issues in the country in which you are operating.
- Be sincerely open in admitting what you don't know rather than adopting a mindset that you have 'been there and seen it'.
- Ensure that the skill sets of your board include professional experience in the legal profession.
- Engage professional accreditation service providers to increase the rigour of your curriculum and its compliance.
- Embrace cloud-based computing systems for school-wide viability and ease of ongoing review.

CASE STUDY – RUSSIA

Several international schools, both English medium and bilingual (using a blended curriculum), have been forced to close their campuses due to a decline in student numbers. It remains to be seen how schools will adapt their assessment and examination models. Should you choose to open an international school in areas of certain political and geopolitical unrest, will your model be robust and be able to see the school through certain key critical global and political moments in time?

---

[34] Abu Dhabi Education Council Private Schools – Policy and Guidance Manual 2014-15.

Governance and Leadership

The Right Governance Model

Challenge
Many schools will operate outside of board models and their structures that you may be used to. This will likely cause a deep-seated distraction, whereby accountability lines become blurred, leading to the potential undermining of the principal's role, where both the board structure and its professional behaviours are unclear.

Solution
Ensure that conversations take place between yourself and the individual you perceive to be the central underlying figure of authority in your school around how the board will operate and who will be accountable for what; the roles and responsibilities of either party should be in writing.

There are multiple models of governance and each comes with its advantages and disadvantages. Corporate-style boards operate very strong structures, where normal members of the public can be approached to sit on a school's board. Here, board members may have some relationship with the school and are somehow either directly or indirectly connected to the school. They know the school from an external lens. 'For-Profit' Schools are often made up of professionals, CEOs, and MBA graduates.

Effective (international) school governance is underpinned by several key responsibilities, including:

- Recognising, connecting with, and promoting an effective school culture.
- Ensuring the clarity of strategic intentions and their implementation, measurement, and progress towards the school vision.
- Ethically holding leaders to account for the school's performance, the educational achievements of students, and the management of staff.
- Providing financial and legal oversight, ensuring a school uses its people and economic resources effectively.
- Representing a variety of stakeholders, including parents, students, staff, and the wider community.

Will Your School Even Have A Governance Model?

- A lack of priority towards the need for a professional board may see it operating as a 'company' with reporting lines and management-style structures.
- The personal interests of the founding owner or group – who may have tenure of a school site – but does not want the oversight of the school to be handed over to a group of people due to the fear of profitability being compromised.
- A lack of professional awareness of school governance may lead to differences of opinion on the need for a board and how a board should be structured.

What Do You Want Your Board To Look Like?

In a Founding School, you may end up inheriting the board model that your owners have operated under in their existing business ventures. In such cases, the owner(s) themselves may not even be aware of the need for a governance model, and the company itself may have nothing to do with education. This may have the advantage of allowing you to clearly articulate what a new and more effective model of governance looks like, and how it might work. The vast majority of our international schools have their own very tight model of governance, which suits how they intend to operate. Family-owned schools can be multi-faceted and layered, and as Principal/CEO, you may not even get to fully explore and uncover these levels during the time you serve, and some may even be deliberately withheld from your eye.

In an increasingly corporate and profit-oriented environment, people who sit on your school board must be people of figure and influence, who can not only affect how your school operates but also have enough influence to gain support for the school and its strategic intentions. This may be at local, regional, or even national government level. You need people who can communicate with the public. If these people have educational backgrounds and are passionate about education, then it can work, but it is not a prerequisite. Next, you need someone who has a good understanding of the legal framework in which your school operates or is likely to operate in, in the future. The third specific skill a board needs is a specialty in finance – to hold the school accountable for its financial decisions. There should also be someone who can liaise with a variety of stakeholders, including most importantly, government educational departments. Finally, your board model needs to include someone who is committed to the fundraising and long-term sustainability of the school. These five roles are crucial to the board structure that you choose to implement.

As a principal, it may seem that negotiating with your owner to choose a board portfolio that allows for the best people to be part of the board is the ideal scenario, but in reality, it may just be a pipe dream. Learning to play the cards you are dealt is not just important, it is critical, especially as a breakdown in relationships between a school board and principal is likely to be the leading factor that your tenure and overall longevity at the school will depend on.

As the CEO of an international schools group involved in the start-up of schools around the world states:

> From a licensor point of view, we establish our governance model that suits our values and our type of school and when we are approached by a partner, we explain that to them ahead of any further negotiations about a contract. A partner might come to us and want us to do it all and we would say 'no'. Some people are investors who want to broaden their portfolio. We advise and we guide with that, but the operations are delivered by people who can deliver and protect what the overall brand is trying to achieve and stands for.

Ask yourself, will your governance model (or lack of it) protect and support your school's value system and overarching philosophy? How will you handle the situation if the governance model acts against your core beliefs?

Key Questions To Consider What Board Model Is Right For Your School

- What is the appropriate size of the board in the context of the school?
- What expertise do the board members bring to the school?
- Is the school a for-profit or not-for-profit?
- What is the rationale for the existence of the board?
- What is the relationship of the board with the Principal going to look like?
- How would the board evaluate themselves (as well as the Principal)?

Make sure sustainability is embedded in all of your considerations.

Governors' Skills Audit
Here, we contextualise each of the five areas of governing body skills and behaviours specific to your international school start-up. You may wish to further develop these within your context.

Skill in focus	Behaviours that support them
Organisational Foundation & School Culture	• Make sure that sustainability is fully understood and reflected in your school's purpose, value, and mission.
School purpose, value, and mission	• Create a culture of sustainability and communicate it with your community and stakeholders.
School sustainability culture	• Implement third-party sustainability inspections to better understand your practice level and get professional advice.
Sustainability audit	• Build sustainability into your education vision. Be very clear about why we educate and what we want to contribute to a more sustainable world.
Education vision	
Sustainable business	• Remember that what you are doing is a sustainable business. Don't do bad things with good purpose, e.g., an overemphasis on green utopia while neglecting a well-functioning school.
	• Have a sustainable finance model to continue providing high-quality education.
Strategy & Implementation	• Put sustainability into strategy consideration, especially the Board of Directors strategy, from the very beginning, to develop full authority on the topic.
Sustainable strategy	
ESG policy	• Create a thorough code of conduct linked to ESG (Environmental, Social, and Governance) elements and match related actions with individuals and the annual plans that support them with detailed actions.
Clear role and responsibility for sustainability	• Have someone whose role is to ensure sustainability is discussed and paid attention to everywhere and at all times.
	• Hold the school and its leaders objectively to account against the school's mission, vision and core values
Accountability	• Annual performance reviews should add at least one clear item related to sustainability to ensure it is on everyone's agenda and calendar.
Performance	
Sustainability (ESG) governance structure	• Set up a robust sustainability (ESG) governance structure to make sure that the strategy, policies, and plans can be delivered effectively with traceable performance indicators and monitoring.
Annual disclosure and communication	• Create an annual reporting system which discloses all aspects of sustainability-related performance and communicate the findings to the whole community to get feedback and support which inform a cycle of continuous improvement.

Skill in focus	Behaviours that support them
Compliance – Financial & Legal Oversight	• Include all risks and performance data in your annual report. Aim for transparency in communicating achievement and areas of focus.
ESG performance	• Be very careful about sensitive areas in data security and privacy.
Data security	• Keep a close eye on local government policy and work to gain more support to have an even greater impact.
Government affairs	
Managing Stakeholder Relationships	• Join and build up a sustainability network for sharing best practices and enlarging positive impacts. • Add climate and environment into the stakeholder list, of who you need to put attention on.
Sustainability practice sharing	• Be honest and transparent about what you achieve and plan to do. Avoid 'Greenwashing' and commit to continuing improvement, which will bring you a long-term sustainable community instead of a short win.
Think bigger on stakeholders	
Transparency	• Take advantage of students, parents, and your community's good will. Everyone is willing to do good things.
Win-win	

Figure 1.3. A Governors Audit for Sustainability

A Founding Educational Consultant Team Member commented:

> When we set up the school in Spain as part of the school's IB accreditation process, we were fully aware that the model of governance we would have to establish, to meet the requirements of the IB organisation and, ultimately, have a school that functions with education as its core purpose. We set up an interim board at the start of the school but were quite dismayed when the board was disbanded by the school's owner, who took on the role of chief decision-maker for the whole project. The decision had a serious detrimental effect on the whole future of the school and its ongoing success.

Get The Right Leadership Team

Challenge

International school start-up teams can if not careful, quickly become bloated, with too many opinions. Engaging a consultant is sometimes done at the wrong time.

Solution

'The core group should consist of people who can work together and who complement each other's backgrounds and work styles'.[35]

Research tells us, of early studies into leadership behaviours, notes Yukl, 'The attention to Leadership behaviours directly concerned with encouraging and facilitating change did not get much attention'.[36] A 2001 study of 87 Portuguese teams across industries found that, when operating under high levels of pressure to innovate, sizeable teams have poorer team processes than sizeable teams without a large necessity to innovate. Unnecessary pressure on your start-up team to deliver may be inhibitive. The New Zealand Rugby 'All Blacks' team currently has a 76%-win percentage. Its success was unrivalled and its 15 'mantras' have been routinely discussed amongst leadership theorists. The existence of core shared beliefs amongst a stable team was found to be a key ingredient of this success. Creating a learning environment and keeping a 'blue head' in the thick of busy international school planning will be vital to your success.[37] 'Don't try to do it alone. Build a team of people who share your vision… Start small and spend at least a year just planning'.[38]

Barriers To Getting The Right Leadership Team in Place:

- Lack of understanding of the scope and responsibility of start-ups and the time constraints involved.
- Budget – Executive searches are costly and time-consuming.
- Increased international school competition for leadership places.
- The fluidity of the market – those involved with start-ups often move on to other start-ups or more established schools.

---

[35] Lake, Winger, and Petty, 2002. P. 13
[36] Yukl, G. (2012), p.67 Effective leadership behavior: What we know and what questions need more attention. *Academy of Management perspectives*, 26(4), 66-85.
[37] Growth Faculty 15 Mantras For Winning Like The All Blacks At Team Culture: James Kerr's Legacy
[38] Lake, Winger, and Petty, 2002. P. 13

Professional Advice On Start-up Leadership Teams
When establishing your core start-up leadership team, take extra time to ensure that your team is aligned, shares the same vision, and has values that are closely interconnected. Some international schools have attempted to do this via psychometric testing. Such tests are designed to gather information on whether people and their personalities are a good fit for each other. There is, however, one deep flaw in such a process if it is used as an overall guiding strategy – it relies on the ability of those administering it to understand and interpret the results generated. Testing and its results may be a part of your overall strategy, to develop the right cultural and values fit for your team members, but always look beyond what the data is telling you.

Be aware of how your own bias can weaken your school's leadership team and undermine the philosophy and values you intend to promote. Affinity bias – the tendency to place higher moral value on those who resemble ourselves in terms of experience, thinking, or membership of professional associations – will damage your school start-up diversity by creating a team of individuals who think and act the same at almost every juncture. As the Principal at British International School – Muscat, Kai Vacher always reminds me, 'Have the confidence to surround yourself with people who are better than you in what they do and how they do it'.

Founding International School Principal Malcolm Phillips advises,

> Ensure you have a team and don't assume because the school is small, that you can do a large amount of the work yourself... The principal's role needs to include oversight of the larger picture and not necessarily always get embroiled in the day-to-day management of the school ... spend too much time on the day-to-day operational management of your staff and students in a start-up and you may compromise your position as the overall figure of authority... The leadership team in a start-up need to have clearly defined roles and staff need to understand what these roles are. In each start-up school, these will be contextually different.

How To Build An Outstanding Start-up Leadership Team

- Establish your core values, focus on what kind of school you want to be and what kind of people you want your students to be.
- Reach agreement with the investors and management about whether the school will be inclusive or selective.
- Establish, agree, and communicate standards of behaviour and performance, then set the highest expectations of yourself and others in how you achieve these.

- Hire for skills that can complement and support each other – such as relational trust; then place a high degree of emphasis on it.
- Identify the needs of your team and provide the best training, development and workplace coaching that you can – especially to leaders in senior positions.
- Anticipate conflict and use it positively as a learning opportunity – deal swiftly and objectively with those who undermine your values and direction.
- Foster individual passion for your shared purpose; gradually increase freedom.
- Communicate your expectations with endless consistency.

> **Serious about sustainability?** Put it at the heart of the Leadership Team's work: how will each member of the team implement sustainability in their personal leadership practices and in terms of making the team itself sustainable?

Determine Your Leadership Options

Top leaders are flipping the hierarchy upside down. Their job isn't to be the smartest people in the room who have all the answers, but rather to architect the game board where as many people as possible have permission to contribute the best of their expertise, their knowledge, their skills, and their ideas.[39]

A decision that faces you is whether to adopt a flatter leadership structure, typically associated with distributed leadership, or a more hierarchical structure with clearer and stronger lines of authority and control, say Chris. It's an issue about vision and your leadership principles which means that you will have to give the context careful consideration. The competence of the leadership team available to you is key. Distributed leadership promotes autonomy and independent decision-making. Are members of the leadership team ready for this degree of responsibility? To begin with, you may need to centralise authority and use a 'command and control' hierarchical model. You can use a phased model, planning a transition from the 'steep learning curve' of the first two or three years, towards a 'mature' leadership structure when routines, practices and standards are embedded. I have followed this process in my post in Beijing, systematically developing leadership capacity around me until I know it is right to delegate responsibility and accountability.

---

[39] Ancona, D. G., Backman, E., & Isaacs, K. W. (2015). Two roads to green: A tale of bureaucratic versus distributed leadership models of change.

It is paramount that you reflect on and systematically evaluate the effectiveness of your leadership structure. Constantly changing positions and personnel is something to avoid in school leadership teams. Staff, students and the community need absolute clarity about who is responsible for what aspect of the school's delivery systems and the time to develop relationships of trust with them. A systematic review on an annual basis will help you to answer two critical questions: 1. Are leadership areas of responsibility aligned with the needs and priorities of the schools and their community? 2. Are the post-holders in these areas of responsibility having sufficient impact and improving outcomes? If the evidence suggests the answer to these questions is no, timely action is needed before the rot sets in and your school culture is damaged.

Learning and 'a culture of learning' should be central to both your vision and your leadership practice. In my UK headship, I rewrote the job description for every post within the leadership team to include a reference to learning and key learning-centred actions for that post, *including* the school HR and Business managers. This meant that evaluations were required to demonstrate evidence about the degree of impact on creating the conditions for effective learning across the school. This strategy also gives a powerful prompt to your school's Board, who involve themselves in discussions about the quality of learning whenever they meet with members of your leadership team, where the job description can help focus their reviews.

There are powerful arguments for considering 'Environmental Citizenship' based around the Sustainable Development Goals of UNESCO to be the most effective paradigm for environmental education. And we would advise a 'warp and weft' implementation strategy of incorporating delegated responsibility for key aspects throughout the leadership team alongside a clear leadership role at a senior level to ensure momentum on the issue and consistency across the whole organisation.

Make something critical to the effective leadership and management of the school the subject of an external evaluation. Staff may feel more comfortable sharing complaints about weaknesses in decision-making processes with a third party, rather than you or their line manager. Equally, on the other hand, talk up the process with your team, as well as the outcomes. Where it is clear that distributed leadership has contributed to better outcomes, celebrate the process and the efforts of those involved, as well as the results. An organisational culture of collective decision-making is not easy. It requires an open and supportive leadership where listening to colleagues is valued. It can be more time-consuming than command and control. It requires leaders at every level who have integrity, trust and respect. It also carries an enormous risk of 'over promise and under deliver'.

The Principal, CEO and Cluster Improvement Partner at GEMS Education, Naveed Iqbal, says of the Founding Principal skills set: '[The Principal] has to be a self-starter and able to start something from scratch (paperwork, write policies, documentation, approvals for regulators, and produce an academic plan etc). You'll need to be organised and compartmentalise your tasks as you're the one in charge.' When it comes to marketing, he asks, 'How are you going to brand your school to maximise student recruitment and do you understand different advertising channels based on your budget?', pointing out that you will need strong project management skills, be able to take calculated risks, and have market awareness in understanding your competitors. He recommends that you ask yourself about your USP – 'What makes us stand out'? Nav also states that 'There's a growing need to understand P&L (profit and loss), the balance sheet, and ensure that shareholders/investors are looked after.' One way to do so, he recommends, is to 'Become a surgeon when it's a turnaround/changes need to be made, or an architect when it comes to the structure of your school'. As Principal, he advises that you'll need to 'Be resilient and able to overcome any imposter syndrome, while gradually building excellence within the school (at the right pace) – being strategic throughout the whole process', noting that having the 'Emotional Intelligence of knowing when you need to focus on being instructional or transformational, is also important.' Finally, he says, 'Go into the business with an open eye. To make improvements and fulfil your requirements, have an honest conversation with yourself – be honest, and be patient'.

SYIS – Start-up Principal/CEO Skills Audit

Wherever you are on your start-up journey/cycle, use this valuable audit to identify where you need help and focus your future hiring on those who can add value and specific skills to your needs.

Skill in Focus	Emerging	Developing	Secure	Substantial
Organisational Foundation				
Build, communicate a start-up school vision, with a clear purpose & direction				
Using, interpreting and responding to appropriate research				
Governance, Business Models & Compliance				
Financial modelling awareness				
Developing short-, medium- and long-term strategic plans				
Infrastructure				
Project Management experience & dealing with timelines				
Design & Build (with a focus on Sustainability)				
Information Management Systems & their context				
Managing a premise that is fit for purpose				
Health & Safety awareness, standards, practices & implications				
Human Resources				
Managing the whole Employee Lifecycle in an international context				
Recruitment, interviewing & finding teachers that believe in your vision				
Managing / minimising staff turnover				
Onboarding / Orientation of new staff				
Developing school culture & wellbeing across students & staff				
Targeted strategic Professional Development to support the school's vision				
Business and Marketing				
Agility for dealing with growth that exceeds expectations				
Parental engagement in a diverse cultural setting				
Competence in a mix of Internal/External Marketing				
Ability to use personal branding to promote the school and its mission				

Skill in Focus	Emerging	Developing	Secure	Substantial
Develop an Admissions Strategy relevant to the school context / selling the school to your customers (parents) to make them believe in your vision				
Educational Programme				
Curriculum design, scope and sequence in an international context				
Inclusivity – systems support flexible/inclusive learning opportunities for all students				
Ability to navigate a wide body of external stakeholders in an international context, including accreditations				
Evaluation of Learning and Teaching and ability to build a learning organisation with constant self- improvement				
Build a Professional Learning Community, growing interdependence through coaching and shared accountability				
Implementation & Accountability				
Manage financial, human and physical resources – sustainably				
Ability to use data to make informed decisions at the right time				
Set & manage expectations, with effective challenging conversations				
School Review of overall strategy & effectiveness				
Management of ongoing change, leading to continuous school improvement				

Figure 1.4 Start-up Principal/CEO Skills Audit

Agree on How You Will Make Decisions

> 'Management is doing things right; leadership is doing the right things'.
> Peter Drucker[40]

Challenge
Making the right decisions (consistently) in our international schools is a very difficult task indeed. The wrong decisions can be costly on many levels.

Solution
Overcome your organisational barriers and improve the overall quality of your decision-making. Separate how you make strategic decisions from operational ones to protect the integrity and sustainability of your school model and its future.

Organisational complexities you face that will impact how you make decisions include profit vs. not-for-profit and competing individual interests, intrinsic motivation; the background of team members; values and motives; personality, culture, and conviction; competencies and credibility; and access to resources.

What Type Of Decisions Are You Going To Make?
Day-to day start-up decisions such as choice of resources, use of space, timetabling and Behaviour models will be your *operational decisions*. Decisions around how your school might develop its curriculum, how you will retain your teachers, or ambitious targets for school growth you set are your *strategic decisions*. Here, we outline several you'll need to be aware of and make in the future.

Operational Decisions

- *Product* – Educational outcomes and curricular decisions. Whole School Behaviour Model. Child Protection and Safeguarding measures and policy.
- *Logistics* – Which services must be immediately in place? Food services, cleaning services, gardening, guards etc. Bussing/transportation for pupils and possibly for staff.
- *IT* – *Systems and models* that serve curriculum (are policies in place?); administrative needs, attendance, assessment, testing,

---

[40] Drucker, P. (2009). Management is doing things right: Leadership is doing the right things. In *US Naval Institute Proceedings* (Vol. 135, No. 4, p. 96).

tracking etc.; staff needs – planning/exposition etc. Communication needs – staff, parents, community and marketing.
- *Finance* – Process, policy and practice. Checks and balances, separation of roles. Preparation for audit.
- *Marketing* – School tours (will this affect the day-to-day running of the school or children's progress?); Open Houses, Exhibitions and School Fairs; Community Communication, and involvement; Memberships (Consuls/Chambers of Commerce/National groups/Expat organizations, etc.); and Principal talks/lectures.
- *Service* – Creating a place within the local community and getting to know them. Building trust for mutual benefit. Building trust for pupils to provide community service and volunteering opportunities.

Strategic Decisions

- *Product* – How will the academic programmes develop and serve both the school's vision and its mission long term? University Counselling and Careers Counselling – at what point are they brought on board? Are long-term systems, rewards and processes being considered – Houses; Prize Giving, Awards, Scholarships and Exhibitions, Events planning – and how will they affect timetables and the calendar?
- *Logistics* – Are companies and services offering the best value for money and service? How will they grow over 1, 3 and 5 years? Do premises issues impact the use of services? How can this be planned for and when do plans need to be put into place?
- *IT* – Are initial systems sustainable? Can they support growth (pupil numbers, staff growth, building expansion, change in focus/needs etc? Will additional services be needed and when?
- *Finance* – Are financial targets in place? Are they achievable, realistic and appropriate for the school's planned expansion? What is the plan for unexpected losses or economic downturn/Force Majeure/tragedies etc? Are insurance policies in place – what is statutory, what is good practice, and what are regional or local expectations or requirements?
- *Marketing* – What processes are being put in place to gather information and build historical data to support marketing over time? What phases/types/changes to marketing will be needed over one, three and five years?

Remember

- Everyone needs clarity on how decisions will be reached and by whom.
- Diverse decisions promote inclusivity / narrow decision-making increases risk.
- Plan to distribute your leadership and create independence as soon as time allows.
- Use your mission to support your decision-making process.

Strategy
In simple terms, the "strategy engine" is driven by four questions:

1. Where should we compete in the future? (The future space we will operate within).
2. How should we compete in the future?
3. What should we be doing?
4. How we should be doing it?[41]

Professional Advice On Decision-Making
In the early phases of a new school, there are many challenging decisions to make and little time to make them. You may find yourself working with a school owner or board that looks to you to quickly deliver on promises you made at the interview. The temptation to 'command and control' will be strong and, at times, highly necessary. Inevitably, collective decision-making is impossible at times. Your job is to quickly ascertain what decisions need more support and where you can 'press on'. Planting the seeds of distributed leadership along the way should be your goal. Remember that habits quickly become 'the way we do things around here' and your team will adapt to an environment of dependency on you for all decisions if not careful.

You need a clear organisational structure and a written code for organisational consultation which you keep growing and nurturing. Work with HR in appointing people to teaching and leadership posts who are comfortable with this way of working, preferably with previous experience in schools run on distributed lines, but who are also going to support key decisions you will need to take. Work with HR to provide professional development that fine-tunes the consultative skills of your expanding leadership team. As with anything you value, keep it under review.

---

[41] Stowell, C., Centre for Management and Organizational Effectiveness – Strategy vs Operations: Understanding the difference.

360-degree evaluations are a useful tool, offering the led opportunities to critically appraise their leaders and decision-making processes. Beware of 'institutional blindness' – the conviction that distributed leadership is working well, everyone seems happy, and that things are getting done – they may not be. Choose your decision-making processes with care.

The Start-up Decision-Making Model
Put your decisions through the following checklist.

- Does the decision sound like it represents our school mission, overarching philosophy, and the guiding values that support it?
- Is the decision based around the long-term interests of the school, or a short-term need/fix?
- What impact will the decision have further down the line, on those who are likely to work under it?
- What would happen if we didn't make this decision? Is deferring it an option?

IDENTIFY WHERE YOU NEED HELP

When you have completed the skills audit above, and shared the results with your start-up team, set about identifying and recruiting for those skills you are going to need. Areas where you most certainly need help will be:

- Local educational licensing and compliance
- Financial modelling and control
- Marketing and networking
- Building regulations and sustainability
- Cultural norms, complexities, and nuances

The Power Of Conversation
One of the greatest sources of information is those who have been there and done it when it comes to founding schools. Gráinne, for example, has been involved in no fewer than thirteen. Current founding school and retired school principals are a great source of first-hand information, yet they are often overlooked and/or undervalued in favour of elaborate high fee-paying consultancies. Whilst consultancies absolutely do play their part (and we include ourselves in this conversation), some of your initial expenses and outlay can be obviated with high-quality interviews and qualitative research. Hearing the pitfalls, snags and routes to breakeven is

fascinating, as we have discovered in the writing of this book. If you plan to talk to any current or former founding international school principals, the following questions may be of use to facilitate and get the most out of the conversations:

Organisational Foundation

- How much time were you initially given? Did that change – when and why?
- Do you feel you were adequately prepared?
- Was the size of the founding team adequate / did it suit the needs of the project?
- What skills were you initially lacking/how did you address those?

Infrastructure

- How many initial designs did you go through before you decided on the final one?
- Were any costs cut during the project – if so which ones and what effect did they have on the overall quality of delivery?
- How effective was your timeline/ what advice would you give about it?
- How did you choose your information management system and was it the right choice for the size of the school?

Human Resources

- What was the average number of applicants per teacher/leader role advertised?
- In what skills were candidates above/below your expectations?
- What challenges presented themselves during the employee lifecycle that you were unprepared for?
- How successfully did you manage to onboard and orientate your staff? What was most successful and would you do it again?

Marketing

- As principal, how much of your working day was taken up by marketing associated activities?
- How did you establish relationships with parents and build your community after you had signed students up for your school?
- What were the most successful marketing activities that you carried out?
- Was the size of your marketing department right for the size of the school you were aiming to be?

Educational Programme

- Did your chosen curriculum fit the needs of your student population and support the school's overall mission and philosophy?
- Did your teachers have the requisite skills to teach it or were there any mismatches that had to be overcome?
- What metrics did you use to evaluate the effectiveness of Learning and Teaching and how/when did you present these back to the board/owner?
- What professional development and training did you provide your teachers with, and how successful was it?

Opening, Implementation and Accountability

- How did you outline/set expectations to staff of working practices and was it effective? What practices did staff have the most difficulty in adjusting to? What might you do differently?
- How smooth was the school's opening day(s)/ week(s) and month(s)?
- What data did you initially rely on and how did it help you to make the right informed decisions? Would any data you didn't have, been of particular use?
- What tools/systems did you use to review the success of what you were doing and how often was this carried out?

TOP TIP

When you interview a Founding Principal, *always* take the time to ask for follow-up recommendations of individuals that would be good to talk to about Founding Schools, or particular areas of research/concern for which you are looking for high-quality information.

Budgets and Timelines

SET YOUR BUDGET

What Is The Role And Purpose Of Your International Start-Up School Budget?

Your start-up international school budget is unique – it details your school's financial plan for the development period leading to opening, the founding year itself and the subsequent years, about anticipated expenditures and revenues from school places. Your budget is the glue that binds 'the intangible missions, operations and objectives into reality by outlining and providing specific programmes and funding/financial terms'.[42] Effective budgeting provides a demonstrable link between your school's vision for academic excellence or outstanding personal wellbeing and the resources that make them happen. As a start-up, the founding team will be involved in discussions about the programmes, staffing and resources that are all competing for financial resources. The key question around all budgetary decision-making processes in the founding process should be 'What are we trying to achieve?' and then formalising this into overall objectives and the operational/strategic priorities that follow them.

What Are The Major Budget Categories For International School/Bilingual School Start-Ups?

Pre-opening
- Demographic research
- Design & Build/Renovation
- Compliance, Health and Safety
- Staffing
- Curriculum
- IT systems
- Library stocking
- Marketing & Admissions
- School Leadership and Support

Post-opening
- Teaching/Instruction & CPD
- Building maintenance
- Energy & Utilities

---

[42] American Association of School Administrators - School Budgets 101.

- Transportation
- IT licenses
- Library Services/subscriptions
- Food Services
- Facilities management

The Capital Works Budget

This includes any capital works funding and should include all costs concerned with the building project – building-related costs, professional fees and a project contingency. According to the Department of Education and Training in Victoria, Australia, standard budget breakdowns look (approximately) like:

- 65-70% – construction, including site-specific costs, external services and landscaping
- 18% – architects and specialist consultants
- 5% – project management and communications
- 5-10% – project contingencies
- 2% – furniture, equipment and ICT[43]

How Much Does It Cost To Start A New International School?

There is no one answer to this question. We have researched schools whose start-up costs have run from a few million pounds to tens of millions. In one international school alone, the marketing budget alone was over 1 million pounds.

What will affect your school start-up costs?

- Cost of obtaining land/building
- Location
- Infrastructure (e.g., architecture/construction)
- Developing the property
- Target market
- School size
- Academic enrolment programmes
- Educational resources
- Staffing costs
- Recruitment costs
- Marketing costs
- Ongoing maintenance (1-2% of build cost)

---

[43] The Victoria State Education Department, Australia – Everything you need to know about a school building project.

- Additional facilities
- Management systems
- Library (Subscriptions: e.g., Turnitin, *New York Times*, Overdrive)
- Delays based on weather, inspections or accidents
- IT resources – Bring your Own Device (BYOD) or not?
- Head office/franchise/royalty payments
- Accreditations – professional & academic

> **Key Note:** One cost you must absolutely be aware of is: wage costs as a share of total revenue

Chris Seal, Head of Senior – Tanglin Trust, Singapore, comments, 'If not careful, you can spend an inordinate amount of money on marketing and advertising. The key thing is making sure that enrolment and admissions are linked – without which it is hard to understand the value of the money that you are spending'.

What Research Tells Us About Budgets

'Both startups I have been involved in have been quite different in terms of costs'. *John Tighearnan, Founding Head, Wycombe Abbey China*

Build, Rent or Acquire?
With the ever-increasing costs associated with construction and labour, on top of the logistics required in transporting vast amounts of people and their capital across the globe, many schools are choosing to rent and repurpose, or in the case of larger established international school brands, are targeting individual schools to take over and re-brand. Whilst building your campus is the preferred route for many premium school brands, it may not always be the most sustainable or the most profitable.

Repurposing and renovating an existing building
Typical renovation costs involved in the repurposing of an existing campus can range from US$100,000 to US$1,000,000. 'Following a brownfield model allows two things to happen from the onset. It allows you to focus on the programme and the people (team) that you are putting in place', says Ariane Baer-Harper, Head of School at Austin International School, Texas. Secondly, 'You can put as much emphasis on the product you are selling, i.e., the curriculum and its programme, rather than a shiny large campus that potentially you might struggle to initially fill', she adds.

As a Founding Principal in Thailand notes, 'The Catholic Church in

America is routinely held up as the warning for schools. They have ended up property 'rich' and cash poor with countless school buildings that are difficult to market as anything other than schools – not only due to architecture and location, but also, zoning'.

Know Your Costs
Good financial stewardship, management and ongoing discipline are the backbone of your school start-up. Outstanding financial management will enable your school to:

- Make sustainably driven decisions that protect the long-term interests of your school, its people, culture and environment.
- Deploy significant adequate investment to your marketing.
- Invest in technology at the right time that can provide a competitive advantage.
- Pay highly competitive teachers' salaries.
- Make rigorous assessments of teaching models and their loads.
- Grow a yearly surplus, to be used for ongoing maintenance of the school building.

I have often heard the phrase 'there is no budget' from principals before, espousing the words of overconfident school owners, who have no idea how good teachers can be at spending money. If your owner/investor or group of schools operates with this mantra then expect to pay significantly overinflated prices for your contractors, when they get wind of this approach. Poor financial management will hamper all of the above and may mean you have to go cap in hand to your partners/investors and move the breakeven threshold.

Are You Eligible For Any Direct Financial Grant Aid?
As a private entity, it may not be the most obvious question to ask, but given the growing importance of education in economic development around the world, there are many incentives for countries and their local education departments to open international schools in their territories, including attracting wealth and investment, providing highly-skilled jobs and the award of contracts to local infrastructure companies and educational suppliers. You, your CFO, Board members, and Market Research Consultants should quickly scan the market, to see if there are financial incentives that can supplement your investment and minimise the risk in the start-up process. For example, are there:

- Direct tax incentives for starting up in one area compared to another?

- Lower rates of income tax for staff from overseas?
- Financial incentives for developing sustainable technologies?
- Development companies prepared to take the financial risk and provide the capital to secure and build the premises as part of a wider overall development scheme?

How To Prepare Your Budget

Review Any Comparative Data Of Partner Schools (If You Have Them)

If you have partnered with an existing overseas school or are part of a group of schools, use their historical data to assist you in developing your budget, explore historical trends, and identify future funding requirements. Your budgeting team must:

- Review the accuracy of previous budgets, spot any inaccuracies and factors that will improve future accuracy.
- Identify and agree where your partner school may have over/underspent.
- Describe general trends (e.g., salaries rising at 5% in real terms annually).
- Forecast likely areas of academic support to increase overall examination results.

Plan For What You Need

What is your school going to need? Use a multi-scenario approach to identify several different income stream models and their costs, determined by the availability of reliable data from consultants, your partner school and local government educational bureau. You need to consider:

- Procurement – How will you source, negotiate terms and make purchasing decisions? (Many schools have been caught out by signing lengthy technology contracts that add little value to a school beyond an initial cycle).
- Strategic development plans – how will you make decisions on investments?
- Accreditation reports – will you have to factor in recommendations?
- Your target class sizes/pupil numbers in each year and overall capacity.
- Changes to your funding streams (e.g., a downturn in boarding students).

- School Fee structures and incremental rises.
- Staffing costs, including bonus payments and local compliance settlements.
- Local government regulations – including social insurance contributory schemes.

Predictive Forecasting
Budgetary forecasting can be developed over a 2/3 or even 5-year cycle. Plan for what you know is going to happen, for what may well happen, and then plan for what is highly unlikely but could still create an enormous black hole in your budget. Professional and active leadership and governance networks will add security to the upcoming financial decisions you are faced with. Use a probability scenario tool to rank events in terms of their probability of occurring and potential financial impact on your school's overall performance and health.

Budgetary Advice To Those Starting A School
Make sure you and your team have a clear and accurate understanding of the financial procedures that govern the school. Get this in writing – translated into English. The core issue of resources is to establish your role in the resourcing process. Depending on where you are from, you will be accustomed to varying defined roles and procedures to control all aspects of resourcing Such systems may need careful adaptation in an international, private school context.

Whatever system of resourcing and procurement you develop in your context, make sure that there are clear lines of communication for middle leaders to resource their areas of responsibility. The system must be perceived to be transparent and equitable. Simple things can quickly become sources of discontent and poor morale in a start-up – like access to appropriate textbooks or photocopying. Make sure logistical problems in procurement do not impact the most vital part of the chain – delivery in the classroom.

Build A Strong Culture Of Accountability
From the start, emphasise the need for 'value for money' by monitoring the educational impact of resources. Staff might hunger for resources that they have previously used, especially in an unfamiliar international setting. Even if available, these may be alarmingly expensive to import. Insist on strong evidence and that more reasonably priced local alternatives be fully investigated. Behind this, a strong culture of self-evaluation, which requires objective evidence of the 'added value' created by resources will support professional decisions on resource acquisition. A strong culture of 'value

for money' also develops sustainability, so look for ways to reduce wastage. Insist equipment is used to the limits of its working life, without compromising health and safety. Equipment considered no longer useful should be re-cycled appropriately. Involve students in this process, so that they gain first-hand knowledge of sustainability as a key concept in finance and resource management.

Avoid the assumption that once set, the budget will implement itself. It won't. It needs strong oversight and the ability to quickly forecast where additional costs may be necessary and how the school will plan to absorb them. Effective financial stewardship and safeguarding of investor funds means accountability starts and ends with you as principal/CEO. It takes resilience and skill to keep directing investment and budgetary decisions back to the question 'How will this be evident in the classroom and our overall school vision?'

Key Budgetary Questions Your Founding Team Will Need Clarity On

- What accounting style/tools will you be using?
- Is there one system for all?
- Does it take into account the academic year/tax year/fiscal year or calendar year?
- What are the accounting/financial rules/laws in your country regarding auditing?
- What are the checks and balances in place to ensure appropriate money management?
- How are you protected?
- What are your responsibilities and does your role leave you open to the burden or threat of prosecution?
- When will the financial year start/end? What if it is out of sync with your partner schools overseas?
- Are there differing interpretations of financial management procedures according to varying positions of responsibility in the school? How will you overcome these?
- When will you (as principal/CEO) submit your budget for the following financial years?
- Who will audit your accounts and do you have the knowledge, skills and expertise within your school board to ask the right questions about fiscal responsibility?

*Note. Although many new international schools are exempt from local government inspections you may need a plan if your local educational bureau rates your school as 'requires improvement' and removes your ability to increase your school fees.

> **Key Takeaway.** The development of your start-up budget is designed to provide an estimate of future expenditure and the manner in which you will attempt to finance it. Your start-up budget– and all future budgets that you go on to develop – should answer one simple guiding question: Is our financial plan aligned to and supports the overall strategic direction – including our mission and philosophy of the school?

Payroll
When will you pay your staff may sound like an easy enough question, but our research has shown some schools have even been hoodwinked into paying their salaries for work that has yet to be completed. Little wonder the temptation of some staff to disappear without a trace with 2 weeks salary, yet to be earned. Traditional salary cycles are paid in arrears of 4-week cycles; some, pay on the 15th of the month, meaning that teachers must wait an initial 6 weeks for the first pay check – a long wait when you consider the costs of international relocation and setting up a new home. Whatever way you decide to pay your staff and whenever you decide to do it, consider whether your school will be able to set up a monthly direct debit for staff to send money back to their home or point of origin, saving an incredible amount of time and energy. When I worked at a school in China, this was their exact policy, which was very popular among international staff.

SET YOUR TIMELINE

Challenge
Timelines for the design and building of international school construction projects are often held hostage to the local authority and their planning requirements.

Solution
Make sure that you have the required people on the ground during the necessary construction period. Remote construction can be a costly error.

Ineffective Timelines:

- Are loosely managed and adhered to.
- Lack cultural competence, awareness and time needed to foster relationships.
- Have inexperienced procurement processes, leading to delays.
- Lead to increased costs

Professional Advice On Timelines
The typical timeline for starting a new international school, from idea to doors opening is between 2-5 years. Bearing in mind that many Western governments operate in four and five-year political cycles, it can be crucial to get your timing right. Timelines can and do change – frequently. Inclement weather, delays in visa applications and processes, and construction deadlines not being met are all challenges that you will have to face. Remember, international calendars operate differently; people take time off at differing times of the year, with the holy month of Ramadan and Chinese New Year being specific examples of where you may face pressure points. The flip side of this of course is that in Asia, Christmas holidays are not traditionally celebrated, so if your start-up team takes a break over Christmas and key infrastructure workers don't, there may be a delay in meeting key deadlines if a proper communication channel is not established and maintained.

Yvonne Fan, Entrepreneur and Founder of a start-up international school in China, says, 'Always think about timing… the geographic location, essential risks you are likely to face and whether you are going to be able to secure the funding and ultimately the license you require in the time you have' – heady advice.

Large project management is a unique field and one that many Founding International School principals I have researched, have not experienced. Leading a partner school in the UK or US does not equip you with the skills you are going to need in developing a multi-million-dollar school from scratch. Talk to people who have been there and done it, in particular retired principals who worked in the first wave of international schools that have been opened in Asia. Use their critical lens in developing realistic timelines that build in buffers into your timeline. Know how to respond to delays.

Successful Timelines

- Are measurable against the key implementation milestones.
- Appoint someone whose specific role it is to oversee the project timeline.
- Are visually stimulating, which serves to increase accountability and improve collective efficacy towards their implementation.
- Anticipate where the workflow speed might be at its optimum/minimum.
- Are used to celebrate key milestones along the way.

SET YOUR SALARY SCALES

Challenge
International school salary scales are often hidden. This can cause distrust and a sense of inequity among staff.

Solution
Publish your entry-level and leadership-level salaries and the knowledge, skills, abilities and other characteristics (KSAOs) needed to gain them.

Research tells us that international school salaries vary considerably – from US$500 to $5000 a month on average.[44] In Dubai, starting salaries for new teachers are around US$30,000 and for experienced teachers, US$42,000.[45] Compare this to Luxembourg, for example, with salaries in the same bracket of between €70,000 and €120,000 Euros. The international country your school chooses to open in, the ability to attract and retain its teachers, and the successful manner in which you can sell school places are likely to affect your salary scales. Whatever scale you choose to operate, a telling statistic that Premier League Football Clubs in the UK have given us over recent years, are wage-to-income ratios. The stretch of which is between 57% in the lowest case and 98% in the highest.[46] As a general rule of thumb a number of financial lenders observe around 36% as a debt-to-income ratio. Whilst in the initial years of international start-up school it may well be higher, it is certainly something to be aware of, if consistently higher than 50%.

---

[44] Understanding Employment Packages - Edvectus.
[45] Salaries and benefits in international schools – Teacher Horizons.
[46] Wage to income rations in the Premier League - Statista.

Salary Scale Options Available

You may choose to 'lag the market' if your new start-up does not have the financial means to match your competitor schools. This may be a risky strategy, since start-ups and fast-paced environments with habitual change have a reputation for increased turnover. Paying people less to experience more disruption to their workflow may backfire. Matching the market by paying similar salaries, is a safe and secure way to establish your salary scales. Leading the market is a bold and competitive strategy that is often aimed at the recruitment of talent directly from competing international schools. The risk, however, to such a strategy is that it becomes a talent drain, rather than a talent magnet, if teething problems and the school's overall leadership and management structure lacks guide and educational autonomy. Think carefully about your adopted salary model and its wider implications.

What Might Disrupt Your Salary Scales?

- Local inflation or a drop in currency conversion rates.
- The discrepancy between local and international hires' salaries/packages for often the same job – the 'split salary'.
- Paying 'golden candidates' over-inflated salaries that distorts and disrupts your salary scale model.
- A lack of coherence and adherence to your salary scale, where qualification, expertise and skills are misrepresented.
- Local (country employment) laws that supersede contract, including a lack of awareness of the tax implications in the international country of your start-up.

> **Key Note:** Remember – when it comes to getting money out of the country, staff will leave if they cannot get money out quickly and cheaply, no matter how much they love your school/job/country.

Professional Advice On Salary Scales

Will your school have group pay scales in place or will these need to be set up? In designing leadership salary models you'll need to carefully assess when and whether changes in the scope of the role fall within its normal expected boundaries. Certainly, your board/owner should be closely involved in setting appropriate pay for the wide number of leadership roles and in general, the approval of wider salaries and any associated performance-related pay that may be due. You will need to have clarity regarding what room your school has for negotiation, since some staff you have appointed may not choose to accept the terms that you have offered. Certainly, you should be aware of local pay agreements/local employment laws about salary levels – these are easy to fall foul of. Since performance-related pay is still a minefield and arbitrarily impossible to manage at times, it may be in your best interests to simply offer your school staff the best salary model that you can provide.

Failure to provide and articulate a clear description of how leadership pay can be progressed may lead to a potential breakdown in communication and understanding between a principal and school board, particularly if you feel (as Principal) you have done enough to deserve an incremental increase. Take the time to carefully articulate what Key Performance Indicators need to be met – or if not met, will they lead to a salary restriction? In international school start-ups it is highly likely that, as Principal, your salary scale will in some way be tied to the school's immediate growth and development of the school roll. Issues surrounding confidentiality are nearly always an issue, so know how and what to communicate to staff. Finally, have a complete number in your head of what the 'package' is worth, as you'll likely be asked this by savvy school teachers and leaders who easily compare schools and their 'like-for-like'.

To Build A Sustainable Salary Model

- Use forecasting tools to predict best and worst-case scenarios – what might happen if the school closes and has to survive without boarding income?
- Centre all future salary negotiations on the value that individuals demonstrate and add to the school.
- Triangulate data and use empirical evidence to support your decision-making processes.
- Ensure appropriate arrangements are designed and in place for salary reviews.
- Add value to your salary models by negotiating preferential rates for teachers and wider staff upon a range of services they are most likely to benefit from.
- Consistently assess your compliance obligations when it comes to severance pay and employee terminations.
- Make decisions that place the long-term financial sustainable health of your school at the heart of your salary model.
- Use an effective decision-making process that is transparent and defensible that adds to the credibility of your school – not erodes it.

SET YOUR FEE STRUCTURE

Challenge
Yearly and termly fee structures are being placed under growing pressure to adapt to market realities.

Solution
You may well need to adopt a flexible fee structure that gives scope and opportunity to increase, particularly during times of economic uncertainty.

What Research Tells Us
New York City is the most expensive metropolis in the world for international schooling with maximum prices up to US$60,000 per year.[47] International schools across Hong Kong are set to increase their school fees by an average of 4.26% throughout the remainder of 2023.[48] The largest group of schools in Hong Kong – The English Schools Foundation (ESF) – is set to increase that fee even further, by around 4.9%. Foundation chief executive Belinda Greer cites the reason for the increase as being able to attract the world's best staff in an increasingly competitive market. K-12 public schools in the US spend $15,230 per pupil per year.[49] Research from Zurich suggests that the United Arab Emirates (UAE) is the most expensive education destination in the world – costing up to $250,000 beginning with two years of pre-school education and including up to 3 years at a UK university.[50]

Challenges In Setting Your Fee Structure

- Your competitor schools may increase (or reduce) their school fee structure, leaving you with little choice at times than to do the same.
- A lack of high-quality teaching talent may force you to increase your fee-model structure to accommodate the desired teachers your parents demand.

School Fees You'll Need To Consider

- *Application Fee.* Non-refundable. Some schools choose not to or are not allowed to charge. For instance, in China, the Price Bureau

---

[47] International Schools Database – New research reveals the cost of international education around the world in 2022.
[48] South China Morning Post. 19.09.2022 – More than 160 primary and secondary schools in Hong Kong to raise fees by average of 3.7 per cent.
[49] US Public Education Spending Statistics. Education Data Initiative
[50] The cost of education in the UAE? AED1m per child.

stipulates you even have to return school fees when a child leaves. Some parents pay application fees to more than one school at a time, to secure their priority, and wait until a place becomes available. Charge a large enough fee to cover your costs, so you don't end up losing money.

- *Registration Fee.* Otherwise known as the 'admission', 'entrance' or 'enrolment' fee – a one-time fee paid for enrolment. In 99% of cases, this should be non-refundable – but check local guidelines.
- *Deposit.* Paid on acceptance of student enrolment. A minimum international school-wide fee ought to be a terms school fee, although this can vary by the demand for your school places. Ensure this is topped up according to your school fee model/the rate of inflation. Think carefully about your policy on reimbursement and what conditions it is subject to. Make that crystal clear upon entry.
- *Tuition Fee.* The school-wide fee model that you plan to charge. How will you charge? When will you collect the fees and through what mediums and currencies will you accept payment in? Will you accept cash? Most international schools have progressive fee structures – fees climb as students get older, limiting the earning potential of younger years you plan to open with. How will you plan around this?
- *School Development Fee / Building Fund Fee.* Many parents are still surprised to pay this fee and believe it should form part of the overall tuition fee. International school buildings are expensive and the general metric to calculate ongoing repair and maintenance is around 1-2% of the overall building cost per year. Our advice: change the name of this to a 'sustainable transition fee' and show parents how their children will be part of an exciting commitment to sustainability and beyond.
- *ICT / Library / Lab Fees.* ICT fees are common, and are an enormous expense to an international school, considering licensing and software upgrades. Library usage/book replacement fees for lost or damaged books. Be explicit on the charges; follow them objectively and use reminders. Add in delivery charges and where books are part of sets that can only be ordered as such.
- *Extracurricular Fees.* This can be an innovative and reasonably simple way in which a school can attract good revenue streams. Fully vetted external providers may offer STEAM classes or coaching, for which the school offers a premium for the right, as many children may look to develop this interest further outside school.

- *Boarding Fee.* Covering accommodation, supervision, activity and dining costs for the period of stay. Some schools tie themselves up in knots by agreeing to have their boarding houses open during holiday weekends and extended breaks and offer a 24x7 service 365 days a year. If you cannot afford to offer this and don't have the human resources to staff it, then don't overpromise!
- *Other fees* including. Peripatetic/Music/Sports Trips/Educational visits and holidays and dining fees, exam fees, uniforms and transportation. Will you include educational trips as part of the overall fee model? Whilst this may suit the 'top tier' international schools, it may mean you face challenges with pricing of trying to secure residentials at peak times of the year. Have a clear policy and communication of exam fees and for those having to re-sit any. Don't lose money on your school uniforms, so choose whether appointing a suitable external supplier directly will save time, money and effort.

> **Key Note:** If you are serious about your sustainability goals and the commitment you will make toward them, then consider charging a 'sustainable development' fee which deliberately targets all revenues it generates at sustainable practices, audits, carbon reduction and carbon-offsetting. Link any school fundraising activities to this purpose and physically show your customers and future market that you mean what you say and can substantiate with hard facts and physical evidence to prove it.

Important Questions You'll Need To Ask About Your School Fees

- Have we carried out the right research on the market that we plan to enter?
- Has someone independently evaluated our educational product and its value?
- How have we benchmarked the services that we plan to offer against local competitors?
- What currency will we accept our school fees in?
- If you accept in the local currency – how will you insure against substantial devaluation in that currency that may take place during the lifecycle of your planning and opening phases?
- Which global banking systems offer market-leading rates for international monetary transfers?

- How will our school fees adapt to the current/predicted rates of inflation in the country that we plan to operate in?
- How will we communicate our fee structure to parents and how will we deal with disputes around the payment of school fees?

Force Majeure is a standard insurance clause that has been adapted to fit private businesses and schools. It covers the school for acts that are considered outside the norm. For example, during recent tsunamis that have caused huge damage, even schools that were not affected needed to be used as shelters or mortuaries. Many international students went home and businesses closed – earnings, profits and clientele at every level were lost. Normal insurance does not cover this. As a Principal in Malaysia says, 'In the aftermath of Covid, parents asked for school fees back and yet still wanted online teaching – a double whammy for schools. We still had to pay everyone, but our income was decimated and we had extra costs associated with the management of Covid'. Make sure your Force Majeure verbiage is clearly presented, proactively managed, and upfront in your start-up.

Professional Advice On School Fee Issues

Anne Dickinson, Director of Marketing and Admissions at Rugby School, Tokyo, Japan talks us through the considerations you'll need to be aware of about your school fees. She notes that when setting your fee structure there are a lot of variables to consider. 'Think about the value of these services that you offer, including boarding, dining options, school uniform and costs associated with exams and residential trips ... Many schools are choosing to offer an 'all in' model which includes all of the aforementioned costs. This can be an easier way of running your finances'. A downside, of course, she says, is that 'Prices can and do fluctuate in less than yearly cycles. If your school and owners have sky-high aspirations of what your school will become and when, but get the pricing strategy initially wrong, you will lose ground in your marketing and admissions process', adding, 'You want to avoid at all costs a situation where you are forced to lower the cost of your school fees, as this could be construed as an obvious sign that what your school is offering is not value for money'.

Examining other schools and their fee structures is relatively easy and, thanks to websites such as International Schools Database, relatively pain-free.[51] If you are planning to charge above market rates for your school, yet don't have the staff capacity or initially will be faced with challenges in recruiting overseas, think carefully. An ideal position you will

---

[51] Data from the International Schools Database.

want to be in is where you can retain a waiting list of parents, who are prepared to hold a deposit with you, should a school place become available.

'In a new start-up one issue you may be pressed with is your ability to offer reduced/subsidised school places to the children of your employees', says Anne. Certainly, as the school grows, you may be placed under more pressure to move away from this model. Thus, in the founding years of a start-up, the offering of free places to your employees' children is a very wise marketing and recruitment strategy, that you can (and should) demonstrate the value of to prospective recruits.

How To Get Your Fee Structure Right

- Carry out extensive market research on the ground and where possible – visit the schools you will be competing against to understand how they add value.
- Adopt a pricing strategy that allows for realistic growth and the flexibility to increase in your current market.
- Develop a parental focus group that explores price and what parents are prepared to pay for / not prepared to pay for.
- Analyse the mistakes of others. Talk to retired principals about their pricing strategy and its overall success and effectiveness.

BREAKEVEN ANALYSIS

The point at which your revenues are equal to your costs – your *'breakeven'* – will broadly speaking depend on the type of school you are planning to open. Athletes have used mental models for decades, to picture success, replay in their mind how to get there and what they can do to get there. In your own mind and those of the founding senior leadership team, marketing team and board members there needs to be an identified number of students that support the school's journey towards sustainability. Take the time to celebrate every new school entry with staff.

If you plan to open a Primary School or will open primary year groups to parents as part of your overall K-12 strategy, you need to carefully consider the effect it will have on your ability to break even. In a founding school, it is easier to attract parents of students in younger years than it is of higher grade levels. That is because the older children get, the less likely parents are to want to move their children to a newer school that may not yet be accredited or have a secure established reputation for academic success. Opening Grades One to Five presents a far greater risk and will likely take longer to reach breakeven than opening a school at Grades 1-2 in year one; 1-3 in year two and 1-5 in year three.

Breakeven Factor Influences

'It will take five years from your first-year investments for the school to even out. If the school is full after three years, it will take seven years until you'll have a more even flow of investments. If you don't know about that, your school will crash!'. *Peter Heddelin,* CEO, co-founder Amerikanska Gymnasiet, Sweden.

The level of financing and liquidity your school start-up has behind it
What is the overall school construction cost/amount of rent you are required to pay for the school building? How quickly are your investors prepared to wait before you need to use your academic results as part of your overall marketing strategy to attract further students in your higher grades? A positive financial margin gives you flexibility to deal with unexpected expenses.

Here, Gráinne explains:

> Breakeven can at times, be almost impossible to calculate. Generally speaking, high school costs are completely different from Nursery costs. Local/bilingual schools are completely different from international schools. Breakeven is usually based roughly on student income against staffing costs. Staffing costs (on average) make up between 55 to 70% of all costs. Premises (again, each school is different) take up between 10-15% – so, often there is not much left to spend on curriculum! If a school is brand new - all costs are projected ones. You'll need to consider rental, management fees and sometimes 'royalty' fees if renting. If you own your building, the improvement/upkeep and mortgage can be significant. Fewer and fewer companies wish to own school buildings anymore.

A former Founding Head in Saudi Arabia notes: 'Some building companies will pay a big 2-year start-up fee to get a good school brand in an overall development and the school off the ground. Then, when the school is established at the 3–5-year mark (usually 5 years) they have a percentage of the profits. That can be up to 12% in my experience – which was my previous experience in China'.

School Structure

AGREE ON YOUR SCHOOL STRUCTURES

How Will Students be Organised?

'When it comes to school structures, the entire structural system is based on the adult's needs and not based on how our students learn best'. *Peter Heddelin*

In any start-up school, the opportunity presents itself to do something different – to be innovative and challenge practices that have remained the same since we started educating our students. Year groups and Grade Levels represent one such opportunity. Given what we know about the impact of differentials and summer birthdays on rates of learning, why not consider breaking your learners into 6-month blocks instead of 12 months in the earlier years? At the same time, why not present collaborative learning opportunities for students to work across more than one grade level in subjects such as Music, Art and IT – subjects where age can often have no boundaries?

CASE STUDY

Harrow School 'Is organised into four sections: Early Years, Pre-Prep, Prep and Senior School, within which is the Sixth Form. The Head of Pre-Prep oversees Years 1-4, the Head of Prep School manages Years 5-8, while the Senior School comprising Shells (Year 9) to Upper Sixth (Years 9-13) falls under the direct remit of the Director of Studies and Senior Housemaster'. (harrowshanghai.cn)

What Are Your Options?

- Can year groups overlay with each other in certain subjects, e.g., Art and PE?
- Are you able to offer some remote or hybrid learning for senior students once a month like Flex Ed, something Kai Vacher at the British School, Muscat has employed?

- Will you have morning tutor/homeroom time, or could this time be used for other purposes?
- Which year/grade/levels will form what aspects of your school?

Give deep consideration to bilingualism and the critical role of languages in learning. Across the curriculum, the learning capacity of your students will be closely correlated with their increasing competence in the two or more languages of the school. In a majority multi-lingual school in the UK, "I found the post of *Literacy Across the Curriculum Leader* vital in developing consistent high standards and expectations across every subject team", notes Chris Nash.

How Will Staff Be Organised?

Challenge
Start-up school structures can be too top-heavy at times with a lack of effective middle leadership.

Solution
Choose your school's structure and leadership model around your current school's curriculum model, size (that allows it to scale) and bottom line. Allow staff to progress and build your ability to retain your staff.

Barriers To Getting The Right School Structure:

- Challenges you face in filling recruitment may mean teachers and leaders must perform a wider range of duties than advertised and expected.
- Small changes in staffing structure suddenly become big, whole-school changes that unsettle an international workforce very quickly.
- Primary and Secondary school staff structures in K-12 schools can be very distinctly separated.

Key start-up appointments are:

- Principal/CEO (or whatever name is preferred)
- Head of Admissions (often one role) with marketing
- Head of Marketing

- Head of HR
- Head of Premises

A generous start-up budget may also include Academic Heads such as:

- Head of Upper School
- Head of Lower School
- Head of Prep
- Head of Early Years
- Cambridge Officer, IB Coordinator

To Get The Best School Structure

- Hire around the curriculum model, size of the school and bottom line.
- Weave sustainability through the job description of every employee, and especially through leadership posts to ensure accountability and delivery.
- Allow for progression and development of staff to become better teachers and increase their overall effect on student outcomes, whilst generating effective ways for them to stay and be loyal.
- Avoid taking staff 'away from the classroom'. Instead, create an even greater focus and responsibility for academic outcomes as leaders progress.

DEVELOP A QUALITY FRAMEWORK

Challenge

Assessing the overall quality and compliance of what you deliver is time-consuming.

Solution

Consider using accreditation frameworks and 'industry standard' best practices to evaluate the success of your school start-up against milestones that are contextual to its compliance, educational outcomes, growth and development.

What Research Tells Us

The great William Dening, who is credited for much of the Total Quality Management (TQM) structures we follow today, highlighted the importance of training on the job, rigorous systems of education and self-improvement for workers, and the removal of a great many barriers that reduce pride, including eliminating annual rating systems.[52] In figure 1.6 below, your school framework may lead from values, through systems and best practices, resulting in a secure and inclusive environment.

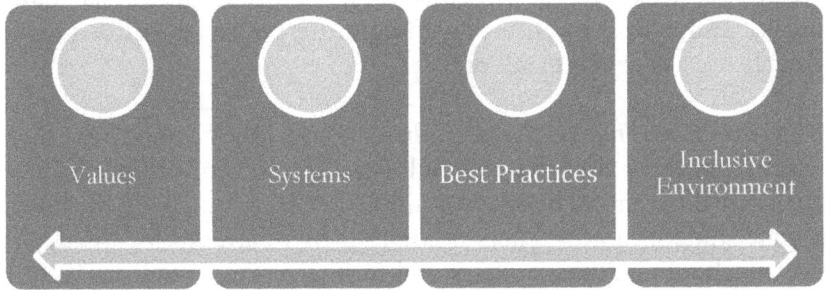

Figure 1.6 Your School Framework.

Values

Underpinning your school's framework should be a set of shared values. These values will form the foundation for your actions, behaviours and all policies and practices that your students and wider stakeholders buy into. When you have decided upon the values system that you will use, you may wish to articulate these into your branded materials, job descriptions, school website and all of your policies. It is also a good idea to have some videos and questionnaires for new staff so they can engage and 'pre-board' and begin to touch and grow in line with your school's overall culture. If you are serious about becoming a sustainable school – here's the place to start, by ensuring it is at the heart of your identified values.

Systems That Uphold These Values

How you attempt to embed your school's values and overall philosophy is important. Monica Sagar, Director/Principal, Shiv Nadar School in India, notes, 'Before selecting a leader, a lot of care needs to be taken to make sure that the value system and the goals are aligned with the leader'.

---

[52] W. Edwards Demings 14 Points for Total Quality Management. American Society of Quality (ASQ)

Best Practices That Sustain The Systems
Where will your best practices that support the systems you plan to use to uphold your values come from? What is the evidence base that you can refer to in supporting you in making highly effective decisions around these best practices? Are these best practices themselves the subject of increasing scrutiny? Have some of them been dispelled or labelled as educational 'myths? How will you ensure that your new teachers and wider staff are aware of them and buy into the use of best practices, and don't just arrive at your start-up with their box of tools for managing behaviour for example, and refuse to entertain integrating your schools 'values-led' approach you are trying to adopt?

The Environment That You Create When A Person Walks Into Your School
Be clear from the outset that you will need to see your school through a consistently different set of eyes – multiple lenses. Keep taking the journey that your students and teachers do. Follow them around for the day and see your school's culture, policies and best practices in action. Walk the route that your new parents will take with the marketing and admissions departments. Sit in the seats of students in your classes. Do everything you possibly can in the lead-up to the opening to identify, connect with and communicate the kind of inclusive environment that your school should be like when the aforementioned stages are implemented. Above all else be inclusive, provide opportunity and in doing so make leadership decisions that are highly ethical and will be valued by others for years to come.

ADOPT A COMMUNICATION STRATEGY

> 'Communication - the human connection - is the key to personal and career success'. *Paul J. Meyer*[53]

In the dynamic and diverse landscape of start-ups, this quote holds a profound truth. Start-ups are a whirlwind of innovation, a melting pot of ideas, and a testament to the power of collaboration. At the heart of this collaboration lies communication – the invisible thread that ties together people, processes, and goals, enabling a start-up to grow and thrive.

However, establishing an effective communication ecosystem from scratch is a complex task, especially in today's digital age. Communication

---

[53] Topic One Communication Theory. P. J. Meyer.wordpress.com/topic-one-communication-theory/.

is no longer limited to face-to-face interactions or written correspondence. It has evolved into a multifaceted entity that encompasses a myriad of channels – from emails and social media to video conferencing and instant messaging apps.

In a multicultural start-up environment, the challenge is even greater. Language and cultural barriers can lead to misinterpretations, creating a ripple effect that can disrupt the entire communication ecosystem. This disruption can erode trust, create confusion, and even lead to significant losses.

The solution? A robust and adaptable communication strategy. One that not only addresses these challenges but also harnesses the power of modern communication tools to drive growth and success. In this section, we will delve into the importance of such a strategy, the barriers you might face, and how to overcome them to create a thriving communication ecosystem in your start-up.

Research tells us that, in today's hyper-connected world, communication has become a complex tapestry woven with threads of various forms – emails, instant messages, video calls, social media posts, and more. As we navigate this intricate landscape, it's crucial to remember that effective communication is more than just a transfer of information. It's about understanding, empathy, and connection. Research underscores the importance of a well-planned communication strategy in any organization, including start-ups.[54] It's the compass that guides your attempts to communicate your vision and culture to your team. But – it's not just about what you say or write. It's also about what you don't say. As Peter Drucker wisely put it, 'The most important thing in communication is to hear what isn't being said'.[55]

In the digital age, the culture of constant connectivity can lead to an additional workload. Answering emails alone can add up to an extra 25 hours of work outside the workplace.[56] This highlights the need for a balanced communication strategy that respects personal boundaries and promotes work-life balance. Moreover, in a multicultural start-up environment, understanding cultural nuances becomes paramount. A personal anecdote from Chris illustrates this. 'Shortly after I arrived in China, a Chinese student's grandparent in my school passed away. In the UK, my approach would have been to share this information respectfully

---

[54] Day, C., Sammons, P., & Gorgen, K. (2020). Successful School Leadership. Education development trust.

[55] Peter Drucker. The most important thing in communication is to hear what isn't being said. interview, Bill Moyers *A World of Ideas* (1989)

[56] L A, Perlow, 'The time famine: Toward a sociology of work time', *Administrative science quarterly 44*, no. 1 (1999), pp.57–81.

and confidentially with the student's friendship group to foster support. However, in China, this was a significant cultural taboo. This experience taught me a valuable lesson – it's not about whether you agree with these 'red lines', but about knowing where they are and how to navigate them. In essence, effective communication in the modern world is a delicate dance. It requires us to balance the use of various channels, respect cultural nuances, and listen to unspoken words. It's a dance that every start-up must master to succeed". Here, Iram Myford takes us on a journey towards effective communication in your setting, beginning with barriers you might need to overcome:

Barriers To Implementing Your Communication Strategy

- *Empathy Deficit:* A lack of empathy or warmth in your communication style can create a barrier that's hard to overcome. This applies to all forms of communication, from body language and casual conversations to formal written communication. Remember, communication is not just about conveying information; it's about connecting with people.
- *Cultural Blind Spots:* Not understanding the nuances of communication styles in your host country can lead to misunderstandings and misinterpretations. It's essential to invest time in learning about the local communication customs and etiquette.
- *Information Mismanagement:* Without a clear strategy for handling important and often confidential information, it can end up in the wrong hands or get lost in the shuffle. It's crucial to establish clear protocols for information sharing and storage.
- *Overcommunication:* While it's important to keep everyone informed, overcommunication can lead to information overload, causing errors and omissions. It's a delicate balance to strike, but essential for effective communication.
- *Disinformation and Gossip:* Rumours and inaccurate information can spread like wildfire, especially in a start-up environment. This can lead to panic, unnecessary questions, and complaints from students and staff. It's important to have a strategy in place to address this, promoting a culture of transparency and trust.

In the face of these barriers, it's important to remember that every challenge presents an opportunity for growth. By acknowledging and addressing these barriers, you can build a stronger, more effective communication strategy for your start-up.

Navigating the Communication Labyrinth: Professional Insights
In the dynamic world of start-ups, your success hinges on your ability to swiftly understand and adapt to your new communication landscape. It's a journey that demands humility, agility, and a willingness to learn new communication skills, no matter how adept you've been in the past.

As a Headteacher in the UK, says Chris 'I navigated a complex communication network that spanned 1,500 bi- and multi-lingual students, their families, a politically divided governing body, local and national politicians with their agendas, and a diverse array of community groups. My tools of the trade? A blend of face-to-face meetings and web communication. However, when I stepped into the vibrant social media-centric communication scene in China, I found myself in a whole new world. The primary platform here was Weixin, better known as WeChat. This multi-purpose messaging, social media, and mobile payment app became my new communication hub. It was a far cry from the communication methods I was accustomed to, and it required a steep learning curve. WeChat was not just about exchanging messages; it was about understanding the subtle nuances of communication etiquette within the app. I had to learn which emojis and stickers would convey the right sentiment at the right time. It was a humbling experience, reminding me that effective communication is a continuous learning process'.

An international secondary headteacher shared a similar sentiment, 'We instituted an SLT meeting before the school day every morning. This allowed us to discuss ongoing issues or identify problems that needed resolution. The goal was to keep the lines of communication clear and open. WeChat became an essential tool in this process, enabling our Executive Principles to liaise with the Board as necessary'. In essence, navigating the communication labyrinth in a start-up is a continuous learning journey. It's about being open, adaptable, and ready to embrace new ways of connecting and engaging.

Crafting Your Communication Strategy: A Step-by-Step Guide

- *Blueprint Your Communication Ecosystem*: Start by mapping out the communication network you'll need within and around your start-up.
- *Identify All Stakeholders*: Your communication strategy should encompass all stakeholders. This includes students, parents, teachers, the management team, the governing body, support staff, owners or investors, local government organisations, and community groups.
- *Know Your Audience*: Identify your target audience and their level of

involvement. A stakeholder map can be a useful tool for planning the frequency and channels of communication for different audiences.
- *Invest in Training*: Equip your team with the skills they need to communicate effectively. Investing in professional communication training can pay dividends in the long run.
- *Choose Your Channels*: For each communication stream, decide on two channels: face-to-face and written communication. This dual approach ensures that your messages reach their intended recipients.
- *Set Your Frequency and Location*: Decide on the frequency of communication and the optimal location for face-to-face meetings.
- *Define Your Purpose*: List the key objectives of each act of communication. This will help ensure that your messages are clear and purposeful.
- *Select Your Attendees*: Be selective about who attends your meetings. Include only those who need to be there.
- *Create an Implementation Plan*: Once you've mapped out your system, you can move on to creating an implementation plan. This plan should prioritise the introduction of new communication systems, allowing time for each one to be set up and tested before full implementation.
- *Assign Responsibilities*: Clearly define who is responsible for managing different communication channels. This will help ensure that your communication strategy is executed effectively.

Remember, a successful communication strategy is not just about sending messages; it's about creating meaningful connections. By following these steps, you can create a communication strategy that fosters understanding, builds relationships, and drives your start-up towards its goals.

Crucial Consideration: Crafting Your Admissions and Complaints Communication Strategy
It's essential to develop a clear and effective strategy for communicating your admissions process and handling any complaints your start-up receives. This strategy should be an integral part of your overall communication plan, ensuring that all stakeholders are informed and that their concerns are addressed promptly and professionally. Moreover, it's crucial to have a plan in place for crisis communication. This could take the form of an Emergency Flow Chart, outlining the steps you will take to communicate during a crisis. This chart should detail who needs to be informed, what channels will be used, and how information will be disseminated and updated as the situation evolves.

Clear and effective communication during times of crisis can help to maintain trust, manage expectations, and ensure a coordinated response. By planning ahead, you can ensure that your start-up is prepared to handle any situation that arises.

Important Reflection: Ensuring Accountability and Protocol Adherence

In the dynamic world of start-ups, you won't always be present when communication occurs. In these instances, consider how you will ensure accountability among those leading the communication. What mechanisms will you put in place to ensure that your communication standards are upheld even in your absence? Furthermore, contemplate how you will handle situations where a team member breaches your communication protocols, potentially jeopardizing the growth and reputation of your start-up. Having a clear plan for such scenarios can help maintain the integrity of your communication strategy and safeguard your start-up's future.

Your Communication Plan Should Include (As a minimum)

- *Parent Handbook*: A comprehensive guide for parents that outlines the school's policies, procedures, and expectations. This serves as a reference point for parents to understand the school's operations and their role within it.
- *Daily Communication Books for Primary Students*: A tool for regular updates on a student's academic progress and behaviour. This fosters a strong home-school connection and keeps parents informed about their child's day-to-day experiences.
- *Class Updates via App*: Daily picture posts for Kindergarten/Primary Schools and weekly updates for Secondary Schools. This provides parents with a visual glimpse into their child's school life, fostering engagement and transparency.
- *Homework Diaries/App for Secondary Students*: A platform for tracking and managing homework. This promotes organisation and responsibility among students and allows parents to stay informed about their child's academic responsibilities.
- *Family Communication Group (e.g., WeChat)*: A one-way communication channel monitored by the Principal and the Director of Admissions. This ensures that important updates and announcements reach all families promptly.
- *Staff Communication Group (e.g., WeChat, WhatsApp)*: A platform for staff communication, guided by clear professional guidelines.

This fosters collaboration and transparency among staff members.
- *Daily Board/Portal or Email*: A system for sharing daily updates on absences and cover arrangements. This ensures that all staff members are informed about daily operational changes.
- *School Marketing Group (e.g., WeChat, WhatsApp)*: A platform for promoting the school's achievements, events, and initiatives. This helps to build the school's brand and engage the wider community.
- *Weekly Principal's Letter/Blog*: A regular school leadership update. This provides insight into the school's direction and decisions, fostering trust and transparency.
- *Bi-weekly Teachers' Newsletter (Lower School) and Monthly Curriculum Overviews (Secondary School)*: Regular updates on curriculum and teaching activities. This keeps parents informed about what their children are learning and why.
- *School Website*: A comprehensive online resource that provides information about the school, its programmes, and its policies. The public face for the school and a resource for current and prospective families, and future candidates.
- *Regular Reports to Leadership*: Weekly reports to the Founder and CFO, and monthly reports to the COO. These ensure that the school's leadership stays informed about the school's operations and progress.
- *Monthly Virtual Meetings with Head Office*: Regular virtual meetings to discuss updates, challenges, and strategies. This fosters collaboration and alignment between the school and its broader organisational context.

Remember, the goal of your communication plan should be to foster transparency, engagement, and trust among all stakeholders. Using a variety of channels and formats, ensures your communications are accessible, inclusive, and effective.

The Master Plan

What Is A Masterplan?
For the purpose of this book, we refer to the 'masterplan' as your central planning and spatial layout tool/document that you will consistently use to configure the land and ongoing development your school forms part of. It is essential that the term is used in the context that it will be applied in, so check for understanding around its meaning and where others may have different interpretations of its meaning and use. Your eventual masterplan is likely to go through several iterations – many may need to be significant and take your school away from its desired outcomes. Brace yourself for what comes; show the resilience and commitment that you will need to get your school start-up to the finish line.

Research from the investment platform Investopedia tells us 2 of the 6 reasons why businesses fail most often are 1. Bad Location, Internet Presence, and Marketing; and 2. Expanding too fast.[57] Executive Headmaster of Wellington College China, Julian Jeffry says: 'Your masterplan may reach mark 1, 2, 3, 4. If the (master) plan has changed so much in terms of your target market and teachers that you might recruit and once the masterplan is disassociated with your vision, you may be explaining changes that are not what you thought, and you will have to get people on side'. He adds, 'It will also most certainly change from planning to reality as it is a long journey and it could be a significantly different product than what you might have been led to believe. Be prepared for that. If you are an international head that wants to go into (start-ups) ... I've had several colleagues want to... driven by high standards, or passion for IB. The reality of endless spreadsheets, and long nights. Very few schools out there can afford to keep dumping money in ... and your ideals can take a real battering'.

What Might Derail Your Masterplan?

- Lack of a clearly defined purpose, and vision of how to get there.
- A lack of or poor communication model, where problems can be identified and brought to your attention.
- An imbalance of the required skills for your start-up team to be successful.
- Inaccurate translation and record keeping.
- A lack of professional socialisation, professional networks and

---

[57] Top 6 reasons why new businesses fail - Investopedia.

knowledge underpinning the organisation of local government educational strategies.

Here, in figure 1.7 below we broadly set out 5 stages, but you should recognise that these may change, some stages may be carried out more than once and even after you have collectively agreed on your purpose you will need to keep coming back to it in the subsequent stages.

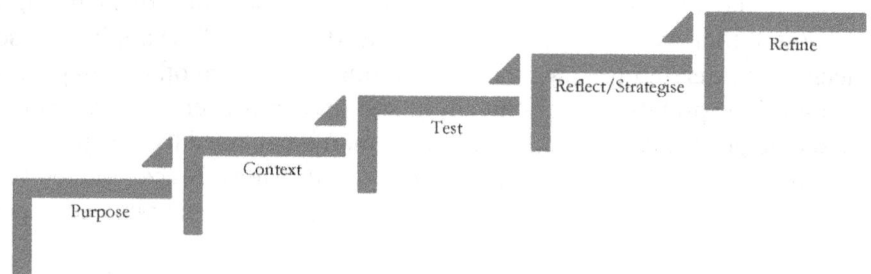

Figure 1.7. Your Overall Masterplan Steps

Purpose
Jayne Harrison – Architect and Founder of *JDH Architects* and Visionary Designer of Educational Facilities, suggests the first step in a school master plan should include 'Pedagogy, People and Place'. Use your purpose to ask the question 'What are we trying to achieve?'. Help forge a narrative of design for your architects. Use the future campus design to instil your purpose, educational philosophy and values. And most importantly, place the pedagogical practices that will take place within your campus at the centre of your design process.

Context
How familiar are you with the proposed school and its context? How will that context fit in alongside your new school's brand and the image you are trying to create? How well do you understand the underlying features of the land and where it lies? What opportunities are there to be bold in the design and where will you need to be conservative – for example in the face of battering rain or drenched sunlight? When it comes to the organisation and arrangement of space, what lessons are there to be learned from others and their projects? Use listening as your greatest device and ask those who have been there and done it – 'what would you do differently if you had your time again'? Finally, make sure that the team involved in the overall masterplan you are putting together has the right blend of skills and where necessary, can hold others to account for the

decisions that they make that will affect the design and build of your school for years to come.

Test
Full land surveys will need to be undertaken to test the ability of various corners of your site to handle the requirements that will be asked of them by planners. One important and expensive afterthought is the external connections between school buildings. How will they look, be easy for staff and students to manoeuvre themselves between and what will happen when there are serious downpours? Will the design of such structures allow for the installation of future solar panels to carbon neutralise the building? How will your outdoor spaces be featured and how will students access them – again during times of inclement weather where indoor space may be at a premium? Think about the connectivity between the buildings and the footfall that they will support. Will your buildings and their design be able to keep up with a significantly increasing student population? Will the campus have features that allow it to be upgraded easily? Will the extension of space be possible and if needed, how difficult will it be to retrofit buildings with technology as and when it comes online?

Reflect/Strategise
How will you be creative in your masterplan? Who will have that license and how? What is off-limits in terms of the design, use of space and overall feel? Which materials are you intrigued by, and which do you want to significantly reduce? Within your strategy will be your design (education) brief. Formulate a series of questions that can help determine how your educational values will be curated in the overall feel and use of the site. Tell your design team what is important, for example:

- Effective use of space
- Significant areas of shade outside
- Eye-catching design
- Classrooms that support collaboration
- Interior light to reduce demand for electricity
- Well-ventilated rooms and walkways that reduce the need for air-conditioning

Refer back to your decision-making model as you will not want to spend days and weeks arguing over what colour the toilet seat lids will be. Try to separate essential and non-essential decisions that can increase the speed and efficiency of the plan becoming a reality.

Innovation may come at a considerable cost. What is that cost you are prepared to go to? And what happens if your attempts to innovate are out of date before the school is even finished? Gathering feedback needs to be done in the right manner, and with the right audience. It is always worth getting experienced town and county planners to look over your master plan as it evolves – even just to point out the most obvious of facts that others have missed.

Refine
Going through steps 3-5 more than once will be a feature you will need to prepare yourself for. Remember that it is often the smaller details that have the biggest effect on a school, its culture, and its ability to live out its core values. Re-visit your purpose if necessary and ask the question(s) How will this design allow our students and teachers to collaborate and acquire the skills of tomorrow, in the space of tomorrow? Or, how will this layout equip our teachers with the right tools and resources to make their overall jobs of educating our students easier? Again, use your 'go-to's' for critical feedback, and make sure they too understand the design brief you are trying to achieve.

If done well, your masterplan may well ask the questions you will likely have in 5, 10 or 15 years, when your school continues to grow and requires a fresh overall approach to the design and way in which people go about their daily lives. Always remember that successful masterplans are about the people and the communities they serve.

Section 1: Review Questions

- What Vision and Mission do you bring to your current post? How do you know that they are the right Vision and Mission for this school? To what extent are these values context-driven?
- What level of confidence do you have in your understanding of contextual issues that impact leadership in your current post?
- Do you know who to go to for accurate and reliable information on issues such as the legal framework for international education in your national context?
- How would you evaluate the depth of your understanding of the different groups that make up your target market?
- Are you confident that you understand the demographics of your school setting well enough to achieve sustainability and stability in your school intake? Can you predict and manage 'pressure points'?
- How well do you understand the range of challenges for your school that come under the heading of 'sustainability'?

- Do you have the outcomes of a recent, reliable sustainability audit to guide a sustainability strategy into the future? Can you engage the full range of stakeholders in sustainability strategies?
- How effective do you think your current decision-making processes are?
- How do you keep up to date with current research and ensure your decisions reflect international best practices?
- Are you a member of a professional network that you can turn to for highly objective and effective advice on a range of leadership issues?

PART 2

DEVELOP YOUR INFRASTRUCTURE

PART TWO – DEVELOP YOUR INFRASTRUCTURE — 96

Project Management — 99
    What Are The Key Aspects of Project Management? — 99

Sustainable School Design — 103
    School Design Principles — 103

Your Boarding Programme — 108

Learning Environments — 111

Sports and Outdoor Spaces — 114

Considerate, Sustainable Construction Practices — 116

Choosing an Information Management System (IMS) — 119

Your Online Learning System — 122

School Transportation — 124

Procurement of Materials, Resources and Suppliers — 125

In this part, we look at the practicalities of setting up an international school so that its opening is successful and serves as a foundation for its long-term future. Central to this is effective project management and also understanding the key challenges and potential barriers you will face along the way.

This part focuses on:

- Project management, its key aspects, and pitfalls.
- Sustainable school design, so that you can create environments that enhance learning and facilitate the collaborative culture you want to develop and curate.
- Creating sports and outdoor spaces.
- How to ensure your construction plan meets health and safety regulations.
- How to resource your international school and the companies who can help you do so.
- Successfully choosing the learning management system that works best for you.
- Information management systems.
- Building your calendar.
- Online learning.
- Resources and supplies.
- School transportation.

Project Management

Challenge
Large Project Management is a unique skill set that a limited number of current International School Principals have.

Solution
Appoint the best and most suitably qualified candidate and make sure that you follow up on references and recommendations of their work, just as you would with your teachers.

There are a variety of pitfalls in choosing a good project manager and being able to oversee the process:

- A lack of or poor communication model, where problems can be identified and brought to your attention.
- An imbalance of the required skills for your start-up team to be successful.
- Inaccurate translation and record keeping.
- A lack of professional socialisation, professional networks and knowledge underpinning the organisation of local government educational strategies.

WHAT ARE THE KEY ASPECTS OF PROJECT MANAGEMENT?

Broadly speaking, there are three central aspects of effective project management. They are:

1. Organising all aspects of work related to your school's new build program in an organised and efficient manner.
2. Managing and integrating change in the project. For example, during design, procurement of materials and the overall construction and methods used.
3. Systematically procuring the right resources at the right time to ensure the maximum rate of progress and minimum amount of economic wastage.

Since your project manager is likely to be working across cultural teams and in some cases procuring and using materials for the first time, they must have outstanding communication skills and be able to present information in a clear, unambiguous manner that puts everyone on the same page.

What Your Project Manager (PM) Needs To Keep You Updated On

- Health and Safety, accidents and near misses.
- All stages of scheduling, upcoming and future planned works and their likely implications.
- The human resources currently involved or who will be involved.
- Equipment and materials to be used, replaced, or upgraded.
- Matters relating to the overall contract(s) you have in place.
- The adherence to design and potential changes to incorporate.
- Significant milestones.
- Costs – including upfront, future financial commitments, cash flow and a financial forecast/planning tool.
- Quality assurance/compliance and what that looks like at the different structures/levels of the overall project.

In addition to the above, we recommend your PM keeps you updated on all aspects of the work culture and how it can be improved to create an excellent working environment in which to deliver the project. Remember your school's culture and ethos don't just start on the first day of school opening. It is evident in the attire of the workers, their ability to collaborate and meet deadlines, and their approaches to health and safety. As Principal/CEO, you have the opportunity to articulate and model the kinds of values that your project manager needs to exude. Also, ask yourself:

- How frequently should you meet with your PM?
- How do you know that your PM/Site Manager is telling you the truth?
- Does your site manager understand the implications of each stage, i.e., what are the implications for marketing/personnel/safety/curriculum provision?
- Does the construction company/site manager understand safety implications if work continues after the school site opens, in part? A very big bugbear for schools and parents.

What Happens When Pieces of the Jigsaw Are Missing?
Consider for a moment what will happen if one of the above aspects of your overall project management is weaker in comparison to the others. What effect might that have on the project's ability to be delivered on time, to budget and in accordance with local compliance systems? If your project manager fails to keep you suitably informed about certain stages of the scheme, that may require a complete shutdown of access to the campus. This may have a knock-on effect on your marketing team, who may have planned visits to certain aspects of the development which will have to be rescheduled. If adherence to your design's overall purpose, philosophy and pedagogical principles are loosely monitored, it may result in extremely expensive steps in redesign or development. Since the project manager is likely to be recommended by the construction firm or architect themselves, you must take the time to develop a highly effective relationship with them.

Professional Advice On Project Management
Quality Control
An essential criterion of your overall project management must be for the regular supervision of the works to be carried out. Fail to carry out regular supervision of the construction site and its works, and you miss valuable opportunities to guarantee the overall quality of the project and the resilience of materials being used to stand up to future everyday school use. Replacing large aspects of a school project can be hugely costly and deemed reckless. Without effective supervision, managing the contracts you have awarded becomes a minefield. Since workers will inevitably be sub-contractors of your main contractors, supervision is wholly necessary to avoid compromising key aspects of the project. It's essential to keep the focus on future projected upkeep costs and to maintain a vigilant approach to the health and safety of the workforce that is aligned with your school's overall mission and philosophy.

Supervision should (wherever possible) form part of a scheduled weekly routine (or daily if already part of an existing site). If you do not have a site supervisor, then agreements have to be made before work begins on how/how often/by whom reports will be made and also permission sought on how to safely enter the site. We have learned of cases of sizeable projects where dangerously obvious things were missed due to a lack of financial resources to dedicate time to supervision. Make sure that adequate supervision forms part of your overall strategy for the construction phase:

- Decide how / who will be responsible for quality control.
- Dedicate appropriate financial resources for suitably qualified individuals to regularly supervise, monitor, and review the quality of workmanship, materials and resources used and approaches to health and safety.
- Raise the awareness of your team who are likely to visit the new build on aspects of supervision and key aspects of quality control they can look out for.
- If you have access to a drone, have someone record regular footage at a height that is inaccessible to you.

Remember

More sets of eyes and a culture where staff are prepared to speak out if they feel the quality is being compromised is a far better approach than one in which everyone waits for your opinion. An advertising campaign properly built around the construction process can build the loyalty of customers already signed up and attract fresh interest in an exciting new project.

Sustainable School Design

SCHOOL DESIGN PRINCIPLES

Although it is obvious, it's important to note that schools and their designs are highly differentiated between countries and their environmental contexts. Huge progress has been made in the design and innovations of educational buildings, but some designs will simply not work in tropical countries, where humidity and moisture and the problems they bring need to be factored in. Equally, vast areas of glass on buildings in the Middle East may not be appropriate. The common use of glass inside school buildings is a growing trend that we urge you to follow with caution. Both Chris and I have experienced 'heat cracking' in our former campuses, where the overexposure of glass to the sun caused large areas of glass to shatter. Here are some essential school design principles your appointed architect should be made aware of:

- The overall school design should reflect the growing needs of an international school and not just be based around the classrooms.
- Spaces should be attractive and likely to facilitate (not impede) learning.
- The building should be inclusive and accessible to everyone, regardless of age or physical attributes, and scaled to the end user.
- The design takes into consideration the local community and supports its existing cultural identity.
- The design is fully conversant with the local climate and can deal with the challenges of heat, light, wind and water that will be presented to it.
- Wherever possible, construction should use sustainably sourced materials.
- The design and corresponding construction that will be required are simple and will not require incredibly highly skilled workers or highly sophisticated and expensive future maintenance.

Key Note
The building should be designed with the need to market and recruit students in mind. What are the 'wow' factors in design elements that are going to attract students and parents? How prominent and accessible are they? Ask your architects and designers to walk the campus as if they were potential parents.

Design For Your Vision

'Our approach is pretty personal and quite fluid'. Jonathan Holland

For many schools, 'The healthiest option is often to use what you've got', Jonathan Holland of Holland Architects tells me, explaining: 'Environmentally, it is the best way to go. If you have an existing building, the whole of it becomes an educational space. With a new school – one of the things we've always focused on in our design is about children who may not be able to cope with the overall design mechanism – making a building inclusive'. He adds, 'Our aims are to make it natural, homely and somewhere everyone feels comfortable in, and allows people to decompress a bit'.

When discussing the design relationship with school leaders, Jonathan suggests this should fit on one piece of paper and reflect the vision you have for the school – what are you trying to achieve? The worst thing to do, he notes, 'Is to tune it to everyone who is there at the school'. Also, international schools often need a sense of place. Be it Shanghai, Geneva, or Buenos Aires, the design may reveal where you are – but subtly.

When it comes to sustainability and energy usage, think of your 'Green Flag Fabric' first. Ask yourself, 'Are you providing something that will have the smallest amount of energy draw?', says Jonathan. Some flaws in design include attempts to be overly clever, wasting materials, or mechanical plant not being used. 'Many contemporary schools are choosing to avoid corridors altogether', he says. Simplicity pays dividends. Here, Jonathan suggests some elements that may impact your choice of design:

- Will rooms and spaces be cross-fertilised?
- A strong theme and an element of playfulness to bring the best out of people.
- Safety. An emphasis on children that need more care.
- Helping the building to not overheat, keeping it cool in the summer.

'Make sure your architects always team up with local architects', says Jonathan, 'In doing so, my job is to become a "design guardian" for the international school client'.

Interior Design And Marketing
The relationship between interior design, furniture procurement, and school marketing is a powerful one, and yet often overlooked. At Kidzink, each new design project starts not with sketching or space planning, but with the team building an understanding of your school's brand, values,

curriculum and pedagogy. Importantly, they also take time to understand and portray each school at just the right point within the local scale of school fees.

A stunning design render is often the first image that the world will see of a brand-new school. Your ideal interior design partner should use these initial images to help you set the scene of student experience and day-to-day school life, as well as to amplify your brand values and help parents understand your offering, credentials and pricing.

Having designs worthy of sharing with local media, on your website and with parents will be the cornerstone of your initial 'student admissions toolkit'. What's more, great designs are fantastic collateral for that other all-important 'marketing' exercise: recruiting your founding cohort of staff.

TOP TIP

As soon as you can 'swap out' renders for 'real' images of the school, do! Prospective parents can be jittery about the progress of a new build school and sharing images of completed learning spaces will be a reassuring reminder that all is well and your timeline is on track for opening.

Green Credentials
Marrying interior design and furniture procurement with marketing and admissions goes far beyond creating spaces that are both beautiful and functional. Choosing a design and furnishings partner with great sustainability credentials means one more positive message for your school marketing team to capitalise on. Gen Z parents are green credential savvy, and many will look at the provenance of your school furniture and resources as part of their school selection checklist. Kidzink's furniture is manufactured to high EU standards and uses only FSC-certified wood. They note: 'For clients that require it, we are also able to offer a full chain of custody on materials. In short, we've done our sustainability homework so that you don't have to!'

Pre-Opening Office
Your pre-opening admissions/marketing office is the next phase of translating your school's brand into its physical appearance. In times gone by, such spaces were simple offices for filling in forms and accepting

payments. In today's globalised and competitive education market, a well-designed pre-opening space is a brochure your families and team can stand in. The design of this space should incorporate all of your brand visuals and typify the look and feel of your future learning spaces. Think of the space at 'stop one' in your prospective parent school tour.

Kidzink's work with The Royal Grammar School, Guildford in Dubai exemplifies this approach. Their partnership provided the school with interior design and furniture, fixtures and equipment (FF&E) that reflected and quietly endorsed their globally renown brand, long heritage and reputation for academic excellence. Alongside these efforts, their renders, space plans, design imagery and beautifully executed pre-opening office proved to be fundamental to the school's early marketing and admissions campaign.

Use the following checklist to help form the foundations of your initial conversations with possible architects who are interested in tendering for the design contract:

- Health and Safety, building evacuation and muster points.
- Design appropriate to climate and environmental factors. Considerations of how space is used in cold, wet or humid locations.
- Separate toilets must be provided for staff and other adults; primary and kindergarten toilets must be adjacent to classrooms.
- Size of classrooms appropriate to the age of children.
- Running water supplied to all primary classrooms/art rooms.
- Natural light wherever possible to reduce the need for artificial light.
- Walkways are covered between buildings.
- Exam room with a Safe – A Cambridge requirement for accreditation.
- Elevator with disabled access to all floors.
- Secure campus, with the capacity to withstand intrusions at the front entrance.
- Library in a cool dry space to prevent light/moisture damage to books.
- Meeting spaces for staff/parents and key stakeholders.
- Entrances to boarding houses are controlled by electronic key cards.
- Science laboratories fitted with gas and water supply.
- Accumulation of water kept to a minimum.
- Appropriate car parking for parents.
- Designated play spaces for age-appropriate children/activities.

- External evacuation meeting points – large enough and appropriate distance from the school building.
- The dining hall is accessible and able to cater to a large number of students and staff.

It's of particular benefit to include a recording studio for professional video and audio recordings and a large auditorium for central school functions.

Professional Advice On Technical Expertise

A school design and build programme, at any level of financial endorsement, represents an enthralling vision but is equally a journey fraught with risk. Your exposure to such risk is exacerbated by a clear lack of technical expertise within your team and partners. Having the wrong skills in place at the wrong time will limit the project's chances of being delivered and handed over on time. Pay close attention to the appointment of your team members and ensure that founding board members can contribute in some way to the development of the school.

Your Boarding Programme

Challenge

Without the right structure, resources, and oversight, boarding schools can quickly become one of the fastest ways that an international school can lose its reputation. As Anne Dickinson, Director of Admissions and Marketing, reminds me of her time spent working for HSBC, 'We were oftentimes reminded that an unhappy customer will tell sixteen of their friends, whereas a happy customer, just four'. The implications of several upset parents of boarding students are therefore self-evident.

Solution

Appoint the most suitably qualified and experienced staff you can to manage your boarding programme. Have clear limits to the number of boarders you will receive in your founding year and grow your boarding programme to scale – do not be tempted to just add more boarding places if you do not have the staff capacity to deal with it.

What Do Others Say?

According to the Harrow International School – Hong Kong, website 'Common challenges children encounter when boarding for the first time' include 'homesickness, struggling to make friends, feeling that they are "different", academic challenges, and issues with personal belongings and money'.[1] Timothy Glare, who helped to set up BASIS International School Guangzhou's Boarding department in 2017 says of the experience: 'The Chinese side didn't have any prior experience of boarding and had a certain idea of what boarding would be, but that was not quite matched to the requirements of a liberal arts school such as BASIS'. In his current school, he adds, 'I had to change pretty much everything, to make it for use in an international boarding school'. In dealing with international students, he found that 'Having a good guidance and advisory programme is extremely important to map out what type of things students at different grade levels should be doing'. 'You need cultural awareness when you are dealing with students from around the world who are stepping outside of their particular cultural background'.

---

[1] The Harrow School - What Common Challenges Do Children Encounter When Boarding For The First Time?

Challenges You May Have To Deal With

'The biggest challenge new schools will face will be finding suitable staff', says Richard Stokes – CEO of The Australian Boarding Schools Association, 'It is a real issue for schools all over the world. Then, ensuring they are trained – teacher training is not boarding training and they must understand the challenging role they hold'.

Other challenges you will need to plan and prepare for are:

- Self-harm
- Alcohol/substance abuse
- Bullying
- Neglect
- Inappropriate relationships and sexual behaviour – opposite and same-sex

The Australian Boarding Schools Association (ABSA) has as its goal: *'To serve its members by providing for their needs - from recruitment assistance to staff induction training, from support around facility design and staffing models to ensuring on-going training is available for staff in critical areas such as mental health and risk, to name just two'*. Oliver Kramer, Executive Principal SCBS School – Shanghai, says 'You need people of the mindset of being in a boarding school. A day school has a very different mindset'.

Professional Advice on Boarding Programmes

With the overwhelming economic potential of students who are part of a boarding programme, you are likely at some point to work in an international school that has or plans to develop boarding. Boarding school positions can often be an attractive career option for teachers and senior leaders looking at principalship further down the line. Any staff involved in boarding need to be embedded in that overall experience. For anyone responsible for leading your boarding programme, you need to make sure that their professional experiences are of at least nationally minimum recognised standards in your country and context. You need good quality Child Protection and Safeguarding policies. At times, staff will need to avoid being too dogmatic in their thinking, as you work together to increase the overall quality and outcomes of your boarding and pastoral care practices. Keep drawing people back to your mission and philosophy and place the students at the centre of your decisions and how you arrive at them. Know what is important, and never compromise the health, safety and wellbeing of the students you are there to serve and protect. A deep and growing awareness of the local cultural context will be important. Identifying and having the right training for staff from the moment the decision is taken to operate a boarding house is vital to the ability to meet local government and future accreditation guidelines.

Key Questions To Ask Before You Begin Your Boarding Journey

- Is there a clear and demonstrable need for boarding? Have we carried out the right research that suggests so?
- What is the local understanding of what 'boarding' means?
- What is the law about boarding – at what age can children board and are we equipped to deal with each age/stage of development?
- How will Child Protection (CP) and Safeguarding work – especially in schools in countries that have little understanding of CP?
- What are expectations of staff regarding supervision – evenings/weekends etc.? Is it paid/expected/obligatory/ part of the package? Do staff live in?
- Does the geography of the school support the safe separation of sexes?
- Can we provide overnight security and security on-site – suicide prevention?
- What wellness support/psychologist support will we need?

Excellent boarding schools have:

- Outstanding staff who are trained and understand boarding.
- Great boarders – who contribute not only to their boarding environment but to the community as a whole.
- A positive climate and culture that includes kindness, tolerance, and respect.
- Exceptional operational procedures, which ensure boarder safety, staff support, cultural awareness and understanding and good record-keeping systems.
- First-class design which provides privacy, safety, public space etc.

Learning Environments

Challenge

How children learn is evolving. Classrooms need to become more fluid and interconnected with the skills future children are going to need.

Solution

Design your learning environments and spaces around their functionality and adaptability.

What Research Tells Us

In 2015, research carried out in the UK by Professor Peter Barrett at the University of Salford and a panel of experts in school design produced robust evidence that effectively designed primary schools can significantly increase children's academic outcomes in reading, writing, and math's. The HEAD Project (Holistic Evidence and Design), as it was termed, concluded that 'differences in the physical characteristics of classrooms explained 16% of the variation in learning progress over a year for the 3766 students included in the study'.[2] Good classroom design, it appears, contributes to the furtherment of academic outcomes. The fundamental implications for design drawn from the HEAD analysis are important to any founding international school and its design team as they reveal the key aspects of design that contribute to these improved academic outcomes. These include:

- Daylight
- Indoor air quality
- Acoustic environment
- Temperature
- Classroom design
- Stimulation

When you consider that the research itself was carried out in 27 schools and across 153 classrooms for 3 years, you may begin to stand up and take note. One company going to great lengths to support schools in their design and, in doing so, produce the highest quality school buildings that we can, is Velux. When it comes to large windows 'Pupils perform better in

---

[2] Clever Classrooms – Summary Report of the HEAD Project link

math and logic tests in classrooms with large windows, a high percentage of windows facing south and adequate daylight control, according to our research into the correlation between daylight and productivity in classrooms across Europe'. [3]

Barriers To Creating Effective Learning Environments

- Your financial model places limited value on interior design and function.
- Inappropriate premises – temperatures, lack of weather protection, safe spaces (lavatories/changing rooms, etc.)
- The height of ceilings, sound distortion, lack of light, basic safety, chemical residue (new building syndrome/new equipment), too close to traffic, no security, too many corners/dark places for bullying to go ahead unchecked, windows that open too far (suicide risk), easy access to roof/high balconies, not enough fire escapes, cluttered corridors/hallways, lack of personal storage spaces.
- Poor flooring – slippage risk. Guard rails/banisters missing on stairs or at the wrong height. Lack of intimate care facilities for young children.
- Lack of privacy in showers etc. for adolescents, in particular.
- Poor layout of dining rooms. Poorly designed boarding bedrooms/dormitories.
- Wrong heights of sinks, toilets, and cubbies for very young children.
- Poorly equipped specialist spaces (no soundproofing or poor acoustics in music rooms, no water in Art studios, etc.).

Professional Advice On Effective School Design

The relationship between highly effective school design and student outcomes is an area that continues to gather research. Advancements in design, technology, materials and construction are all contributing to an increasingly avant-garde market in the design and build of international schools. Fundamental to your interior (and exterior) learning environments is the effective use of space that scales and grows with your school on its journey. A highly effective and well-thought-out plan will mean that your school's lessons and their structure can be tailored to an increasing number of styles and formats when it comes to size. An afterthought in the construction of some school buildings can often be the placement of smaller rooms for the likes of English as an Additional Language (EAL) lessons and counselling. If not careful, this can lead to

---

[3] Velux Commercial Building better schools: six ways to help our children learn.

professional conversations taking place in corridors, poorly lit rooms and outposts of the school building – this can bring both health and safety and the wellbeing of students into question. Make sure that you involve the right people and stakeholders in the design of your school building at the right time of the planning process. Talk to other school leaders who have been through the process and gather important feedback about the effect that design has had on learning environments.

Questions To Ask Your Design Team About Your Learning Environments

- How will your interior design cope with the environmental demands that will be placed upon it in your international context?
- What research are your design team using? Where is it from and how has it guided their former projects?
- What advances in technology can be deployed to limit the impact of noise on learning from activities such as sports or music in other parts of the building?
- What aspects of classroom design do you both hold strong views and opinions on and are these in alignment or need to be brought into alignment?

Sports and Outdoor Spaces

Challenge

Sports and PE spaces can often come in the 2nd phase of an international school opening. Children are often taken off-site to local facilities when facilities are delayed.

Solution

Determine the extent to which PE will support your curriculum and invest in the right facilities that add value to your school and its wider community.

CASE STUDY

When he arrived at Kinabalu International School, notes former Principal Ian Gross, 'I surveyed the staff about what they would change and why they would change it. Our staff told me that the campus could be improved aesthetically. We thought that this would link to how the staff felt at work and make them feel prouder of the overall environment'. He notes, 'We did a lot of work on getting rid of the concrete, tiling and putting more plants into the area. We now have a very green area, but it felt quite drab. We put in a coffee shop which allows parents to meet in the mornings and after school'.

Barriers To Effective Sports And Outdoor Spaces

- A lack of overall budget / smaller campus.
- The value of outdoor education to your school and its group is limited.
- Poor design quality control with dormant/underutilised space.

Professional Advice On Outdoor Spaces

PE and Sports facilities are expensive. If not incorporated as part of your overall design and build strategy, they become incredibly expensive additions – especially when services have to be re-directed, or areas of the school site are closed to access by students and staff. You must take the time to visit other schools that have already experienced design faults, snags and delays. Learn from others' experiences.

Questions To Help Guide Sports Facilities Procurement

- What companies are you prepared to/not prepared to do business with and why? If a company tendering to replace your 3G surface has violated health and safety processes, you are putting your school at risk.
- How will the tendering process put the school's needs at the centre of the tender?
- Are you giving the impression to staff that there is 'no budget'?
- Certain equipment (e.g., Gymnastics) must be kitemarked and have been rigorously tested.

Considerate, Sustainable Construction Practices

Challenge

International standards and best practices have far-reaching differences in benchmarks, approaches to work and the effect of construction on the communities they plan to serve.

Solution

Make sure your contractors are aware of the Considerate Constructors Scheme (CCS) or other suitable industry-standard practices.

The CCS has produced an excellent online resource for considerate construction called the *'Scheme Monitors Checklist'*.[4] We suggest that you download a copy and disseminate it among your board members and, when dealing with tenders and contracts, have your potential contractors demonstrate how they plan to address these three criteria of how they will:

1, Respect the Community and manage their impact on their neighbours and the public to support a positive experience.
2. Care for the Environment, minimise their impact and enhance the natural environment.
3. Value their Workforce by creating a supportive, inclusive, and healthy workplace.

Here we contextualise each:

Respect the Community

- How will your contractors engage with the impacted community to understand and address concerns before the start of site activity?
- How will impacts on the community from construction activity be minimised?
- Will compliments, comments and complaints be sought and proactively managed?

---

[4] The Considerate Constructors Scheme - UK

- Is the perimeter safe and secure, and surrounding areas clean, tidy and free of litter, mud and dust; to protect the community and passers-by?
- How will they identify and reduce the effects of nuisance, disturbance and intrusion on potentially impacted communities?

Care for the Environment

- How does the build identify and manage environmental concerns?
- How are environmental plans and controls communicated?
- Will environmental issues protect the natural environment and watercourses?
- How will your school reduce its carbon footprint, including measurement, recording and publication of performance?
- How will it minimise the use of resources, energy and waste?
- How do they plan to ensure supply chain involvement in the reduction of carbon?
- Will they minimise the use of resources, including minimising carbon throughout the value chain?
- How do you plan to maintain or improve the natural local environment?

Value their Workforce

- Will the competency and legitimacy of the workforce be managed?
- Can they deliver learning and development to encourage construction as a career choice, improving representation from poorly represented groups?
- Are inclusive and diverse workplace practices actively encouraged?
- Will the needs of the workforce drive an improvement in wellbeing?
- Are they proactively addressing safety requirements for the workforce and visitors?
- Will a culture of continuous improvement in health and safety be embedded?

(Edited and updated from the Considerate Construction Scheme – UK).

Professional Advice On Construction Practices
Your mission, vision and values do not just suddenly appear in a building when it is opened to the students for the first time. They are represented through the company that you have hired and placed your trust in to deliver what you hope will be an awe-inspiring campus and education within it. The route you choose to take on that construction path will

inevitably link back to how the school can successfully get to breakeven and develop core sustainable practices (and beyond) that can last for generations. If you cut corners in construction, quality and overall safety, you will likely pay the price further down the road. Think carefully about who you do business with, how you tender the contracts, and ultimately upon which criteria will you objectively decide what contractor is the best fit for your school and its needs. The contractor should be able to demonstrate sufficient liquidity to leverage the people, products and services that they require for a large-scale development such as an international school. Taking on a contractor who has little experience in educational projects is a risk, so if you do choose a contractor with limited experience in education, bring in someone else to support them. Also, be aware that attempting to circumnavigate local laws by bringing in expatriate staff can be contentious.

Choosing an Information Management System (IMS)

Challenge

School data often suffers from poor use in how data is used for its intended purpose and impact. Information Management Systems (when rarely used to capacity) give poor overall value for the upfront costs they represent.

Solution

Carry out a detailed analysis of your options and choose an IMS that grows in scale with your school.

Options available to you include – but are not limited to – Arbor, Bromcom, Compass, Databridge MIS, Ed:gen, ESS – SIMS, Horizons / Pupil Asset, ISA MS, RM Integris, ScholarPack and School Pod. Our advice? Appoint a consultant such as NetSupport, to take you through the intricacies of making the right decision for your school and its size, as well as the overarching purpose you wish to use your IMS for. Investing in sound advice is likely to end up saving you money in the long term.[5]

Dulwich College, Singapore -Principal Nick Magnus comments,

> You have to play safe, and go with what you know… you'll bring with you a lot of institutional knowledge about systems and processes that you had in place. You haven't got time to start dabbling with stuff that you don't know about and integrating new systems. You will have to beg or borrow what you can from previous schools and make sure the people that you employ are familiar with the school information management system. I would never suggest being persuaded by some sales pitch and saying, 'That sounds like a great idea', and rolling it out in a start-up. You have to go conservative (with a small a c). Go with what you know and what you know will work. You can always improve it further down the line.

---

[5] https://www.netsupportsoftware.com/.

You May End Up Choosing The Wrong IMS If You:

- Don't make sure it's fit for your international context.
- Lack objectivity and have ties to one particular system, because that is what you are used to.
- Use inappropriate selection criteria, not based on your contextual requirements.

Professional Advice on Information Management Systems

Al Kingsley, CEO of NetSupport, EdTech Champion and Global ISC Eduruptor, shares his thoughts on choosing the right IMS. 'Before you worry about what curricular maps you're using', he tells me, 'You need to have some form of management information system that allows you to track all the key information. So, what do you log into first thing in the morning? You want to know what students you have on role, what their attendance history is, to track their behaviour and any reports or any wellbeing concerns'. Alongside that, he notes, 'Your statutory reporting requirements for safeguarding, and you want a tool that allows for staff to record all of their assessment output and data, no matter what tools they're using, so that becomes one window on your school ecosystem... One overall tool your staff use for their reporting, attendance, and safeguarding'. But most importantly, says Kingsley, where teachers can do their 'Comparisons and see clearly where the school is at in terms of progress and attainment data'.

According to Kingsley, the market is hugely active because some of the key dominant players are no longer dominant, and many IMS have now moved to the cloud. Schools have been saying for the last few years that 'We want tools that are open architecture – tools that students can access and report into remotely. An open IMS is what you need at the start of your tenure, and everything else should plug into it if it's the right kind of tool'.

He highlights that a popular movement at the moment in tech in schools is for people to want to talk about 'Ped Tech' as 'Pedagogy Informed Technology'. 'That's great when you're in the classroom', says Kingsley, 'But, in the broader organisation of running a school, much of your technology is about effective use of data, frankly. Secure use, but effective use of data. Lots of that is not pedagogy-aligned. It is about operational systems. Does it save time? Does it allow me to have more accurate reporting comparisons? Does it make staff jobs easier?'

Choosing an Information Management System (IMS)

Finally, Kingsley notes that,

> Often what schools have is an absolute mass of data they're recording, but poor analytics of how that data is being used for purpose and impact. And so, lots of the conversation, now you tend to have two halves. One half is about data, privacy, and protection. What data do we store about students? Where is it stored, how long do we keep it and who has access? On the other side, we have - What information is purposeful that will save staff time? If you can link these tools to your IMS, you may then want to consider some other things.

Questions To Consider When Choosing Your IMS

- Will it actually reduce teacher workload?
- Do they have pre-existing formats for reporting to parents?
- Do they allow you to take voice notes rather than written notes?
- Do they have an open interface, so that all those other tools we use are there?
- Does it streamline our process?
- Are they quicker and easier for us to report a concern about a child or a behaviour record against the child?
- Does it give you the right data?
- Does it save the school money?
- Does the system improve parental engagement?
- Does it streamline overall processes?
- Will your data be transferable to other systems?
- Does the vendor provide the appropriate level of training and ongoing support?

Your Online Learning System

Unless you have been on Mars for the last three years, you will likely have experienced an online learning system of some sort. You will need to be able to integrate your online learning system into your everyday approaches to learning and teaching – as fast and effectively as you can.

When selecting your online system, think about your location, ease of use, and the location of the overall server that supports it. Many schools complained of a 'lag time' or poor download speeds and even inaccessibility of the programs they used. Make sure this is not you.

As Founding Principal, you need to answer the following questions about your online learning system.

- What system will we use? How will we agree on that system, and will we use the same system in the lower / upper school?
- What training and development will you provide to your teachers for them to use it successfully?
- How often will you test your system?
- Who will monitor the online learning platform and what will quality look like?
- How will your online learning cater for your students with Individual Education Plans (IEPs)?
- Could teachers deliver one particular aspect of the school's curriculum online?

Macur, in his book *Teaching Online for Kindergarten and Primary Teachers*, asks several guiding questions that you will need to consider on the appropriate use of your online learning system.[6] They include:

- What opportunities are there for you to enhance your practice through the use of platforms?
- What role do parents play in online learning? How can they support you and what are they worried about?
- What are some of the core ways to support student welfare when online teaching?

---

[6] Macur (2023) *Teaching Online for Kindergarten and Primary Teachers*. Routledge.

> **TOP TIP**
>
> When conducting your interviews, consider having teachers present something basic to you to gauge their pedagogical awareness of a certain platform.

School Transportation

The transportation systems and infrastructure you create for your school are a clear and obvious statement of intent about how you intend to work towards the Sustainability for Development Goals (SDGs). Allowing 2000 vehicle movements in the morning and afternoon is not sustainable. The simple act of car-sharing between those who live close together should be actively encouraged and managed. Effective covered storage for students wishing to cycle to your school should be provided.

Key Questions When Deciding Your Transport Providers

- Is there a demand for such a service?
- What is the most effective route it can take in the shortest possible journey time?
- Who will be responsible for the safeguarding of your students on the bus?
- How will you award and renew the contracts to those who want to operate the service?
- Have you carried out due diligence on any company you contract to supply transport services?
- Are you satisfied with the company's safety record and that students will not be exposed to any forms of prejudice?
- Are there clear procedures to be followed in the event of such incidents?
- Is the transport fully accessible not just by current students but also by any future students who might be differently abled, e.g., wheelchair users?
- Is the company offering the most sustainable local solution available, preferably using zero-carbon transport?
- Is the service offering value for money?
- Is the service fully flexible to meet all anticipated needs? For example, after-school events, weekend activities and school outings?

You will want to take up references from any existing partners, and possibly ask the local police office if they have any concerns. Listen to your parent and community voice – after all, it's your school's reputation that's on the line in the event of an accident – and they do happen.

Procurement of Materials, Resources and Suppliers

Challenge

Resources can often take months to arrive from overseas at an international school. Some may arrive in poor condition and some may not arrive at all, or even be banned by the country you work in.

Solution

Allow additional time for the procurement and delivery process. Choose a reputable provider.

CASE STUDY, CES HOLDINGS

CES Holdings has a 40-year history of supporting international schools and over the years has helped administrators and investors deliver school development projects to the highest standards all over the world.[7] Their project expertise extends to various educational settings covering classrooms, technology workspaces, libraries, dining spaces, sports halls and more. Whether the undertaking involves renovating, refurbishing, fitting out an educational space or constructing a new building, CES has solidified its position as a reliable project partner.

Their largest project to date involves a total fit-out for a brand-new High-Performance Learning (HPL) School located in Saudi Arabia. This remarkable project comprises nine school buildings, an administration building, a theatre, two stadia, two libraries and two sports halls, establishing it as one of the largest international school campuses in the world.

Here is what Artan Consulting and Educational Services, who own and operate The Doha British School, says about them: 'We have worked with CES Holdings for over 20 years. CES's extensive knowledge of the education market for furniture, fittings and equipment has been essential to Artan and equally their willingness to go the extra mile and to think

---

[7] https://www.cesholdings.co.uk/

outside the box. Their willingness to listen and to be part of the Artan team has been invaluable'.

The Founding Headmaster of a school in Malaysia, who used a different procurement process, comments on his experience:

In Malaysia, we went through a central ordering company in the UK, whose name escapes me. All of the equipment arrived in 2 enormous shipping containers. I vividly remember being told to empty and store the contents of both containers, by myself, in 24 hours!! I ended up having to get six of the construction workers to help me, as we had no time to check each item individually. We put all of the equipment and resources in two senior classrooms and two prep classrooms and locked them. When we came back to finish the job the classrooms were open – our worst nightmare, with equipment missing or we presumed, having been stolen. Some two years later we were still finding various pieces of equipment that we'd ordered. I do remember that we spent a colossal amount of money on starter resources ... maybe as much as £1 million (in today's prices). But we likely lost some of this between arrival and our school opening through theft.

Resource Issues
Bear in mind that resourcing may be negatively affected by several factors, including:

- Underestimating the cost, shipping and access to the country your school resides in.
- Underestimating the time it takes for items to be shipped.
- A critical lack of understanding of your students and where they are at on their learning journey – which may be caused by an ineffective admissions process or an overestimation of ability.
- A lack of understanding about restrictions/limitations/banned items entering the country.

When in Senegal, Ariane Baer-Harper, former Founding Assistant Head, noted, 'The first thing that we learnt very quickly from experience, was not to give all resources and equipment out at the same time – try and keep it for years ahead', adding, 'When I returned to the school, I had founded some twenty years later, I was amazed to see that a number of the school's resources were still in use!... We made the expectations to students clear about how they should look after their books, computers and other resources. We used local tailors for uniforms, but we had to order some specially made items from Turkey'.

Professional Advice On Procurement
There is nothing worse than staff arriving at an under-resourced school, especially when it comes to the right textbooks and other teaching equipment. When your staff arrive, they need to be on your side and you want them to be happy. A lack of available resources will hamper that. However, as a principal, you do not have the time, nor can you afford to be the pilot for educational products and services that you and your staff are likely to have a limited working knowledge about.

Ariane notes, 'Any Founding Head needs to first procure what the school community is prioritising. This requires the head to scan and survey what the school has and to plan what you are buying and when. The danger in buying resources because you simply have the budget for them, may mean that they end up being underutilised'.

Sourcing and acquiring safe, purposeful and sustainable teaching resources in our international schools can represent a challenge. In my first school in China, the order and delivery of Jolly Phonics resources from the UK took a substantial amount of time. In some countries –for example, Malaysia – where Amazon does not fully operate (at the time of writing), teachers who are independent in resource procurement may struggle at times. International resource shipment is expensive – especially when not logically thought out and if items of poor quality or have been damaged in transit, need to be returned.

Before you order any resources and equipment for your start-up, ask yourself:

- Are there already resources in your community that can provide the service of quality that we are looking for, for a much lower fee and/or can be shared in partnership with the school?
- Do the resources/equipment directly match/serve the academic goals of our chosen curriculum?
- Is the cost of shipping and customs worth the method of procurement that we plan to use?
- Is the equipment safe and will it promote the safety of its user?
- Will the equipment/resource add value to the school and promote learning outcomes? Can the manufacturer prove this or provide evidence?
- Are the products durable and sustainable?

> **WARNING!**
>
> An increasing number of furniture and resources you will order are likely to contain the chemical **formaldehyde**. This is found in paints, resins, and sealants and is an active ingredient in the glue used in the production of furniture. Formaldehyde is linked to cancer[8] as well as other respiratory problems. As CEO of a school and group of schools, you must be aware of it and take the necessary actions to limit its potential effect. All furniture and materials your school procures will need time to 'breathe' in open well-ventilated areas before it can be used by staff and students.

Resources You Are Likely To Need

- *Books* – A library with fiction and non-fiction books in English and local and other languages. It also needs to hold levelled readers, classroom books, UOI's etc.; branded curriculum core texts and exercise textbooks; teachers' resources; and home/school communication diaries.
- *Toys* – Small and large play/discovery equipment; home/role play equipment; consumables; numeracy games and equipment; manipulatives; indoor soft play equipment to develop gross motor skills; and outdoor play equipment – bikes, Lego/blocks etc.
- *Literacy Development Games/Equipment* (wet weather activities) – Science/Our World games; equipment display materials for classrooms; sand, and water trays; gardening equipment (for children's use); and Listening centres.
- *Science Equipment/Lab Resources* – Cambridge accreditation states a minimum of 3; Art equipment and supplies for specialist rooms and classrooms; Building, construction resources (bricks, Lego, recycled materials etc.)
- *Borders and Displays* – This includes paper, card, fasteners; multi-cultural play resources; festival resources; Badges, awards and prizes.
- *PE Equipment* – Both indoor/outdoor equipment that caters for a wide range of abilities and interests; and swimming equipment (safety)

---

[8] Formaldehyde and Cancer Risk – American Cancer Society

- *Music Room/Performances* – A range of instruments for children), keyboards for teachers, music stands, microphones, mixers for IT programmes etc.
- *Furniture and Fittings* – For classrooms, shared spaces and specialist rooms, including soft furnishings, fabrics, cushions etc.
- *IT Equipment* – For classrooms, including Interactive White Boards (IWBs), laptops, iPads etc.; equipment IT lab; and for school/administrative offices.
- *Offices* – Admin and principal's furniture, fittings and hospitality. Office equipment such as printers etc.; teachers' workspace/staff room with furniture and fittings, including hospitality items like a coffee machine, kettle, fridge, and microwave etc.; a meeting room with furniture and whiteboard(s)/glass board(s); a reception area with furniture and soft furnishings; and a parents' room, again with furniture and soft furnishings, as well as hospitality items.
- *Stationary* for each year level, offices and marketing activities.
- *Branded school* uniforms and polos for your marketing team, as well as tie options.
- *Entrance Displays* – Showing staff, company leaders and other schools in the group, as well as branded company info and news and branded room names.
- *School Nurse and Infirmary Room* – Stocked with first aid equipment, a small fridge for medicines, scales, bed, linens etc.
- *Lavatories and Showers* – Stocked with soap, shampoo, paper towels or equivalent, etc.
- *Cleaning Equipment and Supplies.*
- *Compliance/Health & Safety* – Guards/Security equipment – compulsory/in line with licensing; fire equipment (mobile) – mandatory in line with licensing.

Section Two - Review Questions:

- What level of expertise do you / could you bring to the area of project management? If this is currently an area of relative professional weakness, what's your strategy to develop greater insight and rigour?
- Sustainability is a critical concern in modern school design. Do existing school infrastructures need to be updated to bring them in line with zero-carbon strategies? How up-to-date is your knowledge and understanding of sustainable design techniques and technologies? Do you know where to go to find reliable sources of internationally recognised thinking? Can you identify and explain successful case studies of schools that have made the transition to zero carbon?
- Do you understand the essential contribution of sport and exercise to student wellbeing? Do you understand the health and sporting culture in your local context? Do you have strategies for enduring inclusive approaches to healthy student lifestyles?
- Where would you go to get accurate, reliable information and advice about Health and Safety legislation relevant to your local context? How would you ensure the effective management of the Health and Safety aspect of any school infrastructure project?
- How would you evaluate your knowledge and understanding of the competitive field of Information Management Systems (IMS)? What criteria would you apply to select the best system for your school? How would you evaluate your level of competence in using such systems? How would you ensure that the whole school community of students, teachers, parents, and investors/ owners get maximum value from any such management system?
- Have you done a recent sustainability audit for your resource supply lines (e.g., catering) and school transport? What are the significant strengths and weaknesses of current systems in terms of their carbon footprint? Do you have the knowledge and leadership skills to drive both reductions in carbon emissions and better value for money for investors?

PART THREE
HUMAN RESOURCES

PART THREE - HUMAN RESOURCES   133

A New Vision for HR   134
    Your Approach To Talent Management   135
    Establish Your Code Of Conduct   137
    Build Your School's Culture   139
    The Employee Lifecycle   143
    Advertising Your Roles   146
    Interviewing   150
    Safer Recruitment   156
    Contracts   160
    Generating Key Performance Indicators (KPIs)   165
    Onboarding Your Staff   167
    Orienting Your International Staff   170
    Diversity, Equity, Inclusion and Justice (DEIJ)   173
    Documentation and Record Keeping   176
    Exiting The Workforce   176

A New Vision for HR

Returning to a school that I helped to found some twenty years earlier has taught me that the areas of human resources have been the area that has been the least developed and most undervalued. If you take the time to get it right from the beginning, by right, you will be investing in the development of your people and creating a sustainable system for years to come. A head can come and go, but the common language that embodies what schools represent are the things that last. Ariane Baer-Harper – Head of School, Austin International School.

Human Resources is evolving. People, their purpose and how to fulfil an individual's potential matter more than ever before. Here, we present the traditional mindset of HR and those that are required for our adaptive and agile schools of the future.

This section will help you:

- Identify the constituent parts of your school culture.
- Understand compliance in your international school context, including (but not limited to) the employee lifecycle, safer recruitment and increasingly, the need to develop inclusivity of practice.
- Design effective Job Descriptions that are underpinned by KPIs that are aligned with your school mission, vision and values that support it.
- Manage the onboarding and orientation phase and reduce the incumbent risk of staff turnover.

You will also learn about international school start-up strategies from three sources: professional research on a variety of organisational foundation issues; school and non-school contexts; and powerful professional voices of principals who have experienced school start-ups, or who are currently working in them.

Your Approach To Talent Management

International Schools as we have known them are changing – and changing fast. Teachers are quick to understand what a school is all about and how it operates. The way that you recruit, develop, and attempt to retain staff will be significantly shaped by your overall resources available and your ability to deliver on the key student numbers that will lead to breakeven. Managing international school talent takes poise, attention to detail and an overall awareness of your staff's key motivating factors. Human Resources are an integral part of this. If your school is a highly values-led one that espouses equality and inclusivity, there will be a huge gap between your staff and their behaviours if you choose to adopt performance management practices that show little compassion or opportunity for coaching, development and collaboration.

Professional Advice On Human Resources

Human Resources, its management and the management of your people represent a golden opportunity to maximise the human resource potential of your employees – when linked to student outcomes, it can be transformative. The stronger your working knowledge of HR and its overall functions, the more likely you will be able to work with, collaborate/coach, and potentially influence the decisions that your school's HR team adopt. In my own experience, principals often assume that the actions and practices of their HR departments are compliant and usually consist of the right course of action during the Employee Lifecycle. However, when these assumptions are made, risk is added to the Employee Lifecycle itself. HR practices I have experienced in both Malaysia and China are not what they are in the UK. Although they continue to develop, there are often errors in advertising wording and the consequent communication procedures that follow a successful offer being made after an interview.

As a principal, you must be aware that HR practices may not be on par with what you have been accustomed to. To counter this, plan on allocating a dedicated amount of time with your HR Leader to ensure alignment with the school's vision and how HR will articulate it in their interactions with staff. In *Leading Your International School* we continually advocated for the use of 'culture conversations' – regular positive interactions between HR and school staff to gauge the attitude, mindset, and ability of staff to carry out their role successfully. [1]

---

[1] *'Leading Your International School'* (2023)

Finally, as and when your staff do decide to leave, try to make it a smooth and pain-free exit as possible; in doing so, use your staff who do decide to move on as another free external marketing opportunity, happy to promote your school, wherever they go. Here, we present the traditional HR mindset versus that of the future. Decide where you want your school to be and set in motion a plan to get there.

Traditional HR Mindset	HR & People Leaders of The Future
Boundaries Works within prescribed traditions of HR. Little flexibility for creativity and innovation. **School example:** HR sticks to recruitment, retention and corrective action.	**Multidisciplinary** Works with a wider number of stakeholders across school disciplines, including the principal, board and CFO and heads of department to identify school needs. **School example:** HR part of discussions on strategic direction and the talent requirements towards its goals.
Culture Ambassador This is our culture – staff sought that fit it. **School example:** 'In this school we …' 'This is what our culture looks like'.	**Culture Curator** This is our culture and these are the cultures of our people. How can we develop them together to become a competitive advantage? **School example:** Culture continually measured across multiple variables; refined to add value. Work-placed coaching to maximise potential.
Execution Focus on compliance. Limited strategic input. **School example:** Here is the absence and wellbeing policy.	**Team Decision Making** Contribute to overall strategy with their knowledge of people, their talent and school culture. **School example:** Here is what other schools' absence and wellbeing policies are. Here are some ideas of how we can improve ours. Innovation groups on policy.
Reactionary Responds and deals with work place issues on a 'case by case' basis when they surface, e.g., Performance Improvement Plans (PIPs). **School example:** Teacher turnover is high; we need to recruit further talent. Focuses on problems, not innovation and creativity.	**Diagnostic / Proactive / Iterative** Uses school goals in the management and measuring of talent. Employs school-wide coaching to develop skills, capacity and future performance. **School example:** Quarterly 'check-ins' with school staff. Move staff to different roles to aid performance/ maximise potential. Innovation department. Exit interviews to identify future 'brand ambassadors' for the school.

Traditional HR Mindset	HR & People Leaders of The Future
Distance from Teachers Deliberate distance between HR and school staff after hire. HR only deals with problems.	**Collaborates with Teachers** Actively involved and interested in staff development and growth, PD and collaborates with staff on school needs.
School example: HR office away from teachers. Teachers go to HR, but not HR to teachers.	**School example:** HR as internal consultants, teachers and leaders can engage with.

Figure 3.1. Human Resources: Present And Future.[2]

In any international school, central to the induction, performance and evaluation of staff, will be your schools code of conduct – critical in a start-up school. Next, we discuss how to develop it.

ESTABLISH YOUR CODE OF CONDUCT

Challenge

Ensuring that the Code of Conduct policy is aligned with local standards in the context of your school should not be an afterthought. Your international school will have domestic staff and staff from a wide range of previous backgrounds. The right policy is key to getting consistency across all staff.

Solution

Work closely with your HR team – a key aspect of people leadership. HR should be familiar with local laws and cultural norms regarding what school employees may or may not do. Use HR to develop an integrated and progressive Staff Conduct Policy.

Your code of conduct will be limited in effect when:

- A lack of clarity about what is acceptable both on campus and off of it is evident.
- Communication is lacking. Vital guidance documents must be translated and made available to all employees in a language they readily understand.

---

[2] Double and Cook (2023)

- There are 'grey areas' – where there is ambiguity in how laws and expectations should be interpreted. These are challenging to resolve at times.

Professional Advice On Codes of Conduct

Don't develop the Staff Code of Conduct Policy as a last resort, when a disciplinary case arrives on your desk. The Code of Conduct (CoC) should be worked into the school culture, so that everyone understands, accepts, and actively lives by it. Avoid being draconian or rule by fear. Expectations of your CoC should be regularly re-visited in meetings, literature and Professional Development sessions, especially at the start of each term. Emphasise the benefits of staff implementing the CoC correctly, including a smooth-running school, a glowing reputation for the school locally and among its stakeholders, and the successful integration of international staff into local life.

Ask staff to recount stories of successful travel both in the national context and in other countries where cultural competence was valued. Engage HR to contribute to CoC updates, keeping abreast of changes in the law as they affect international residents. Ensure HR includes an understanding of local laws, their compliance and cultural expectations in the onboarding process for all new staff and double-check this has happened in your review meetings with new employees. The first rule is always: 'ignorance of the law is no excuse'. Finally, make sure that HR has immediate access to relevant legal expertise if things go wrong. Offer staff appropriate protection, but protect the reputation and integrity of the school. A 'lose-lose' situation is one where a member of staff is found to have broken the law and it subsequently becomes public knowledge that the school took insufficient measures to prevent this unacceptable behaviour from occurring. Require all staff to sign a document to ensure they have received, read, and understood all relevant CoC information – critically important in the worst-case scenario.

'I am very much about trying to create an empowering culture and not a compliance culture', notes Liz Free. 'We expect staff to be on time and marking has to be returned within two weeks… If we find it's not working the first question we ask is "Is it because it's (the policy) not right"? Always link it to policies and practices and what is respectful engagement'.

How To Get Your Code of Conduct Right

- Align all expectations for international employees and domestic employees.
- Increase your professional knowledge of where 'grey areas' are likely to occur and advise your staff to always err on the side of caution.
- There has to be a clear, objective and fair disciplinary procedure alongside the Code of Conduct – and you have to show that you apply it rigorously.
- Demonstrate consistency. Treat local and international staff equally.
- Take bias seriously and make sure your actions and decisions are above such doubts.
- Make sure it is written for the reader, not the individual who wrote it.

BUILD YOUR SCHOOL'S CULTURE

Challenge

Affinity bias – the tendency for leaders to appoint staff who act and think like themselves affects decision-making – it also deeply erodes a positive school culture.

Solution

Use your school culture as your biggest inoculation against the debilitating effects of an increased and dysfunctional level of staff turnover.

What Research Tells Us

A positive culture is created when the people in an organisation believe in the mission of the organisation and are motivated to do so by the leadership.[3] 'The principal shapes a school culture by fulfilling five roles: those of "symbol, potter, poet, actor, and healer".[4] In 2018, at the National Institute for Urban School Leaders at the Harvard Graduate School, Ebony Bridwell-Mitchell noted that school culture comprises core beliefs, connections and behaviours of students, families and teachers.[5] Fullan

---

[3] Six Tips for Building a Better Workplace Culture. Harvard Division of Continuing Education.
[4] Deal, T. E., & Peterson, K. D. (1990). *The principal's role in shaping school culture*. US Department of Education.
[5] Five Characteristics of Effective School Culture - Marigold International School.

argues that school culture can be defined as the guiding beliefs and values evident in the way a school operates. 'School culture' can be used to encompass all the attitudes, expected behaviours and values that impact how the school operates.[6]

CASE STUDY, ICS LONDON

Alec Jiggins, currently Head of School at ICS London, previously recruited and coached a high-performing team, building a market-leading boutique international school in the heart of Singapore's Central Business District, breaking even in 18 months. One of the key ingredients to his success, he tells me, was knowing what types of people you want on board. As he says: 'How does what I've got, affect what I need to get?' and 'Now I've got this candidate, what's the counterbalance?' Before he finally found the right candidates who would fit the school and complement the strengths of other staff, he readily admits to me that, 'I went through about 30 Art teacher applications before finally arriving at the one that would help develop the school and its culture we wanted to build'.

Barriers To A Successful School Culture

- Not being self-aware of how you are showing up as a leader and a human being.
- Inequitable hiring, development and recognition strategies.
- Accountability lines that are lacking, poorly understood or carried out with little regard to their intended purpose.

Professional Advice On School Cultures

Developing a successful school culture takes resilience, reflection and self-awareness. Great organisational cultures are those in which employees, students, parents and wider stakeholders find it hard at times to separate their personal and professional identities – such is the strength of feeling. Your culture is represented by the beliefs, actions and values that your staff hold and set about reinforcing. It is hard to quantify and measure. Many have tried and failed, but they know what many of the

---

[6] Fullan, M., (2007) The new meaning of educational change, Routledge, New York.
School Culture: Creating a unified culture of learning in a multicultural setting Darlene Fisher IB Regional Conference October 2012

successful ingredients are that help to establish and develop it. These ingredients – such as a clear manner in which teachers and students interact with each other – are fostered by a true respect for the learner and the individual learning path that they are on. The conversations that are held between staff represent your culture. 'Self-awareness affects how we show up in a conversation', notes Alec. Wellbeing should always remain a key priority, but effective principals find ways to focus conversations on learning; they hold on to the belief that the core purpose of our international schools is to develop the potential of every student (and every member of staff).[7]

Culture is represented through various artefacts, ceremonies and processions. It is reinforced through great narratives and powerful stories. Aligning staff from a variety of cultures from around the world to your school vision is not an easy task. Ultimately, as Chris firmly believes, 'It is your school's culture that must aim to persuade teachers that the investment in learning and teaching is meaningful.'[8]

To Develop A Successful School Culture

- Ensure anyone involved in the recruitment of your staff and students, as well as the development of stakeholder partnerships, are in alignment with your school's vision and values, and recruit people who think and act differently from you.
- Be the leader of questions – not answers.
- Use HR to catch people's dreams; and support them in how to get there.
- Develop high-quality opportunities for staff to self-actualise and reach their potential with your school. This doesn't always have to be financial.
- Use a workplace coaching approach, across and between staff and governors.
- Use your policies to communicate not just what you expect from your staff, but what staff can also expect from you.
- Use true distributed leadership – hire the right people / get the right people around the table.
- Do not under any circumstances display or tolerate any form of discrimination, sexual misconduct, workplace bullying, or actions that bring your start-up and its values into disrepute.

---

[7] Jason A. Grissom, Anna J. Egalite, and Constance A. Lindsay. 'How principals affect students and schools', *Wallace Foundation* 2, no. 1 (2021): pp. 30–41.
[8] Double and Cook, 2023. Leading Your International School. P.66

Wellbeing – The Core Of A Successful International School

'I first started using the hashtag #WellbeingFirst shortly before I became an international school Principal in 2017', writes Matthew Savage, 'In an attempt to intentionally centre wellbeing as one of my school's three strategic priorities. After all, we were a school "where every child can thrive", and I recognised that, without positive wellbeing, our students would not be able to do so. This is why it had to come first. In the words of the late Stephen R. Covey, "The main thing is to keep the main thing the main thing".[9]

Savage continues:

> I am proud now to be one of the architects of Thrive, a bold new movement for wellbeing in the international schools sector. We recently had to postpone our first attempt at a face-to-face conference focusing entirely on wellbeing in international schools because there were simply too few registrations. Whilst I know that travel is more complicated now, and enrolment is down in many schools, I also came to the sobering realisation that not enough schools yet put wellbeing quite first enough to put their money where their marketing mouth is.
>
> Professional learning budgets are not infinite, and investing in pedagogic or curricular training is immediately appealing. However, whether one looks to Maslow or the tenets of trauma-informed practice, it is obvious that, unless a child or young person is well enough to learn, the rest will never fully and sustainably take root.
>
> Through a concept I call #TheMonaLisaEffect®, I work with schools across the world to help them shift that paradigm, and I am encouraged by what I am starting to see. The message I communicate to schools is threefold. Firstly, we must be humble and curious enough to accept that our students are wearing manifold masks, thickly and well, as a means to perform in a relentlessly performative space. Once we acknowledge this, we can seek creative ways to help them safely take off these masks. Many of my conference keynotes make this point.
>
> Secondly, we need to use data and assessment to create a wellbeing net so tight that no child or young person can fall through it. In other words, we need to measure wellbeing. Much of my work explores this specifically and in detail. As well as leading a recurring course for ECIS (the Educational Collaborative of International Schools) on Data for Wellbeing, I have developed my own model which I call the 'Wellbeing Data Wheel'. This offers a framework for wellbeing measurement that

---

[9] Matthew Savage is an Assessment, Wellbeing and DEIJB Consultant.

every school can and should adopt. Crucially, we must make sure the data we create is as 'warm' and 'street' as it can possibly be.

And thirdly, we need to do something with all of this new information. Apart from anything else, students will, and do, quickly grow cynical about efforts to learn about their wellbeing that are not coupled with intentional strategies to enhance and support their wellbeing as a result. This might, for example, be through a UDL (Universal Design for Learning) approach, finding the 'spikes' to their wellbeing and designing the 'curb cuts' to defuse them; or through reviewing our support capacity, in terms both of our counselling team and our Mental Health First Aiders, staff and students.[10]

THE EMPLOYEE LIFECYCLE

The Employee Lifecycle recognises and responds to the varying stages an employee will go through at your international school. They include: how you attract talent; your recruitment policy; employee onboarding and orientation; professional development staff will receive; and your approaches to retention and separation (how staff leave/exit the school).

Before you start your recruitment process, get clarity on:

- Do you have a profile in mind that outlines the knowledge, skills, abilities and other characteristics (KSAOs) that you are looking to attract?
- How will you be honest with prospective employees about what will be required of them in an international school start-up?
- How much time will we leave between making our final decision and a subsequent offer? We know of several principals who act within 24 hours.
- How will we ensure that we always have a diverse pool of candidates?
- Have those who will be carrying out interviews (including you as principal) received appropriate training about what is compliant in your context?
- Do you know how to answer candidates' questions about the start-up experience?
- Do you have adequate information to give/reassure them about the process/location?

---

[10] Matthew Savage

Designing Effective Job Descriptions

Challenge

Job Descriptions (JDs) rarely allow the employee to fulfil their potential. In international schools, it can be easy at times to get drawn into non-essential roles.

Solution

Design JDs with empathy for the role itself. Review them continuously, and use them to communicate with your staff what they can expect from you.

What Research Tells Us

A recent study in the US carried out by Allegis of 1400 employees and 13,000 jobseekers found that whilst 72% of hiring managers believed they had provided accurate JDs, only (36%) of the job seekers said they were provided with clear and accurate JDs.[11] A lack of clear documentation and description of duties can lead to employee dissatisfaction.[12] JDs can help in simplifying the recruitment process, placing the right teachers in the right posts, helping staff to achieve their potential and guiding teachers through your appraisal process.[13] However, Job Descriptions, although a critical success factor, are often either missing or incomplete.[14]

Poorly Designed Job Descriptions Feature

- A lack of awareness of the overall role, its central functions and core responsibilities, from an ineffective job-analysis process.
- A lack of cultural experience and differences in work styles.
- Inflexible expectations or awareness of complexities that founding schools face.
- An over-simplistic view of what the purpose of the JD is.
- Text written by professionals outside the jurisdiction and regulatory

---

[11] Allegis Group Announces Findings From Its Global Benchmark Study

[12] Ramhit, K. S. (2019). The impact of job description and career prospect on job satisfaction: A quantitative study in Mauritius. *SA Journal of Human Resource Management, 17*(1), 1-7.

[13] Switasarra, A.V. and Astanti, R.D., ' Literature Review of Job Description: Meta-analysis', *International Journal of Industrial Engineering and Engineering Management* 3, no. 1 (2021): pp. 33–41.

[14] Double and Cook, 2023

environment the school operates in, causing considerable compliance issues.
- JDs that are too explicit and distinct causing staff to fear stepping outside of their own JD and across others.

Professional Advice On Writing Job Descriptions

Put your best team and talent together when writing Job Descriptions. JDs are highly valuable marketing and represent the importance that you place on the people who work for your school. Whilst many international schools have worked hard to differentiate these (including the Nord Anglia group) they can remain dry, overly generic and limit the capacity for those who have them to be successful in their roles. Effective JDs are a foundational pillar for all staff in their roles.

Job Descriptions rarely allow for reflection and iteration in their application. A simple strategy when meeting new recruits is to ask them to bring their JD to an informal meeting and gauge their opinion on what they are most excited about and identify any areas in which they may need future support. In *Leading Your International School,* my co-author Warren Cook noted, 'The Job Description itself should be the result of an extensive job analysis process in which Human Resource professionals and subject matter experts who understand the role and responsibilities of the position and can collaborate on the development of an accurate description of the work to be performed.'[15] Ensure you combine the talents of both in their design.

Finally, the JD should be the basis upon which all discussions surrounding performance and the employee's overall contribution to the school are held. Allow staff the time and space to reflect on their own JD and discuss with a school-wide coach where they feel they have added value to the school. JDs add value to the continual conversations between HR staff about the success and challenges they may face. I've worked in some schools where JDs were a closely guarded secret and staff had to second guess what others were responsible for. All JDs – regardless of level or responsibility – should be available to your staff. You are unlikely to build a culture of trust and respect if they aren't. Effective JDs have a good O.V.E.R.V.I.E.W.

- **Organised.** Guidance on what staff should be spending their time on.
- **Values-based.** They represent your school's mission, vision and core values.
- **Editable.** JDs are living and breathing documents.

---

[15] Double and Cook, 2023, p. 136

- Receptive to feedback.
- View skills and behaviours as key aspects.
- Inclusive individual difference; not universal collective conformity.
- Evaluative. Can be used to review performance against criteria.
- Walks the talk. It will support and guide employees to meet your expectations.

As a minimum, your Job Descriptions should include position details including,

- Title / Reports to / Classification (Full Time / Part Time)
- Contracted time
- Work Location / Salary / Level
- General Purpose of the Job
- Essential Duties and Responsibilities/Additional Position Requirements
- After-school clubs/marketing events/boarding duties
- Supervisor Responsibilities
- Qualifications: Education/Experience/Various Skills Sections Required
- Knowledge, Skills, Abilities / Other Qualifications/ Characteristics (KSAOs)
- Physical Demands
- Approval Section for Management

ADVERTISING YOUR ROLES

What Research Tells Us
In Warren Cook's experience – nearly thirty years in Human Resource Management – the cost of a bad hire can be anything up to one-third of the annualised salary. This is when you take into consideration flight allowances, initial hotel costs, onboarding materials, professional development, time off to complete visas and paperwork, re-advertising the roles and the time taken to re-interview.

Where To Advertise Your Roles?
TIC Recruitment was set up in 2005 by experienced international school educators whose desire was to help teachers and leaders find great positions in international schools.[16] Many of their current team have

---

[16] https://www.ticrecruitment.com/

worked overseas as teachers and have first-hand experience with the rigours and demands of international teaching. Their website describes how they work:

> "We are passionate about providing a quality and personal recruitment service to teachers and leaders. TIC Recruitment works with teachers and leaders to ensure they find the best possible placement for them in leading international schools across the world.
>
> Our team is small and efficient. We can be flexible and adaptable to your needs. To find our teachers and leaders the perfect overseas jobs, we listen to their needs. TIC Recruitment doesn't send mass job alerts and we do not fill vacancies for the sake of it. Our priority is to provide advice and support for teachers and leaders looking for their next position in an international school.
>
> We regularly visit international schools that we hire for. This means we can guarantee we can offer teachers and leaders positions in the highest quality schools across the world. We have already visited over 100 international schools so far. We are also proud associate members of BSME, FOBISIA, and COBIS."

Other places to advertise your roles include:

- TES Jobs
- Your website – very helpful for those keen/waiting to join your organisation.
- Teach Anywhere.
- Specialist search consultancies for high-level and leadership positions. These include TIC, Anthony Millard Consulting (AMC), and Edward Clarke.
- Compass
- flyteachers
- Search Associates
- Teachaway
- Teacher Horizons
- Teacherfolio
- ISS EDURecruit

Common Advertising Mistakes

- Advertising in the wrong places.
- Adverts that are written by people with a limited scope and

understanding of the role, leading to the wrong pool of applicants and subsequent poor hires.
- Lack of clarity or even misleading information about the role, the functions of the role and the expected outcomes.
- Written in a manner that uses complicated jargon and is hard to understand, with a lack of overall clarity, which will be confusing to potential applicants and risk reducing your talent pool.
- A basic lack of awareness of the overall costs of advertising.

Professional Advice On Job Advertisements

Job advertisements are your external marketing. When written supremely well and innovatively, they help to enhance your school's reputation and widen your overall search for top and upcoming talent. When written poorly, they have the opposite effect and staff are quick to point out, 'that wasn't in the job description'. A growing trend has been to cover an increasing number of overall responsibilities that are either unrealistic or simply unobtainable. The goal for your school when writing job advertisements is for potential applicants to understand and relish the fact that they will have some professional autonomy around some of their wider roles.

Key Questions To Ask When Advertising Your Roles

- Will the advert attract the right candidates who fit the role?
- Is it clear who they will work with and be accountable to?
- Is it clear what sort of previous experiences and qualifications you are looking for in candidates?
- Have we highlighted the essential functions of the role?
- Do we state the school's mission and core values on our template?
- Are our job advertisements compliant in the countries we will place them in?
- Are the role expectations clear - what outcomes do you expect from the appointment?

Know Your Context!

In France, it is forbidden to publish in any medium (print, online or other) a job advertisement that: contains false or misleading information on matters such as the existence, availability, nature and description of the job, the pay and other benefits offered, and the place of work, sets an upper age limit for candidates, except where required or permitted by law, mentions the sex or family situation of the candidate sought, is written in a language other than French (if the job or work concerned can be described only with a foreign term without a French equivalent, the advertisement must contain a detailed explanation of this term in French).[17]

ATS, CVs or Both?

The Curriculum Vitae (CV) is perhaps one of the great social and educational dividers. Anyone can make a CV look, sound and appear incredible. The accuracy and validity of such information can often be questioned and, because they are also a huge source of bias within our international school, many are choosing to move away from them. The Applicant Tracking Systems (ATS) used by such schools as the English Schools Foundation (ESF) and Harrow are one way of ensuring that the candidate's information is collected objectively. It also allows staff to check the all-important safeguarding boxes such as 'Have you ever been the subject of disciplinary proceedings?' or 'Have ever knowingly been subject to an order that might prevent you from coming into contact with children?'.

Invariably, CVs will make their way across your desk as international recruitment agents fight for your custom. Know how to review them, using Situation, Action, Results (SAR).

What did the candidate do, what actions led them to be successful and how were those results documented? Beware of CVs (especially in leadership positions) that are merely a repetition of the job description.

Filtering Candidates

The quality, standing and financial muscle of your school is likely to affect the number of interview rounds you operate. The process of filtering candidates is designed to ensure that you have the best, most suitably qualified candidate for the job. Air dropping previous colleagues from your former international schools into positions of senior responsibility is not an ethical leadership behaviour, yet is a surprisingly common occurrence in the world of international education. Anyone who applies to your current school must follow the same processes that all other candidates do. Here's Liz Free again, 'As a school that focuses on Diversity, Equity and Inclusion, the International School Rheintal has trialled blind recruitment. What I want to see is getting as many diverse views as possible… will they fit into this school community? What we are learning through this process is that we have biases – both known and unknown bias. Our latest pool of recruitment was the most diverse we have ever had … we managed to remove the Anglo-American bias', she adds.

---

[17] Croner-i Employment Law in France: In-depth

INTERVIEWING

When and how will you be involved in the interview process? Barry Cooper, Founding Principal of The Global College, Madrid, always takes every first interview with a candidate. During the interview he sets out exactly what the school is about 'They are shorter interviews, 20-25 minutes, to get a sense of people and get to know them' he said in the recent Leading Your International School podcast.[18] 'It is never that I am the end-level boss ... I am at the front and I am always very honest with people ... if you go forward from here, this is what we are about' adding, 'If you can see them teach, it's very important to see how they relate to your students. Finally, he says, 'You need to write a list of things that you are not very good at and they become your job description ... that's what I did with the recruitment of the leadership team'.

Questions You May Want To Ask During Interviews

General

- What is your understanding of Child Protection and Safeguarding in our school context – how does that show itself in the day-to-day context of a school?
- How would you want to expand and improve your understanding and experience of this area?
- What expectations do you place upon yourself and how do you endeavour to meet these?
- How do you react when you disagree with a policy or directive you have been asked to implement? This question is designed to elicit an open response about whether the prospective candidate can accept decisions going against them.
- How do you promote social, emotional and academic wellbeing in students and teachers?

Teachers

- What does a highly effective curriculum do?
- How can you further help us to meet the aims and values of this school?
- Are you able to explain how your students have become better learners? Take me on that learning journey.

---

[18] Cooper, B. Leading Your International School Podcast. 2023, Episode #2 https://leadingyourinternationalschool.com/podcast.php: Vision, Values and Virtues

- In an international school setting, relationships with local culture(s) are essential. How would you lead a culturally sensitive school?
- How do we keep learning the primary focus in our busy international school?

Senior Leaders

- Successful school leadership depends upon the quality of stakeholder relationships. What evidence can you share of successful work with any of these groups?
- Explain and analyse a school improvement strategy you successfully led. What do you think were the critical factors in its implementation? What barriers did you overcome and how?
- How do you currently report underperformance, what would you do if a teacher were perceived to be failing and what strategies have you used when dealing with it?
- Many high-performing leaders visit other leaders around the world. Who would you like to visit and why?
- In your opinion, how can schools use the data they have effectively for purpose and impact in improving student outcomes?
- What are the major future risks and challenges you see that we may face and what contingencies should we be making for these?
- What measures can we introduce to reduce staff workload/improve wellbeing?
- Tell me about a difficult conversation you have had to initiate with a teacher; what was the outcome?

You may/or may not ask the following question, depending on your context, so remember to check your local compliance situation.

- Are you aware of anything that may currently or in the future may limit your capacity to perform the central functions of the role? (Check European Context).

Interview Do's and Don'ts

Do

- Be very clear and honest with potential recruits about what to expect – focus on resilience and how it will be needed in a school start-up. Start-ups are hard work.

- Get candidates to exemplify areas of professional resilience they have shown.
- Use a data capture form to capture the same (objective) information from each candidate, and avoid potential bias.
- Follow the same interview format for each candidate that applies for the same open position – regardless of whether they are an internal or external candidate.
- Reinforce flexibility and a need for staff to contribute to the school in a variety of potential ways – not just in the areas they are being specifically hired for.
- Be aware of your own bias, how it may be evident, and what you can do to limit it.
- Probe candidates if you are unsure, may have misinterpreted any information, or feel that the response to the question could be elaborated on.
- Allow the candidate to take notes.
- Ask the candidate what they would expect from you as an employer.
- Remain professional, courteous and wherever possible give brief written feedback to each candidate within 48 hours.
- Make sure that your interview panel is diverse and that for every position there are at least two interview members.
- Ensure the interview questions are linked to the overall description of the job.
- Make sure technology is accessible to your candidates from around the world.
- Allow plenty of time for the candidate to ask questions at the end of the interview. A generally accepted number before wrapping up is around three.

Don't

- Deliberately withhold information from a candidate that may place you and the school in bad light.
- Make promises that you are unlikely to be able to meet.
- Put answers into your candidate's mouth – the interview is a professional conversation, not a cosy supportive chat.
- Always assume that because a person spent a small amount of time at a school, it was necessarily a bad experience.
- Have unnecessary people on your interview panel, that causes the interview to lose its form and function.

Selection & Hiring
Hiring decisions should always take into account the school's philosophy, overarching values and expectations you hold for teachers and staff. Hiring for the skills you need and the behavioural qualities that are likely to implement them is, in our opinion, likely to lead to stronger candidates being appointed. In our combined experience of over forty years in education and its leadership, and as my previous co-author Warren Cook states, 'past performance is nearly always a good predictor of how good a teacher will be at getting the job done'. Always avoid the temptation to hire someone who is 'readily available' and might be a good fit, but for whom a position is unavailable and unlikely to be in the immediate future. Be aware that the international school world is still a relatively small one and a large number of teachers and senior leaders follow their principal when they change schools – some in more than one school. If you are serious about your reputation and that of the school, pay close attention to how you select and hire. International start-ups can have higher turnover rates in their founding years, so give this careful consideration too. As your school grows, its hiring needs will change and your highly committed, resilient starters –or 'builders' as they are often referred to – may give way to more established teachers keen to develop themselves professionally – the 'settlers'. Here we briefly explore one school in Hong Kong and their start-up journey.

CASE STUDY – KELLET SCHOOL HONG KONG

The Kellet School had a rich 40-year history as a Primary school. In the mid-2000s, a decision was made to expand into a through school on another campus. 'Huge political conversations needed to happen with the community', said Matt Seddon, the school's former Deputy Head. Where the end goal previously was students travelling to other schools around the world, 'We had to re-purpose our why, to keep families and their children in Hong Kong'. Once the school secured the land and was granted a site, a timeframe of around 4 years was established. In that time a re-purposed government building was to be used as the school's campus. The school opened up to Year 7, then added subsequent years. The school developed 'a clear vision as a family-based school for academic excellence. Convincing people of serious wealth to stick around with no track record of secondary examination results was a key challenge, notes Matt, adding 'We had to deliver a very bespoke experience and parents initially had a very big impact'. In 2013 by the time the school opened its new campus, by which time student numbers had trebled and staff numbers quadrupled.

Finally, he says, 'Opening a new campus when nobody knows how things worked – how the building worked and functions and the culture that you are trying to adopt was incredibly difficult. Trying to induct staff into a new building that you only got the keys for a few days ago... and you don't know how the aircon works can be unsettling'.

Looking back and reflecting on the school's growth and success, says Matt, the advice he would give to founding principals is 'We had some hard but successful decisions to make. As the school started to build from one subject teacher to a point where leadership roles were created, we made the decision that all new leadership positions would be reviewed after the first two years. This meant staff (including myself) needed to reapply for leadership positions. On average around half of those reapplying retained those positions. This meant we weren't having to have to make even harder decisions further down the line. We were committed to having the best people we possibly could, and this was our way of achieving it'. How might Kellet's approach to selecting the best staff affect you? Here, we explore some further challenges around hiring.

Hiring Challenges You'll Need to Overcome

- Agents/recruitment partners who are not educators may not understand the remit.
- Recruitment programmes take place too late in the academic year, resulting in a smaller pool of suitably qualified and experienced candidates.
- Cultural differences in the meaning of 'teacher' and expectations of the role.
- No experience or understanding of the scope of start-up or the flexibility needed to be successful.
- An increasingly competitive recruitment pool and lack of/availability of suitably qualified teachers.
- Lack of true understanding of the IB philosophy.
- Lack of familiarity with external examination systems such as Cambridge, IB and IPC.

'When you hire teachers, if you're a start-up and you want your first year to be successful and each year after that, it is very important to get a sense of the person's character'. Adam Neufield - Co-Principal at Shanghai United International School Qingpu Campus.

To make the best hiring decisions you can, remember to:

- Follow all safeguarding and safer recruiting procedures scrupulously, especially when the candidate seems 'too good to be true'.
- Appoint the best HR leader you can; use their knowledge to guide you, and give them the best support, mentoring and coaching you can around education.
- Be rigorously clear about who and what you're looking for. Make sure the appointment panel have a shared understanding.
- Develop an accurate job description and profile of the skills and values that will enhance the candidate's overall appeal.
- Focus on value. Both in the sense of individual values and the overall value that individuals can bring to your school.
- Be scrupulously objective. You need hard evidence of previous achievements in similar posts in schools in similar circumstances.
- For teaching appointments, ask teachers to submit a video about their teaching philosophy; show them a clip of teaching in an interview and get their feedback.
- Set up an interview process that gives you the evidence you need. The right interview questions generate the best quality responses.
- Have someone who represents and knows the local culture on your panel. They might spot the critical weakness that you as an outsider to the culture are blind to.
- Rigorously self-evaluate your hiring procedures after each appointment cycle. Did you get the right person – why? – Do more of this? Did you get the wrong person – why? Change before the next appointment process.
- Supplement curriculum knowledge with the character and skills needed to work with colleagues and students from around the world.
- Advertise your vacancies in the right places. If you only advertise your vacancies with agents, ask yourself how it will affect the overall quality of the applicant pool.
- Get the right organisational balance between hiring for existing talent and the potential of those you hire to become outstanding.

- Have an interim strategy for managing until you make the right appointment. Don't make compromised appointments because you can't fill the vacancy.

In 2018, Chris Nicholls, Master of Wellington College International School Bangkok, chose to fly to the UK to watch every possible teacher to be hired teach, before making a final offer. Whilst it might sound an expensive and elaborate strategy, and may even no longer be possible, its attention to detail helped paint an enormously successful picture of the overall quality of teacher the school was attempting to recruit and the standards for excellence it was trying to achieve.

SAFER RECRUITMENT

'We have made several appointments over the years, pending background checks and satisfactory references, and there have been some serious cases which have proven appointed individuals to be unsuitable to be working with children – these offers were subsequently rescinded. Police checks (although necessary) are not enough. We always contact schools that a member of staff has worked in for the last 5-7 years depending on how many schools they have worked in'. *Principal, Eastern Europe.*

Challenge

Recruitment practices are not standardised internationally and some countries are far behind others. As educators, we have a responsibility to go above and beyond local legislation.

Solution

Use your available filters to identify possible risks, prevent the wrong candidates from trying to apply, and reject unsuitable candidates that do. Develop rigorous policies around onboarding and supervision of your staff. You must not in any way compromise.

Risks in Your Recruitment Strategy

International recruitment is full of inherent risks including the background of teachers, their qualifications and work history. It may surprise you that we have learned about false qualifications and fictitious employment histories being offered for sale. As Principal/CEO you are responsible for the hire of every member of staff. Inherent risks in your recruitment strategy include:

- A poorly designed application, screening, hiring and onboarding process.
- Allowing applications from unsuitable candidates who are unfit to work at your school and who present a clear risk to students.
- The length of time it takes. Haste and speed can undermine the process.
- Reliance on agents. One of the key differences of recruitment in an international context. Be very cautious and always look deeper.
- Failure to plan for contingencies you must be ready for, such as staff shortages.

Build The Right Filters Into The Following Stages

Job Application Process

- Collect the full name history of the candidate; include 'legal name'.
- A 'check-box' that asks staff to disclose if they have received any criminal convictions (and) cautions.
- A signed statement to say the candidate has not been subject to any disciplinary procedures concerning their ability to work with children.

Prevent Unsuitable Applications

- Thoroughly appraise your application system, packs, questions and data that you capture – ask the right questions.
- Scrutinise the applications through more than one set of eyes.

Carry Out Pre-Employment Checks With Fidelity

If your school develops a reputation for not carrying out the appropriate background checks, it will quickly attract the wrong staff who may be unsuitable to work with children. Our research suggests that in some cases anything up to 50% of background checks in some larger schools are not satisfactorily carried out. The deeper and more rigorous your checks are, the more compliant your practices will be and the risk that your children are placed in will be substantially reduced.

- Always contact former employers to gauge a candidate's suitability for working with children.
- Carry out the right checks, and if not satisfied, carry out further checks.

- How prepared are you in dealing with candidates you are unable to suitably screen, given their international background and context?
- Do you have a single central record (SCR) that manages employees and volunteers, including the dates checks were carried out, that you can demonstrate to potential accreditation/membership bodies?

Onboarding and Supervision

International schools are busy places, start-ups even more so. Make the initial observance of staff hires a process that includes an observation of the appropriateness and manner in which staff interact with young people. Develop internationally recognised standards of expectations and take time to explain, reinforce, and address any cultural variations and misinterpretations of your Code of Conduct. Explain to staff that they must report any concerns over child protection and safeguarding protection they may have. An adequate Whistleblowing Policy is therefore essential. During onboarding and supervision:

- Provide the necessary documentation, policies and contact details of important designated people.
- Include mandatory safeguarding training on an annual basis – without exception.
- Be clear on role boundaries (particularly in the boarding house); spell out clearly what unsafe/unacceptable practices are.
- Set clear expectations of behaviours. Here, Chris explains.

Professional Advice On Safe Recruitment

You must have a very deliberate and clear strategy for safer recruitment. As a Headteacher in the UK, I took a 'hands-on' approach to all appointments to ensure a consistently high-quality of teacher and to make a personal link with each employee. I have continued this as an International Headteacher. I work closely with an HR manager who always subjects applicants to my scrutiny. International teaching agencies will tell you that they 'screen' every teacher on their list, but you cannot rely on that. I came very close to employing an individual highly recommended by an international agency and it was only when I insisted on knowing why he was not currently in employment that I found out he had been dismissed for fraud. Agents' work is insufficiently regulated because the private international industry is relatively new. Be very upfront with any agents you choose to work with and get terms and conditions relating to safeguarding in writing. Mandate your terms if they want to do business.

Once you have identified possible candidates on paper, use all of your safeguarding antennae with your HR. Interrogate every piece of information you have about the candidate for warning signs. The process may take longer and you will take a pass on a few good candidates who take up jobs with schools with lower thresholds. Have rigorous monitoring procedures once teachers are on campus. Be aware that one poor hire can destroy your school, your career and worst of all a young person's life by the time procedures kick in. When hiring, I investigate the quality of the school and meet every candidate invited to interview either in person or online. I have identified and mentored in my team highly reliable responsible teachers who have a deep, intuitive understanding of Chinese characteristics and advise me on interpretations of what candidates say in Chinese, where I might get the literal meaning, but not the inferences.

Safer Recruitment Summary

- The responsibility for ensuring the development and implementation of rigorous procedures around recruitment lies with you.
- Be intentional with your language at every stage of the employee lifecycle, including the follow-up.
- Ask the right questions and capture them in ways that reduce your risk and likelihood of hiring unsuitable candidates.
- Always assess a candidate's overall suitably to work with children as a part of your interview and selection process.
- Beware that references can be inaccurate, so challenge suspicion by contacting schools by telephone.

One of the best resources you can access to inform your safer recruitment strategy is from the International Task Force on Child Protection. Figure 3.3 shows the Core Practices for reference checks. Download the whole document in the footnote below.

Reference Checks			
The school has a clearly written statement of its hiring procedures including the process by which the institution reviews and validates references. The candidate provides specific minimum information for each referee.			
Core Practices	Y	N	Notes
The candidate provides at least three confidential *professional* references			
One or more of the confidential references is a direct supervisor of the candidate (minimally at the Assistant Principal level).			
At least two confidential references are secured from the last two positions the candidate held during the past 6 years, with one or more of the references supplied by an assistant principal or principal.			
At least two supervisory references are contacted directly, either through technology (e.g. telephone, Skype, etc.) or face to face.			
Questions in direct exchanges include: • Do you have any concerns about the candidate working unattended with children? • Did any of the candidate's colleagues, students or parents express such concerns? • Would you rehire the candidate? (why or why not according to the response received)			
Recommended Additional Practices			
The candidate provides at least two *personal* references (to verify candidate biographical information, including place, nature and timing of employment).			

Referee Verification			
The school has a clearly written statement of its hiring procedures including the process by which the institution verifies the identities of referees.			
Core Practices	Y	N	Notes
Referees are contacted through business email addresses (if possible, e.g. retired) or personal electronic account (e.g. WhatsApp)			
Referees are contacted through business telephone numbers (if possible, e.g. retired).			
Recommended Additional Practices			
Personal numbers are checked through available online directory services.			
Referee identities and contact details are checked using professional directories/sources.			

Figure 3.3. International Task Force on Child Protection (ITFCP) – Recommended Screening and Assessment Practices for International School Recruitment[19]

We now move into one of the most important topics for any founding international school principal/CEO – contracts, and in doing so hope that we can support you through the process. Whether it be in negotiating your own, or those of others'. If you need help, talk to Gráinne.

CONTRACTS

As Principal/CEO, and with the support base you have, you will need to decide on the length of the contract and, where applicable and permissible, the length of probationary period you will give to your teachers and wider staff. You must carefully do your research on the types of contracts and probationary periods you are allowed to offer by law. Generally, the more senior the role, the longer the probationary period is allowed to be. Although the probationary period means the employee is essentially in a period of 'trial', how you word and articulate this needs to be carefully considered. You also need to remember, in our experience, the cost of replacing a teacher will amount to roughly 1/3 of the annualised salary, after factoring in re-advertising the role, recruitment fees, flights, relocation allowances and costs associated with potential cover, and onboarding and orienting the new staff member.

---

[19] Council of International Schools (CIS) International Task Force on Child Protection.

Probation

It may surprise you to learn that there is still a great deal of confusion about what probation is and how it can be managed. During the probation period, you must formally assess the knowledge, skills, abilities and other characteristics (KSAOs) the candidate has presented during the interview and application to see whether they are accurate and in alignment with and support the school in establishing its overall mission and philosophy. During such a time, it is (technically) easier to dismiss a member of staff, as a considerably shorter notice period is required. In our collective experience, where international schools can and do go wrong in this process, there is a lack of collaboration between Human Resources and senior leadership regarding who is responsible for the effective observance, management and documentation of the performance of new hires. The tools that schools use to effectively and sufficiently evaluate staff need to be fair and just, and demonstrate humility in line with your overall guiding values. As founding principal, you will be incredibly busy marketing, talking with parents, ensuring the dining hall runs smoothly and that your buses arrive and leave on time. Getting the support of your wider leadership team is critical. Carefully manage:

- How teachers and wider staff interact with students and safeguard them. Do not accept any circumstances which place your students at risk.
- Staff who deliberately contravene your agreed working practices or whose actions damage your school's culture.
- Staff who are repeatedly late, or who flout arrival/departure times and cause unrest with other staff.
- Staff whose priorities may be repeatedly distracted by the local international landscape and all it has to offer.
- Those who fail to meet reasonable academic deadlines, despite timely communication, support and training.

One of the responses that your staff will most likely state as and when problems surrounding probation arise will be, 'You didn't give me the right training and support'. Make sure that as a school, you document your training, communicate it effectively, and – of increasing importance – have staff acknowledge the training. Use a coaching and mentoring scenario as soon as possible to allow staff to relay that training or convey any misunderstandings or mismatches they may have in their role.

The Contract

Standard international contract lengths, based on our research, are two years for teachers and up to three years for school leaders, although these can and do vary significantly by context. Some schools have moved forward to three-year models for teachers, and some have even moved onto flexible one-year rolling contracts. Each has its pros and cons for you to consider. When deciding the contract lengths you will offer, it may help to answer these guiding questions:

- Is our educational license valid, in place and secure for the length of time in which the contracts will be valid?
- Are we confident in our overall ability to secure the quality of teachers that will add value to our school?
- How large is the candidate pool likely to be and will it expand/contract as the school grows, making it easier/harder to retain or attract staff?
- Will we have the time and resources to develop our staff and provide them with opportunities to develop and lead?
- Are the positions and corresponding skills for which we have hired, potential areas of future growth or decline, according to your natural student intake curve?

'In Sweden, it is very hard to replace underperforming teachers. In international law, the student comes first, but in Sweden, the law (LAS) of protected employment means that no matter how bad a teacher is, the right to employment is stronger than a student's right to learn'. Peter Heddelin.

The more confident your answers are to the questions above, the longer the length of contracts you may be able to offer.

1-2-or 3-year Contracts: What model works best for whom?

Contract length	Pros	Cons	Most suitable for
1-Year	Highly flexible; easy to replace underperforming teachers;	Heavily administrative; lack of sustainable thinking; may attract wrong type of candidate; teachers always looking for other jobs.	Schools in areas of economic uncertainty; lesser experienced staff.
2-Year	Standard international school model; aligned to others.	Teachers often begin searching in year 1.	All international teachers in their first contract.
3-Year	Long term view – more focus on strategic goals; provides longer-term job security.	At times restrictive to the flexible/modern teacher; performance management needs to be carefully managed; higher risk in uncertain economic times.	Founding principals, senior leaders and experienced teachers; schools with strong financial resources/ reputation.

Figure 3.2. International Contract Lengths

The Principal/CEO Contract

As a minimum, when negotiating and accepting your contract, the following need to be understood and agreed upon. Failure to arrive at clarity in any of the following is likely to lead to a breakdown in trust and accountability lines, and ultimately negatively influence the overall longevity of your tenure.

Principal/CEO contracts and remuneration – what to consider.

- Do you have a basic understanding of the law in your country/part of the country?
- Are you in an area of the world that favours the employer or the employee? Remember – you are classed as both in most countries, as principal.
- Have you negotiated an appropriate salary for a start-up? Start-ups are 24/7 for at least the first year – are you being recompensed appropriately for that?
- Does your salary package/contract cover yours/your spouse/family) needs? It is unlikely that you will be able to renegotiate after. Have you looked at:
  1. The exchange rate (especially if you have commitments/ mortgage to pay at home).
  2. The strength of the currency in which you are going to be paid.
  3. The laws regarding home purchase in the location.
  4. Tax laws in both the country you are going to and your home country if you own/rent out a property.
  5. Ease of sending money out of the country and whether there are limits on that amount.
- What is your bonus (if any) predicated upon? If it is numbers generated – how realistic is it that you will ever reach that number? Bonus amounts usually only stay static for one to two years and are often raised incrementally on an annual basis, never quite allowing them to be claimed!
- Are bonuses taxed in that country? How and when are they paid?
- How long is your probation period – how is your success defined and measured and, importantly, by whom?
- Are you liable for repayment to the company of moving/ relocation/housing etc., if let go during probation?
- What financial penalties are applied if notice is given (by either party) before the end of the contract?
- If in an 'at will' country or state, are expenses paid to repatriate you and your family if let go (not for cause) unexpectedly?

- Are leases (car/apartment etc.) still outstanding to be paid by you if you are unexpectedly let go?
- If you are let go, can your children remain at the school (if you wish them to) until the end of the school year/exam period or will you be expected to remove them immediately?
- Is there time in the salary/contract negotiations for you to consult with your lawyer regarding the contract and to raise issues?
- Moral turpitude – Are you aware of the laws in the country to which you are going regarding women's rights and independence? Gay/lesbian rights? Rights of partners/spouses? What does a moral turpitude clause cover in that country?
- Does the company pay for DaO[20] insurance and does it indemnify you?
- Does the company have Key Man insurance?[21] It is worth understanding what this is and why a company might have it.
- When will you 'age out' in that country – particularly important for professionals over the age of 55.
- Salary (and how its paid), bonuses if any –and why they are paid.
- Package, term of contract (number of years) and contracted days per year.
- Scope of expectations.
- Notice period required (for both parties).
- Terms of dismissal (moral turpitude etc.).
- Expectations of company/country (ethics, laws etc.).
- To whom is one responsible and how?
- How will you be judged and by whom?

> **Key Question.** Do you have the right to present the contract to your lawyer?

Remember

If you are an international school principal and would like to receive expert advice about any aspect of contracts, do reach out to us.

---

[20] Directors and Officers is a standard protection for owners/directors/board members in The USA in case the school is sued, you are covered for the costs involved.

[21] Key Man is insurance that covers a key player, to cover all the costs associated with that person not being there.

GENERATING KEY PERFORMANCE INDICATORS (KPIs)

Challenge

As a leader, you need to be able to measure progress in every aspect of your new school's development towards its objectives. If you can't tell this story reliably, using evidence from your key performance indicators, others will – for instance, investors not convinced you were the right person for the job or competitor schools anxious to keep your school out of the marketplace.

Solution

You need evidence-based self-evaluation built into every part of your school programme. Differentiate the evidence base from the objectives the KPIs will sit alongside. KPIs will be a mix of the quantitative and the qualitative. The KPIs answer the critical question: What does the school look like at the various milestones in your journey from opening to excellence?

What Research Tells Us

According to *ClearPoint Strategy,* 'Nine out of ten organizations fail to execute strategy'.[22] Many schools that are part of a chain of schools that have a monitoring and evaluation system choose to grow their own KPI system, which has the great benefit that you can align the KPIs closely with your values.

Barriers To Implementing Your KPIs

- You are likely to be operating outside of a standardised evaluation and monitoring system. The framework you work with will take time to readjust to.
- Home-grown KPIs are not standardised. What looks like excellence to you, may only be satisfactory in comparison to similar schools in similar circumstances.

Professional Advice On KPIs

Here's Chris, sharing his thoughts. As an instructional leader, the quality of Learning and Teaching is of critical importance. My vision was for the quality of learning and teaching to match the best in the world. Therefore, I needed a set of international standards to replace the national OFSTED standards which I used in the UK. I found this from

---

[22] Clear Point Strategy. 9 Reasons Your Strategic Planning Process Fails.

Cambridge Assessment International Education (CAIE), who publish standards based on their work with schools around the world. These standards can be used to set milestones for the whole teaching team and individuals at different stages of professional development in their teaching careers. Teachers can also use them for self-assessment. They must be 'owned' by everybody working towards them. Discuss these standards with your team during implementation and add any measures of local educational culture.

The second set of KPIs is totally different. Our school measures the developing attitudes and values of our students. How do you set standards in this area? One way is through attitudinal surveys. Cambridge Assessment International Education has one of these, too. Our school is very focused on the development of Chinese characteristics which we didn't think was measured well enough, so we designed our system of indicators for student progress in these areas. Measure the impact of your work as a team of teachers to cultivate your agreed values – such as the sincerity with which students study. This evidence is qualitative and brings together the observations of teachers about the behaviours of students and the outcomes of 'tailor-made' attitudinal surveys focused on these same values.

You need an eco-system of diverse KPIs, including external standards so that you can measure progress in your school against the best international standards, and internal standards, to measure progress against your values. You need a diversity of 'quantitative measures' – hard numerical data – and 'qualitative measures' of the attitudes and feelings of stakeholders captured in surveys and interviews.

Remember

The value of any KPI system is that it helps you as a leader to give an honest, objective account of the school to anyone who wants or needs to know. The more your school grows and applies its KPIs, the more you need to work with independent, external consultants who can 'moderate' your evaluations, confirm where your self-evaluations are correct and, crucially, help you to identify where your KPI judgements may need further work.

The 5 KPIs Every Founding Principal Needs To Know

1. Numbers, numbers, numbers
2. Efficacy of marketing (conversion rate)
3. Accreditations (setting everything up in place and ready effectively)
4. Relationships with parents
5. Building trust and credibility

ONBOARDING & ORIENTATION OF YOUR STAFF

Challenge

Onboarding and orientation are often didactic: we are told what to do, when and how to do it. We retain little information and quickly lose our motivation.

Solution

Onboarding programmes should be 'strategic, thoughtful, engaging, and interactive' – then staff are more likely to benefit from them. [23]

What Research Tells Us

Organisations often report that employees are receiving more onboarding activities than the employees themselves suggest.[24] Research suggests 86% of employees make a decision as to whether they will stay in the first few months of a new job.[25] A staggering low number of just 33% of American workers feel engaged, which Gallup has estimated costs the 'U.S. $483 billion to $605 billion each year in lost productivity'. The International Schools Review (ISR) is a subscription-based service that lists over 416 schools in the Middle East and 4,900 Director and Principal reports from around the world. Many criticisms on the site come from ineffective onboarding and orientation practices. A recent HBR study found that onboarding can often 'make or break a new hire's experience'. [26]

---

[23] Double & Cook, 2023
[24] H.J. Klein, B. Polin, and K. Leigh Sutton, 'Specific onboarding practices for the socialization of new employees', *International Journal of Selection and Assessment* 23, no. 3 (2015): pp. 263–283.
[25] State of the American Workforce. 2017. Gallup.
[26] https://www.gallup.com/workplace/238085/state-american-workplace-report-2017.aspx; Onboarding can make or break a new hire's experience. Harvard Business Review, 2022.

CASE STUDY – NETFLIX

There's a reason Netflix's infamous 'Culture Deck' of slides has been viewed tens of millions of times. Its onboarding and staff welfare programmes are notoriously successful. There was a time in the international school world when, after your hire, you waited with bated breath to see whether the member of staff would turn up. Thanks to the likes of Netflix, this is more and more a thing of the past. Netflix has five essential pillars that make up its onboarding. They are: 1. *Preboarding;* 2. *Onboarding buddy;* 3. *Onboarding sessions;* 4. *Project assignment;* and 5. *One-on-ones*. By the time staff hit the office floors, they are already bathed in the Netflix culture, supercharged when it comes to professional working capital, and have developed effective working relationships that can be further strengthened and developed. jobs.netflix.com/culture

Take the time to align your new staff to your culture and values, and save a lot of time when boots arrive on the ground. Share important curriculum documentation and allay fears, and staff will begin to get their heads around what they will be delivering and their approach to teaching and student learning. Probably the most effective aspect of Netflix's approach to onboarding that you could do well to implement are the one-to-ones. These could be in the form of any number of discussions around approaches to work, the school's culture and your expectations of staff in their daily professional lives, and importantly – in the communities they serve and represent.

Barriers To Onboarding Your Staff:

- Hiring the wrong staff who lack the required skills and abilities and end up negatively engaging in the process, lacking commitment to its purpose, and ultimately – leaving.
- Inaccurate Job Descriptions or those that are overly generic; fail to set out basic expectations or articulate what success in the role looks like.
- Loosely managed onboarding. For example, your people leaders have taken leave before or during the process and communication between them is ineffective.

Professional Advice On Onboarding

At the first start-up school I worked at in China, the owner took the time to fly every new hire across the world to meet in the UK – a very smart (and expensive move) indeed. This. however, was because the entire international teaching cohort had left in the first year. For those of us who met in the UK, it was a great opportunity to meet, learn about each other, and gel. Unfortunately, the principal didn't take the opportunity to meet with us individually and share our experiences, professional backgrounds and further ambitions, something I think would have been entirely welcome.

Onboarding awareness, its standards and its practices differ tremendously around the world and from school to school. I know of some schools where the onboarding that you receive is the taxi ride from the airport. Challenge the mindset and narrative you and others might have of employee onboarding – it can be anything up to six months.

Onboarding Best Practices

- Use the *Netflix* approach to 'preboard' employees; get essential paperwork out of the way and share key information in plenty of time.
- Ensure training and development that you and all senior leaders receive is befitting of your organisational aspirations and equips you with the right professional and socialisation networks to overcome challenges.
- Make onboarding *practical* and *interactive*; link any learning material to real-life school strategic examples and assess staff on their knowledge of it later.
- Plan key milestones that new staff can work collaboratively on together – such as opportunities to embed the school's core values in teaching and learning.
- Use a buddy/mentor system that can establish a high-quality relationship between new and existing staff, problem-solve, and develop leadership skills in the mentor.
- Incorporate your school's culture in progressive onboarding steps.
- Plan steps carefully and succinctly – avoid bombarding staff with information and always centre the information around the key functions of the role hired for.

Handing future colleagues a copy of this book will ensure that their minds are tuned in to what you are thinking. By all means contexualise the content further to your situation.

You will likely be required to ask your staff to provide the following during your onboarding process. This should be requested as soon as the candidate has been hired.

- A full-colour scanned copy of their passport that includes the photo page.
- Digital photos and up to 8 physical photos for staff that arrive.
- Degree certificates, notarised from the relevant host country embassy.
- Colour scanned copies of all certificates, including all degree certifications, teaching certifications and any other relevant academic information that the candidate was offered the position subject to.
- A fully updated resumé with a complete work history and any gaps accounted for in chronological order (newest first) and on a Word document.
- A signed letter of employment for at least the last two years of prior employment, that must include: position, dates worked, subjects taught and the contact details of at least 2 references that can be sought at the prior employer.
- A signed health statement, where required.
- Non-criminal record and authentication (issued within the last three months).
- Marriage status (again where legally required for Visa purposes).

Note

The extent of the information you require the candidate to provide and gain approval of will vary between country and context.

ORIENTING YOUR INTERNATIONAL STAFF

It has not been uncommon in my experience for international school leaders to fail to acknowledge the difference between onboarding and orientation. Orientation practices vary drastically in quality and implementation in our international schools. The term orientation describes the activities and practices carried out by HR. They include (but are not limited to): an insight into the school's history, culture or way of working; elements of your school and services you offer; academic guidelines and information; your school's salary practices; and an overview of additional financial/non-financial benefits. Use your orientation process to enrol staff successfully (e.g., in international healthcare schemes), provide emergency safety training (e.g., in Science on the use of specialised equipment), or provide quality training. Anything appropriate for staff to receive training on or be inducted into can appear during the orientation process. In international schools, this is often the first day or a series of consecutive days before the formal school calendar begins. In *Leading Your International School*, Warren 'Highly recommends members of the executive team participate in the orientation by introducing themselves (live, by video or recording); this is a good way to set the stage for trust in their leadership'.[27]

Perhaps the most critical leverage tool you have for orienting your staff successfully is the detailed information you can give to staff on the curriculum you are using, its aims and objectives and how it should be taught. Fail to do this and you will have an army of dissatisfied teachers.

What Hampers Effective Orientation?

- Human Resources capacity, training and the overall role of HR themselves.
- Conflicting interests from senior leaders and HR.
- A lack of strategic approach that fails to use school priorities or embed the cultural expectations and behaviours of staff.

Professional Advice On Orientation

Your onboarding activities with staff can take place anything up to a year before they step foot in your school. They are designed to align staff with the culture and prepare them for the environment they will find themselves in. Orientation encompasses the tools, practices and procedures that your staff carry out when they physically arrive at your school.

To get the most out of your orientation, our advice is to listen as much as you talk. Communication is a two-way process and by allowing your teachers to share their professional experiences, career highs, special interests and passions, you will be laying the groundwork for your professional learning communities and their future collaboration. Keep reminding yourself, your senior leaders and your HR team that learning is an active process – especially when it comes to orientation. One of the best orientation activities I ever took part in was at my former Academy in the UK. Each year we participated in a 'Car Rally' in fancy dress, where we navigated ourselves around the town, collecting various pieces of information, and observing numerous cultural landmarks along the way.

---

[27] Double and Cook 2023, p.153.

Whilst such an activity might not necessarily fit your school's context, think outside the box about how you can orientate your staff, build the school's culture, and create an atmosphere that people will want to be a part of for years to come.

What A Highly Successful Orientation Programme Looks Like

- People-centred. Orientation combines the successful blend of organisational know-how with individual expectations, coaching and support.
- Focused on the Job Description, the school's values system and the central functions of the role that will allow staff to be successful.
- Gives teachers enough time to plan quality lessons.
- Lays the foundation for a collaborative culture and highly effective teams.
- Sets key milestones and goals for staff to meet, which they have ownership of.
- Has the right relevant, succinct information available at the right time.

During your start of school year orientation, make sure you consider your objectives for the week. For example:

1. Successfully Onboard and Orientate new staff.
2. Identify the school's key core aims.
3. Engage all staff with a key whole school priority, e.g., language & learning.
4. Ensure staff are prepared for the first week back.

> **Key Point**
>
> Staff arriving at different times of the year in your international school may slip through the net and miss key onboarding and orientation information and activities. Be conscious of the fact that teachers may be so eager to get up to speed that they overestimate themselves and perpetuate an image that says they don't need any orientation as they have 'been there and done it'. This is a red flag – particularly when it comes to your expectations, safeguarding, child protection and working practices.

Diversity, Equity, Inclusion and Justice (DEIJ)

Challenge

International schools can still act in ways that do not project their outwardly divergent thinking – such as their approach to hiring talent. Research from the Council of International Schools revealed "A leadership team member is three times more likely to be white than of any other ethnicity".[28]

Solution

Follow statements of intent with action – show you mean what you say when it comes to diversity: they are fruitless unless acted upon.

What Research Tells Us

The State of Diversity Report revealed that only 50% of companies have 'defined strategies and processes on setting and calibrating your diversity goals'.[29] Most businesses, it suggests, are 'barely scratching the surface' when it comes to diversity in the workplace.

DEIJ is affected by:

- Historical and systemic discrimination: Your job is to know how and why.
- School policies, practices, legislation attitudes towards progress – are you and your group of schools prepared and ready for the challenges ahead?
- Your leadership and decision-making models; ingrained personal and systemic bias.
- Social taboos. DEIJ is still taking hold in certain societies and cultures.
- Education, cultural competence and a lack of awareness from your stakeholders.
- Challenges from investors to overlook certain aspects. You may face pressure from school owners or parents to refrain from employing certain teachers.
- Media and Social Media platforms that promote hate-speech.

---

[28] What the data tells us about diversity in international school teaching staff and leadership. Alejandra Neyra, CIS Data Analyst and BI Manager
[29] The 2021 State of Diversity Hiring Report (2021). Human Capital Institute.

Professional Advice On DEIJ

Unfortunately, as we have now become only too aware, diversity doesn't just happen. It needs intentional leaders who mean what they say and act like they mean it. International schools in some cases help to serve and protect the interests of those who benefit most from them. You will need to prepare yourself to face such challenges and answer tough questions about your hiring practices. Diversity in the workplace covers the workforce, their background, cultures and belief systems. Set the tone for your school in a different way so that it welcomes every member of your school community, and makes your language simple for people to understand. Look at your overall recruitment strategy and how it can support the propulsion of DEIJ.

Wellington College China has taken on board such future challenges with their ongoing commitment to feed and support the local leadership pipeline in China. Training local Chinese teachers and leaders to undertake professional qualifications is now an underlying part of the school's strategy, recognising the growing need and responsibility as an employer to drive change and improve the futures of all of their employees – not just international ones. Other schools are looking at the ever-growing need to bring their salary models together, thanks in part to the ongoing work of Dr Liam Hammer to bring to the fore of our mind, the notion of the 'split salary' where international (expatriate) school staff receive larger salaries for performing the same work.[30] Be intentional with your approach to diversity and inclusion.

Create Diversity In Your New School By:

- Building it into your recruitment strategy and talent acquisition programmes.
- Exposing children to a broad range of staff, their backgrounds, accents and appearances.
- Having divergent curriculum opportunities that present authors, global icons and advancements in technology from individuals, cultures and perspectives around the world.
- Having Admissions policies for students that are inclusive, holistic and based on potential, just as much as prior academic performance.
- Continually evaluating and improving your culture, policies and overall approach to diversity.

---

[30] Exploring the Ethnic Gap in Teacher Salaries in International Schools – Dr Liam Hammer, 2021. Proquest.

Improve Equity By:

- Identifying and addressing disparities that exist (e.g., challenging salary gaps between local and international staff.
- Delivering quality educational experiences to all students.
- Understanding disproportionate discipline.
- Using data effectively to identify challenges and provide actionable solutions.
- Creating an open culture and being transparent in your leadership and decision-making processes.
- Allowing individuals to speak up and out in the face of such inequality in the workplace.

Equity policy and diversity statement – Teacher Horizons
'Teacher Horizons is committed to challenging all forms of discrimination. Our vision has always been to build an international community of educators and offer a free, transparent, platform to enable all teachers to make more informed decisions about the schools they apply to. We regularly review our processes and take steps to identify and eliminate bias. This is especially true of the language we use, particularly with regard to the way we advertise vacancies.'

Committed to equity and diversity, our initiatives include:

- Creating a focus group of teachers, headteachers and advisers to discuss and identify areas within the sector that can be improved and how we can most effectively advocate for change.
- Ensuring transparency at all stages of the recruitment process between the hiring schools and the candidate teachers.
- Creating a collaborative community experience by building a safe environment for teachers to feel personally supported by advisers that they trust.
- We understand that we do not have all the answers but are committed to challenging attitudes and bias – both internally and also for the organisations that we work with.'[31]

As we come towards the end of this section, we now look at the importance of record keeping and how to deal effectively with teachers and staff when they depart.

---

[31] Reprinted from www.teacherhorizons.com.

Documentation and Record Keeping

Effective and accurate record-keeping in your new international school is an important tool in the chain of your new school's development. Accurate record-keeping breeds confidence and develops internal and external accountability of who you are, what you do and the adopted culture in the manner in which you do it. It also means you meet compliance laws in many international contexts and that you can defend your decisions and how you arrived at them. The following are critically important areas that will need to be effectively documented at your school.

- A Single Central Record (SCR) of all staff pre-employment checks undertaken by your school, on all staff. For a good example of what to include in your SCR, Al Kingsley's book 'My School Governance is a good place to start.[32]
- Training and development records for all staff.
- Senior Leadership Meetings.
- Board of Governors meeting minutes.
- Incidents of bullying, and racism or gender discrimination.
- Performance Management meetings (especially where capability issues have been outlined).
- Salary statements.

Remember

Email is recoverable and in most cases for years (if not decades) after a teacher leaves a school.

Exiting The Workforce

When handled badly the processes and procedures surrounding the exit of an employee can be a marketing disaster. Every departure should be seen as an opportunity to learn about your staff, and school culture and pinpoint areas in which you can further develop.

Effective Exit Procedures are hampered by a lack of awareness of the time constraints involved in the overall process. Ineffective performance management systems that have not been communicated effectively, often leave staff with unexpected surprises. A complete avoidance or lack of

---

[32] Kingsley, A. (2022). *My School Governance Handbook: Keeping it simple, a step by step guide and checklist for all school governors.* John Catt.

overall strategy can leave staff feeling undervalued and searching for places to take their skills and knowledge elsewhere. As Karen, International Principal in Dubai, notes:

> International teachers have an increasing desire and need to be heard. Their opinion matters. Make sure that the process for leaving your school is as painless as possible and ensures nothing but a positive experience that virtually eliminates any possible friction and ensures both parties leave on good terms. If staff are unsure about the type of reference they are going to get, handle this with care, early.

Online School Reviews

International Schools Review (ISR) and Glassdoor are online international school feedback websites, based on schools and their leaders. Many teachers, leaders (and now increasingly parents) use such sites when considering where they want to work or send their children. Our research in the writing of this book suggests that some schools even openly discuss online reviews during their interviews. Whether that is a good strategy or not remains to be seen.

Why You Should Monitor Online Reviews?

As principal, you need to know what is being said about your school. Quotes and articles written online can quickly be taken out of context. One comment about a particularly bad experience may quickly become two. Research from Market Connections suggests that it may well be the silent workers who present the most threat to your school and its reputation. While silent customers don't complain to management, they most certainly will share their experiences with their friends, neighbours and co-workers. A dissatisfied customer will tell between 9 and 15 people about their experience, with over one in ten telling 20 people about their bad experience'.[33] Manage the overall experience that your staff receive when leaving your school to minimise the likelihood of staff leaving a negative review on a review website.

---

[33] What's More Dangerous Than a Dissatisfied Customer? A Silent One. Market Connections.

Section 3 Review Questions

- How well do you understand your school culture? The culture of any complex organisation is made up of many components – can you analyse your school culture by these parts? Which components do you manage well and communicate with fluently? Which components are more difficult and why?
- Does your school comply with local and international educational regulations and standards? In which areas does it strongly comply? Where are the areas of possible weak compliance? Do these areas pose any threat to the long-term sustainability of the school?
- What do you understand by 'inclusivity'? How inclusive do you believe your school is? Are there any 'reality gaps' between your aspirations to be inclusive and your actual practice? How do you measure and audit inclusivity? Is inclusivity a value shared by all of the investors and owners of the school or might they be prepared to compromise inclusivity in pursuit of profit?
- How well do job descriptions at every level in your school contribute to outstanding teaching and leadership? What core values are threaded through every job description?
- Is there an explicit reference to 'learning' in every job description? Are job descriptions routinely evaluated and updated?
- How confident are you that your staff recruitment procedures 'get the right people into the right seats on the bus'? Do you routinely review the recruitment process? Have all participants in the recruitment and interview process been trained to the same professional standards? Who is responsible for the different parts of the onboarding process for new staff? Do you carry out 'exit interviews' to gather evidence to help reduce staff turbulence?
- What are your key takeaways from the section? What did you learn that you will apply in any future start-up where you are involved?

PART FOUR

BUILD YOUR EDUCATIONAL PROGRAMME

PART FOUR - BUILD YOUR EDUCATIONAL PROGRAMME — 181

Academic Plan — 182

Curriculum — 183
   Your Curriculum Aims — 183
   Agree on Learning Outcomes — 188
   Choose Your Curriculum — 191
   Developing Your Curriculum — 198
   Develop Your Assessment Policy — 201

Provide Effective Professional Development — 205
   What Professional Development Will You Provide? — 205
   Curriculum Training — 206
   Build Your Calendar — 209

Design Your Timetable — 210

Creating Policies and Procedures — 212

Accreditations, Authorisations and Memberships — 218
   What Are Accreditations? — 218
   What Are Membership Organisations? — 220

Academic Plan

The focus in this section is on your academic plan. Here we highlight key requirements for building an educational programme that is 'fit for purpose' in terms of educational outcomes and the development of your school, its staff and students, including how to:

- Link your school curriculum to your Mission, Vision and Values.
- Choose the curriculum that is most likely to support your school and students to grow, to achieve their potential, and to develop your educational brand.
- Provide effective professional development that is evidence-based and linked to your school's overall strategic direction.
- Measure the implementation and impact of what your teachers teach, and the outcomes that your students achieve in your specific context.

Key learning outcomes include:

- Acknowledging the importance of a specific learner profile to develop your overall academic culture, support the behaviour of students and teachers, leading to responsibility of action.
- Understanding the decisions that schools face and the questions they ask/answer before they agree on their educational calendars and timetables.
- Knowing what assessment looks like in an international school and how you (as principal) are the key driver on student outcomes, second only to the class teacher.

Curriculum

Your Curriculum Aims

Challenge
Articulating curriculum aims can sometimes be done as an afterthought. Exams and university final destinations often take priority. This causes a 'blind spot' in the thinking of the principal.

Solution
Use the aims behind your curriculum to help your decision-making process around which curriculum best fits your context.

Embracing Sustainability in International School Operations
Here, Grace Hu examines how sustainability can be incorporated into your curriculum.

Challenges and Pathways to Success
In recent years, sustainability has emerged as a critical global concern, with individuals, organisations, and governments recognising the need for sustainable practices to ensure a viable future for our planet. As the world becomes more interconnected, the role of education in promoting sustainability has gained significant importance. International schools, being hubs of diverse cultures and ideas, have a unique opportunity to foster sustainability principles and inspire young minds to become responsible global citizens. However, integrating sustainability into the operations of international schools presents its own unique set of challenges. Here we explore what sustainability entails and discuss the hurdles faced in its integration, along with potential solutions to overcome them.

I have been working in the field of sustainable development for 15 years, and have served the world's top 500 companies, NGOs and foundations at home and abroad. No matter which institution I go to, the questions I get asked the most are: What exactly do you do? What is sustainable development? So, 'What is sustainability?'.

At its core, sustainability refers to the practice of meeting present needs without compromising the ability of future generations to meet their own needs. It encompasses three interconnected pillars: *environmental stewardship, social responsibility,* and *economic viability.* Achieving sustainability requires a holistic approach that considers the environmental impact of our actions, embraces social justice and equity, and promotes long-term economic stability. The popular reference these days, ESG, stands for 'Environmental, Social, and Governance'. It is a framework used to evaluate a company's performance and sustainability practices based on its environmental impact, social responsibility, and governance structure. ESG factors have become increasingly important for investors, as they seek to align their investments with companies that demonstrate responsible and ethical practices, making a positive impact on society and the environment while maintaining strong governance standards.

While we see sustainable development is valued and practised by more and more governments and institutions, we also see many challenges in operational integration. Here are some examples of challenges in integrating sustainability into international school operations:

- *Awareness and Mindset Shift.* One of the primary challenges in integrating sustainability into international school operations is raising awareness and fostering a shift in mindset among the stakeholders. Sustainability should be seen as a fundamental value and a shared responsibility rather than an optional add-on. Educators, administrators, students, and parents must understand the urgency and benefits of incorporating sustainability principles into everyday practices.
- *Curriculum Integration.* Developing a curriculum that integrates sustainability across various subjects is crucial for embedding sustainable practices into the fabric of an international school. However, achieving this integration requires dedicated effort and collaboration among teachers from different disciplines. Incorporating sustainability into existing curriculum frameworks can be challenging, but it can be achieved through interdisciplinary projects, case studies, and experiential learning opportunities that highlight the connections between subjects and real-world sustainability challenges.
- *Infrastructure and Operations.* The physical infrastructure and day-to-day operations of international schools often present obstacles to sustainability integration. Outdated buildings, energy-intensive systems, and wasteful consumption patterns can undermine efforts to reduce the carbon footprint of a school. Retrofitting buildings with energy-efficient technologies, implementing waste management systems, and promoting

sustainable transportation options are some strategies to address these challenges. However, budgetary constraints and resistance to change can pose hurdles that need to be carefully addressed.
- *Community Engagement.* Sustainability efforts can only thrive when the entire school community is engaged and actively participates. Communicating the importance of sustainability to parents, involving local communities, and collaborating with external organisations can create a supportive ecosystem. By organising workshops, awareness campaigns, and community service initiatives, international schools can foster a culture of sustainability that extends beyond the school premises.
- *Evaluation and Measurement.* Measuring the progress of sustainability initiatives is essential to understand their effectiveness and identify areas for improvement. Implementing evaluation mechanisms, such as sustainability audits, tracking energy and resource consumption, and conducting regular surveys, can provide valuable insights. However, developing suitable metrics, ensuring data accuracy, and interpreting the results can be complex. Schools may need to seek external expertise or collaborate with sustainability-focused organisations to overcome these challenges.

On top of these challenges, there is one overriding logical challenge, which I think is the most significant and possibly the root cause of all difficulties. If we compare other departments, such as procurement, HR, etc., to firefighting departments, we find that they will work wherever they are needed. The content and needs of the job are preceded by the job content. Just like in Western medicine, which identifies which part is sick, the right medicine will be prescribed and the disease will be cured once the medicine is taken. Sustainable development, relatively speaking, is a process that needs to be 'set on fire' and then tackled through 'fire-fighting'. It is a 'systemic therapy of traditional Chinese medicine' that spans various functional departments, identifies problems, 'reforms' and 'innovates'. As a result, many people will feel worried and retreat because they cannot see short-term benefits and results. This leads to hesitation and a lack of smoothness in the advancement of work. Therefore, when dealing with these challenges, the priority is leadership and firm awareness. Starting from this, I list some relatively feasible coping strategies for your reference:

- *Leadership and Commitment.* Effective leadership is vital in driving sustainability integration in international schools. School administrators should champion sustainability initiatives, allocate resources, and provide professional development opportunities for

staff. A top-down commitment combined with a participatory approach can create a strong foundation for sustainable practices.
- *Professional Development.* Investing in professional development programs for teachers can empower them with the knowledge and skills required to integrate sustainability into their teaching practices. Providing training on sustainability concepts, curriculum design, and pedagogical approaches can enable teachers to be effective sustainability advocates.
- *Student Empowerment.* Students are key stakeholders in the sustainability journey. Engaging them in decision-making processes, encouraging student-led sustainability clubs, and providing opportunities for hands-on projects can foster a sense of ownership and empower them to become sustainability leaders.
- *Partnerships and Collaboration.* International schools can leverage partnerships with sustainability-focused organisations, NGOs, businesses, and universities to gain expertise, access resources, and share best practices. Collaborative projects, joint research initiatives, and exchange programs can enrich the learning experiences and amplify the impact of sustainability efforts.

Overall, integrating sustainability into international school operations is a complex endeavour, but one that holds immense potential for shaping a more sustainable future. By addressing challenges such as awareness, curriculum integration, infrastructure, community engagement, and evaluation, international schools can embrace sustainability as a guiding principle and inspire the next generation of global citizens to become advocates for a sustainable world. With strong leadership, commitment, and collaborative efforts, international schools can be at the forefront of promoting sustainable practices and nurturing environmentally conscious individuals who will drive positive change in the world. Remember: Together, we make a pioneering impact.

CASE STUDY – THE EDUCATION IN MOTION (EIM) SCHOOLS GROUP.

'Learning: Across our schools, we aim to continue delivering a holistic education with our five-year education strategy. We have seen Dulwich College Shanghai Pudong and Green School Bali shortlisted for the World's Best School Prizes in the areas of sustainability-focused and wellbeing-focused education respectively.
Planet: On a group level, we are cooperating with suppliers to improve sustainability within our supply chain and advancing our Carbon Roadmap Strategy.
People: We have deepened our commitment to building a rewarding employee experience by refining our Employee Value Proposition, establishing a Wellbeing Strategic Working Group to develop a groupwide framework for a proactive approach to wellbeing and continuing to offer our award-winning Accelerate Middle Leadership Programme (which has so far seen 250 leaders graduate since its inception).
Policy: We launched the "Responsible Supply Chain" project in 2022 to develop systematic strategies and policies to guide responsible sourcing practices across the group, ensuring greater adherence to good labour practices throughout the supply chain by enhancing our capability to collect Scope 3 emissions data in the future'.[1]

EiM has created an ESG report. When you want to invest in an environmentally friendly company, where does the school's money that they invest go? The sustainability conversation needs to be had at that level, too.

Laurence Myers, K12 Service-Learning Coordinator at the American School of Dubai, notes,

> I don't think it's fair for schools to not do something because they think that the children choose it. For example, some schools are reluctant to make changes in their menus at lunchtime because it is what the 'children enjoy or want to eat'. In my time in Malaysia, we went down the curricular path towards sustainability. However, we realised that we needed something more tangible and contextual, that children could relate to in their everyday lives.... Moving forward we are getting our

---

[1] EiM Environment Social Governance Report, 2021-22

students to contribute to the conversation around sustainability within and through their service learning.

Kathy Burger Kaye, former Consultant at the IB, when talking about the service model for their CAS program, comments, 'Studying about sustainability is not enough. A five-year-old is not going to have the same process as an eighteen-year-old. We are all about trying to build and develop change-makers. Anything sustainable we need to create a learning space around it'.

Professional Advice On Sustainability
Catherine Copeland of the consultancy Global EDGEucation shares her views on the importance of aligning the Sustainable Development Goals to the work that you will carry out in aspects of your school. 'Our future schools have to look at sustainability starting right from our mission and then how we look at bringing the sustainability perspective into our curriculum and teaching approaches', she says. 'Sustainability should be the basis or foundation of our systems thinking, so operationally, academically and community-based and beyond', she adds. Finally, she says, 'It isn't just a topic or a course that you are developing, but instead an actual culture of thinking'.

Feedback from the 'Take Action Global Climate Action Schools Program' was that 'teachers felt that they weren't prepared and didn't have the resources to teach about the Sustainable Goals Development Program'. Accreditation organisations are now increasingly moving to adding sustainable standards to their accreditation standards and expectations and this is something you will need to be prepared for.

AGREE ON LEARNING OUTCOMES

Just as you base your curriculum decision on best fit looking back to the prior learning experiences of your intake, you *must* anticipate their future learning needs. I learned very quickly, notes Chris 'that the majority of my students were focused on gaining admission to Russell Group universities in the UK and that many of them had a preferred option for STEM courses – Sciences, Technology, Engineering and Maths. I was influenced by arguments that the IB gives students a better overall set of learning skills and makes them reflective learners. Hard-headed common-sense thinking told me that 3 good A Levels and an English language qualification could get them admission to their target universities. Having opted for IGCSE as the 14-16 qualification, there was every reason to move directly to the complementing A levels. I was also confident in one fact from my own education experiences. The depth of study on A level courses means that students can move very comfortably into undergraduate studies even at elite universities like Oxbridge or the London School of Economics. And so it has proved. In eight years of university cohorts, we have had zero 'dropouts' because every student has found the step from A Level to university manageable'.

If you are moving from a standard national curriculum to an international setting you need to put yourself through the learning curve of understanding the full range of available courses and their benefits. Coming from a UK curriculum background I found myself utterly ignorant of the American Advanced Placement ('AP') courses. These are quite different from A Levels but are accepted by UK universities and can be used very strategically to improve a student's admission profile. In Economics, the second year of A Level is notoriously challenging because of the essay-style assessments. The equivalent AP course covers the same content but the end assessment uses multiple choice questions and short written answers instead of the A Level essay, which is much better suited to the needs of most bilingual learners. Be open-minded and prepared to think more widely than your former national curriculum straitjacket.

Choosing The Best Curriculum For Your Context

- Which course is the best match to the needs of your intake?
- Which curriculum is best suited to the skills of your teachers?
- Which curriculum best prepares students for future challenges?
- Analyse the curriculum that students follow before entering your school.
- Find the best fit between the curricula available to you and the prior learning.
- Make sure students can transition as seamlessly as possible from one way of learning to the next, with minimal learning loss.
- Be ruthlessly pragmatic. As a school leader, you might have the deepest possible attachment to a particular curriculum, but if you can't get the teachers to teach it, it's a lost cause.
- Analyse the school location, the salary scales on offer, the local competitive market for teachers and work out pound for pound (or 'rmb for rmb') which teachers you can attract and retain.
- The most important implication of this is that teaching quality is more important than curriculum content.

> **Key Note**
>
> 'The IB Primary Years Programme (PYP) is a framework, not a curriculum. Many schools use the IB PYP as a framework and embed one or more curricula into the framework. The Diploma Programme (DP) is a curriculum with set books and set course options to choose from', notes Gráinne.

CASE STUDY

DUBAI. YOUR ACADEMIC PLAN – THE KNOWLEDGE AND HUMAN DEVELOPMENT AUTHORITY (KDHA)

Here is an example of how one regional authority, Dubai's KDHA, regulates international curricula. By looking at this example you can prepare yourself to answer some of the curriculum questions that will be raised in whatever context you work in. The KDHA publish guidance for prospective private schools in Dubai. Key information you will need to set out includes:

- The type of school you are planning to be.
- Your proposed curriculum – refers to the type of curriculum and he phase/year levels to which it will be offered.
- Gender, Grade/Year groups – what are your expectations on roll numbers after five years of opening?
- Instruction time. Here you must set out the number of teaching delivery days and teaching delivery per day.
- The language (or languages) of instruction you intend to use for teaching.
- Language(s) of instruction: Number of hours.

Key focus areas for KHDA evaluators:

a. If the applicant has a plan for extending the school's Grade range, is it manageable and coherent? Does it follow the KHDA-prescribed model?
b. Do the target numbers match the accommodation available, as shown in the site plan?
c. Is the proposed class size appropriate? Is it based on international best practices?
d. Is the total annual instruction time in line with KHDA expectations? Minimum 20 hours per week for Grades 1-2, minimum 25 hours per week for Grades 3-12; around 190 days per year for all Grades.
e. Is the admissions policy in line with the school's vision and mission, as stated in Section 4.3 of the proposal? Does the proposal include appropriate procedures for admitting students with special educational needs?[2]

Choose Your Curriculum

Research released by Dubai's Knowledge and Human Development Authority (KHDA) suggests that, 'Seventy-three per cent of students attend Indian curriculum schools rated Good or better, and the proportion of students attending 'Very Good' schools has increased to 42%, up from 37% in 2019-20.'[3]

---

[2] Dubai's Indian and Pakistani curriculum schools show great improvement. KDHA 2nd March, 2023
[3] Dubai's Indian and Pakistani curriculum schools show great improvement. KDHA 2nd March, 2023

Use the following table when deciding what curriculum model you will consider implementing. You may wish to design your measurement criteria.

Curriculum	Australian	American/AP	British GCSE/A-Level	IB	Indian	OPC
Standardised						
Wide range of subjects						
Creativity						
Collaboration						
Critical Thinking						
Communication						
Implementation						
Student experience						
Flexibility in approach						
Sustainability /SDG focus						
Assessment Outcomes & Quality						
Cultural relevance						
Cost						
University value						
Standard course length						
International recognition						

Figure 4.1. Choosing Your Curriculum Matrix.

Before Implementing the AP Curriculum, Conan Magruder Suggests You'll Need to Consider

- Cost. Implementation is expensive for new international schools and often requires textbooks, training teachers, and administering exams.
- Time commitment. AP courses are demanding for students, requiring significant time and effort outside of regular school hours. When you consider in-class practice, test prep like Albert.io, students possibly hiring outside tutors, and the sheer number of tests students take (one of mine is taking seven this year) – you will find it may affect performance.
- Rigidity. While AP offers some flexibility, it can still be relatively rigid in terms of what is taught and how it is assessed, which may

not be a good fit for all students and teachers. It can be difficult for administrators to understand the process and for teachers who are familiar with other curriculums to adapt.
- Lack of cultural relevance. Designed for an American audience and may not always be relevant or applicable to students from other countries and cultures. In the US, not all students can take all tests (indeed several states ban AP African American History) and in China, some tests must be taken in Hong Kong or Singapore.[4]
- Emphasis on standardized testing. AP Places a heavy emphasis on standardized testing, which can create stress and anxiety for students and may not accurately reflect their abilities or knowledge. AP test preparation is difficult for some students who do not take preliminary classes in the subjects they test in.

Before Implementing the Cambridge Curriculum, According to Chris, You'll Need to Consider

- As a British pattern curriculum, it might not give the best possible preparation in some academic areas.
- It favours application of knowledge to problem-solving in its examinations. This demands an element of skills development in the teaching, for example, critical and creative thinking, and can be challenging for inexperienced teachers.
- Apart from Mathematics and Sciences, A Level courses have higher English language competency demands. Multiple choice questions are not used in A Level exams, unlike equivalent AP examinations. In A Level Economics for example students will need to be able to write coherent short answers, which are not part of the AP assessments.
- Every curriculum and assessment system contains bias. Although there is zero explicit bias and a genuine commitment to international relevancy, courses and examinations inevitably contain British references and contexts that are occasionally puzzling to international students.
- The courses and assessments are not 'plug and play'. Inexperienced teachers need training to be able to deliver high-end results. Syllabus content and assessment criteria are clearly and methodically laid out, but demand to be carefully read by teachers

---

[4] At the time of writing, In China you need to go to Hong Kong to take AP Histories or book with the same company in Singapore. You can't take AP Comparative Government in China with that company.

before any teaching of the courses and may be challenging for bilingual teachers or teachers without a UK background.

Before Implementing the IB Curriculum, You'll Need to Consider. Here's Sabah Rashid to explain

- Cost. There are budgetary considerations for new international schools, including annual programme fees, a minimum professional development requirement for teachers, the appointment of a Programme Coordinator, and administering exams. Some schools expect students to pay for their exams.
- It can be an issue finding activities/providers/sponsors/hosts that are safe (in unstable countries) or available (in countries that do not have a tradition of youth community service).
- Commitment. The DP requires students to study six subject groups and core components across all disciplines. Through subject selection, students can tailor their course of studies to meet their needs. While DP offers subject choices and level choices, there is less flexibility due to the compulsory breadth of study required. Students study a minimum of 2 courses. The DP is a two-year curriculum and assessment system. There is considerable work and study needed.
- Acceptance by colleges and universities. Colleges and universities may still have very high minimum score requirements for entry into their institutions. A score of 38-40+ can be considered well-received by selective universities. The highest total available for DP students is 45 points. Scores are based on the grades of 1-7 for each of the 6 subject areas for a total of 42 possible points. There are up to 3 additional points for core components.

You really have to communicate the program effectively to your stakeholders', notes a former Head of Secondary, 'Constant communication around the values, goals and expectations was necessary to get parents to buy into the IB'.

Before Implementing the Finnish Curriculum, You'll Need to Consider

'Essentially, there are two main models of international education – the British and the American, with the IB sitting somewhere in between'. If you find yourself working in a future international school in Turkey or Brazil, then there is a chance that the adopted curriculum may be from Finland. The aim of Finnish International Schools 'Is to convert many existing international and bilingual schools into Finnish international schools. As well as being a local brand, powered by Finnish International Schools to bring the international element, whilst continuing to deliver the national curriculum', says Alejtin Berisha, the group's Chairman. Before implementing any aspect of the Finnish Curriculum, you'll need to consider:

- The quality of teachers that you will need to hire to support the overall philosophy.
- How you can justify a curriculum that is based more on informative assessment than standardised testing to parents who may not be wholly aware of its structure?
- The Finnish curriculum has to be developed around your context and the framework from the *seven transversal competencies*. It cannot simply be exported and replicated in other countries/contexts.
- Choosing your global education partner carefully who will be able to take the best of the Finnish education model and make it fit for the global education market.
- Attracting Finnish teachers – who themselves are in high demand and are extremely well supported and developed in Finland itself – may prove challenging for you to rely on as a founding model.

Here's Alejtin again, 'If you want your children to have a holistic education – not merely focusing on academics, if you want your students to learn by doing, and understand the world around them. And if you want your child to be happy and healthy, you should choose the Finnish education model'.

Other curriculum models you will need to consider

- Australian curriculum schools
- Chinese curriculum
- Indian curriculum schools
- Singapore curriculum schools
- The International Primary Curriculum (IPC)

Special Educational Needs (SEN)
In some countries there are no official agreed standards as to what constitutes a Special Educational Need. It may be that within the educational framework in your local context, the concept doesn't apply at all. This then translates into problems of provision:

- There may be no locally trained experts in the various needs you want to meet.
- Parents and students may not understand the logic of SEN and feel that the school is labelling or disadvantaging the child.
- Locally trained teachers may lack the knowledge, confidence and expertise to offer inclusive teaching.

You must understand the local culture and framework around SEN. You need someone with SEN expertise on your team, and it's even better if they also know the local framework. If not, get them trained up ASAP. Start by carrying out a needs analysis. What are the most pressing needs among current admissions? If students are transferring in from external schools, what knowledge and information is coming into their records? If you can improve data transfer from 'feeder' schools, do so.

Talk to your teachers, during interview and after hiring them. What barriers to learning have they experienced in the international classroom? Don't forget that high-achieving students can also experience barriers to learning. Our collective experience of international schools suggests this can be a feature of certain private, fee-paying schools. Hot housing and other high-stakes parenting styles can translate into psychological and behavioural barriers to learning and well-being.

Based on your needs analysis, get your SENCO (Special Needs Co-ordinator) to draw up a costed, time-referenced SEN Action Plan. At the heart of this Action Plan is likely to be professional development (PD). There will be two streams to this: 1. Awareness raising and understanding – i.e., 'Understanding the student with dyslexia in your classroom'; and 2. Classroom management and teaching strategies – i.e., how to provide for the student with ADHD in your classroom. Be clear and consistent on the difference between SEN and ESL. Provide Language Awareness training and clear statements on bilingualism to minimise confusion and wasted resources.

Strategise 'Alternative Provision' based on your needs analysis and carefully balance the need for inclusion and well-being against the gains of extracting children from mainstream classes for 'special education.' Ask your SENCO to monitor and analyse both quantitative and qualitative data to justify the benefits of 'withdrawal' programmes.

Cast the net wide to source more specialised services. Therapeutic psychological counselling will be challenging to locate but can be tracked down. You may need to engage with local medical services to find sources of support.

Remember

SEN provision demands ongoing and rigorous scrutiny. Assumptions can become institutional practices that damage vulnerable children irreparably. An outside set of eyes keeping a focus on SEN is advised, possibly a member of the School Board/Governing Body. Students with SEN should not be invisible nor should they be overly visible in patronising celebrations of their progress. Weave powerful stories about all sorts of people overcoming all sorts of barriers in life into the school culture and avoiding labelling anyone or any one group as 'special'.

Barriers To a Holistic, Student Centred, Learning Centred Curriculum

- Pressure to maintain 'high academic standards' may narrow your curriculum vision and approach to sustainable education.
- A predominate 'university-centric' model of education that ignores a wider variety of educational skills and entrepreneurship.
- Competing school interests that shift the focus away from your overall educational vision.

How To Choose The Right Curriculum Model for Your Context.

Use an effective data-gathering system to highlight key workforce and entrepreneurial skills of the future. Other success criteria can include the curriculum:

- Enables all students to achieve in line with or above predicted targets.
- Motivates and inspires high-quality learning for all learners
- Is well-matched to the social, cultural and political local context.
- Enables all students to become lifelong learners, well-equipped with the skills needed for success in both higher education and life in general.
- Teaching and its assessment are all clear, well-understood and supported by the school stakeholders.

We now move into how you will go on to develop your chosen curriculum.

Developing Your Curriculum

Challenge

The curriculum is a core part of the international school as an institution. It commands considerable resources – teachers, a timetable, and course books. Continuing with a static curriculum runs several risks, including denying students exposure to important new areas of knowledge and understanding; losing market competitiveness; and the 'fossilisation' of both the curriculum and its delivery with an attendant gradual loss of enthusiasm and motivation from both teachers and students.

Solution

Carry out a formal curriculum review every year and be ready to ask hard-headed, objective questions to reach an evidence-based decision as to any curriculum updates.

Curriculum Review
The annual curriculum review must be a formal process. It should be both 'top down' and 'bottom up'. Heads of academic subjects should carry out a rigorous curriculum review of service and delivery within their subject areas. This must be evidence-based, using examination data, formative assessment information, lesson observations and student satisfaction surveys. You can think of it like this: every year the school is investing in all of the services provided by the department and the annual review is a justification for why the level of investment should be maintained, expanded, or cut.

The report must then be submitted to a senior leadership team member for review – either an attached senior line manager or the Deputy Head of Curriculum and Learning. It is best practice to include an element of external scrutiny which can be achieved by including school governors, parents, or an external consultant in the review process.

Finally, the whole school overview will be presented at a Senior Leadership meeting for decisions and executive actions. The senior team may want to ask Heads of Subject to attend the Curriculum Review meetings to develop discussions if needed. A critical element of the Review process is the outward-looking 'horizon scanning'. Your subject leaders and your curriculum leader must be aware of external threats and opportunities. This means being well informed and ahead of the curve on both curriculum changes from outside, e.g., new government frameworks or syllabus changes from examination boards and developments in curriculum delivery, such as new technology or teaching methods. Timing is critical here. The further ahead of changes your school is, the better the implementation process will be.

What inhibits curriculum success?

- The conservative mindset of teachers, students, parents and or school owners.
- Curriculum regulations at national or local level.
- The availability of resources – teachers, course materials and even time.
- 'Faddism' – Well-intentioned, ineffective solutions that demand a lot of attention.

Professional Advice On Curriculum Reviews

In my leadership of a Middle and High School in an international context, notes Chris, 'I've kept the curriculum and its delivery under ongoing evaluation and review through the simple question: Is it fit for purpose? That purpose was to prepare students rigorously for successful admission to leading global universities, typically in the US, UK, Canada or Australia. At least that was my initial framing of 'fit for purpose', until I realised it was not challenging enough. As believers in life-long learning, we should be examining whether our curriculum is a fit and proper foundation not just for short-term goals like university admission, but longer-term objectives such as empowering students to successfully manage the challenges of international university study and then accessing meaningful careers beyond that – a curriculum for life. To gather evidence for this, I set up an 'alumni association' so that the school can stay in touch with students in their international destinations and gather evidence about strengths and weaknesses in university study and the sorts of careers they enter. Through this, I have a constant 'feedback loop' so that I can develop the curriculum to reflect real-world opportunities and challenges. An example of this would be the increased teaching of research skills in all areas of the curriculum to 'close a gap' which some students experienced in their first-year transition to university study. If you get this right your alumni themselves can become the messengers, passing essential advice to future cohorts via video or live-streaming presentations.

This question of fitness for purpose goes wider than academic preparation. There are a wider group of future needs for your students, including 'citizenship', by which I mean the knowledge, understanding and skills required to contribute to society and its improvement. In the mind of every international principal should be the question, 'How do we best prepare our students to become environmental citizens who will make their contribution to reducing the threats of climate change, loss of biodiversity, unhealthy lifestyles and economies based on harmful patterns of resource use and waste'. 'Future-proofing' your curriculum by its very definition is challenging. When you try to anticipate future needs, you accept that there are no 'off the peg' curriculum solutions. As a leader, you must be prepared to put in the extra hard work and risk of being a 'pathfinder'. You may find some imperfect, but 'best fit' solutions to such gaps in the curriculum including, for example, the 'Global Perspectives' course from Cambridge Assessment International Education, which gives sustainability a credible entry point into your curriculum and offers accreditation in environmental citizenship skills to your students. However, to meet objectives such as the Sustainable Development Goals of the United Nations you will have to do some pioneering curriculum innovation, with the risks that this carries'.

How To Successfully Develop Your Curriculum

- Make sure each subject area has a written curriculum plan, used to 'on board' new recruits and which is a working document.
- Make sure there is regular and rigorous curriculum review. This means stress-testing the curriculum both internally and externally. Internally you will measure the curriculum's effectiveness in delivering the broad range of school mission statements, not just narrow academic targets. Externally you must judge the effectiveness of the curriculum against international best practice- is it competitive?
- Systematically listen to and respond to the views of the two critical consumers of the curriculum - students and parents.

Remember:

Be constantly sceptical; demand a reliable evidence base for innovative projects. Wherever possible, insist on a trial period before implementation. I was approached by an American company wanting to sell me the 'definitive' solution to IELTS English through online tutoring by US undergraduates. It sounded feasible. They wanted a minimum one-year contract. I insisted on a two-week free trial period and that was enough to show up a plethora of problems that saved me from wasting not only a lot of money but more critically – precious learning time.

Develop Your Assessment Policy

Challenge

Future Knowledge, Skills, Abilities and Other Characteristics (KSAOs) are evolving. Yet many children lack the basic fundamental basic skills to lead independent lives at their universities.

Solution

Develop innovative forms of assessment that measure collaboration as well as individual achievement; support your students to be able to live independent and enriching lives, whilst forging links with employees that visualise the skills they are going to need.

What Research Tells Us

The University of Birmingham in England recently published guidance to parents on 'Seven lessons to teach your kids before they go to uni'. Incredibly, they featured skills like how to use a washing machine, change a duvet cover, and make a basic meal.[5] Pearson, 'the world's learning company' suggests we need to 'build a culture of employer engagement with education'.

The Singapore Ministry of Education (MoE) provides a number of fantastic resources for schools on its website. Here, Oasis Primary School – Singapore outlines its 'Purpose and scope of assessment':[6]

- Assessment is the process of collecting, analysing and interpreting information to assist teachers in making decisions about the progress of their students as well as about their teaching.
- Assessment should provide evidence of student performance relative to learning outcomes and assessment standards as described in the MOE syllabus.
- Assessment should be both formative and summative and should be used to provide feedback to students that supports and enhances their learning.
- Formative Assessment could include a range of appropriate activities such as projects, oral presentations, written reports, demonstrations, performances, investigations, practical work, and creative writing.

---

[5] Seven life lessons to teach your kids before they go to Uni. The University of Birmingham.
[6] Qualified to Succeed: Building a 14-19 education system of choice, diversity and opportunity. Pearson's report into the Future of Qualifications & Assessment in England.

- Summative assessment (e.g., Semestral Assessment (SA) and Continual Assessment (CA)) must be designed to measure student achievement and report evidence of student learning relative to the assessment standards for each specific learning programme or subject.[7]

Barriers To Getting The Right Assessment Policy In Place

- Outdated beliefs and values-systems of what effective assessment is for.
- Overemphasis on standardised assessment systems that lack local references and fail to measure skills and competencies values in the local context.
- Issues with bias, reliability and validity.

Make sure you can train domestic staff to be able to accurately and consistently apply the assessment criteria of the Examination bodies you choose to adopt.

Professional Advice On Assessment Policy

Your school's assessment policy and its delivery will be influenced by and have a significant impact on the overall school culture. Staff leading assessment in your school are key appointments to get right and need significant professional development, training and support. The Standards for British Schools Overseas relating to assessment and the 'Quality of education provided' state that a school:

> 'demonstrates that a framework is in place to assess pupils' work regularly and thoroughly and use information from that assessment to plan teaching so that pupils can progress'.

A well-structured Table of Specifications (TOS) helps ensure that assessments are valid, reliable, and aligned with your teachers learning objectives. It will also enable you to be specific about the cognitive level of the assessments and their questioning.

All assessments need to be branded and standardised in their appearance, format and the evaluative system in which marks are awarded. The Cambridge curriculum has some very good templates and extensive resources for assessment that will help smooth the process of assessment in a new Founding School.

---

[7] Assessment Information. Oasis Primary School.

In 2015, PISA looked at the 'purposes of assessment' (both standardised and teacher-developed assessment). They were, to:

- Guide students' learning
- Inform parents about their child's progress
- Make decisions about students' retention or promotion
- Group students for instructional purposes
- Monitor the school's progress from year to year
- Compare the school to district or national performance

Be clear on why you are assessing, what you are assessing and how assessment fits into your school's overall academic journey. When it comes to assessment, make sure that key dates are on your school calendar, your teachers have plenty of time to prepare for them and that students realise that it is equally the process and manner in which they approach them, as the outcomes themselves that are important in building positive lifelong learning habits.

Key Questions When Designing Your Assessment Policy

- What is the purpose of assessment?
- What knowledge, skills, abilities and behaviours do you want to assess?
- What types of assessment will you use, and how will teachers be supported in their design and implementation?
- Will some assessments be more important than others? If so, why?
- How will you seek the views, input and professional concerns of all stakeholders?
- How will assessment data be stored securely and who will have access to it?
- How often will you assess your students?
- Do you have the appropriate space in the design of your building for exams and assessments – especially when your school grows and develops?
- How will you increase the diversity of your curriculum, its framework and assessments?
- How will you ensure that sustainability and sustainable practices are woven into your assessment policy?
- How will you use the data from assessments for continuous improvement?
- How will you evaluate the success of your assessments?

> **Key Point:**
>
> Communication around assessment is a critical component of establishing a successful founding school, with a good reputation for academic excellence. Consider developing a specific communication plan about how you will inform parents – new to your school, about all aspects related to the manner in which you assess your students.

Provide Effective Professional Development

WHAT PROFESSIONAL DEVELOPMENT WILL YOU PROVIDE?

Challenge

There is a wide disagreement about what successful Professional Development is in our international schools. Research that supports it is often inconsistent and contradictory.[8]

Solution

Ensure Professional Development fits your context and is focused on your whole-school goals, linked to students' outcomes. To work, it must be followed up, reflected upon, and sustained.

Research On Professional Development:

In 2013, a synthesis of professional learning research revealed that 'Most professional development today neither changes teacher practice nor improves student learning'.[9] As Thomas Guskey points out, by 2014 a summary of approximately 900 math's-related professional development showed that there was 'Very limited causal evidence to guide districts and schools in selecting [an] approach or to support developers' claims about their approaches'.[10] A meta-analysis of 27 professional development programs revealed that 'PD programs had no significant effect on student learning'.[11] A study of 10,000 teachers and 500 leaders across 3 school districts in the US revealed that, despite a huge investment in teachers, most do not appear to improve year on year and that our schools as systems fail in their efforts to articulate how teachers can improve; even when teachers did improve it was virtually impossible to say PD was the contributory factor.[12] Yet a 2020 research study from the Council of British

---

[8] T. R. Guskey. 'What Makes Professional Development Effective?', *Phi Delta* Kappan 84, no. 10 (2003): pp. 748–750. https://doi.org/10.1177/003172170308401007 .

[9] A. Gulamhussein, in T.R. Guskey, 'Professional learning with staying power', *Educational Leadership* 78, no. 5 (2021).

[10] Gersten et al., in T.R. Guskey, 'Professional learning with staying power', *Educational Leadership* 78, no. 5 (2021): pp. 1–2..

[11] Kahmann, R., Droop, M. and Lazonder, A.W., 2022. Meta-analysis of professional development programs in differentiated instruction. *International Journal of Educational Research*, 116, p.102072.

[12] Jacob, A. and McGovern, K., 2015. The Mirage: Confronting the Hard Truth about Our Quest for Teacher Development. *TNTP.*

International Schools (COBIS) showed that 56% of senior leadership respondents noted 'Enhanced Professional Development' as a strategy for improving retention.[13]

CURRICULUM TRAINING

You must provide consistent, adequate training and development around the core tenets of the intended curriculum model you intend to use. Without doing so, you risk a series of misaligned approaches to curriculum understanding, design and execution. Here are some examples of curriculum training you will need to provide.

- IB PYP Exhibition training undertaken by the IB Coordinator.
- Exam training for IGCSE's and policy/ practice must be defined.
- A Level training of policies and processes in place.
- University Counsellor in place as soon as IGCSE's are approved (accreditation) and numbers permit.

Some schools have moved to delivering their own internal PD. Here we discuss.

CASE STUDY – THE NORD ANGLIA GROUP

The Nord Anglia group of schools uses a range of professional development strategies to upskill its staff, build professional collaboration, and ultimately enhance student outcomes. One such strategy is an online university with between 500-1000 online courses, including mandatory safeguarding training that all employees must attend. Teachers often lead PD in other schools and each year there is an annual conference with individual hosts and features 'jobalikes' – opportunities for teachers in similar roles or those who share common interests to collaborate on when meeting and highlighting challenges and how they might overcome them. As one teacher said to me, 'PD is really difficult to get right … you need choice … at times you need to be conscious of the fact that many teachers simply don't want PD or are unmotivated to receive and implement it'. As a Founding Head, an awareness of such issues will be valuable to the professional development journey model you take.

---

[13] COBIS Annual Research Survey 2022.

CASE STUDY – BRITISH SCHOOL AL KHUBAIRAT, THE BRITISH EMBASSY SCHOOL IN THE UAE

Nigel Davis, Head of Secondary, speaks about the transition in staff performance development that has taken place at the school during the last five years. Teaching and Learning is now referred to as 'Teaching for Learning' with the key question in focus, 'How do we create more learning'? The school offers a menu of PD opportunities to its staff, including subsidised master's degrees; a full suite of National Professional Qualifications (NPQs); online training from Evidenced Based Education (EBE); and The Chartered College of Teaching (CCT), for example, 'The Certificate of Evidence Informed Practice'. Nigel says, 'Creating a culture in which our teachers strive to be better teachers year on year, is at the core of what we do'. Lesson studies often involve staff working in triads in an attempt to create lessons that have a higher learning effect. In partnership with the Teacher Development Trust (TDT), two staff are facilitators for the NPQs in Senior Leadership and Leading Behaviour and Culture. 'Staff retention is very very high', notes Nigel. BSAK is currently the winner of 2 'Best School Awards' from the schoolscompared.com Top Schools Awards in the UAE. They were judged outstanding in every category by the local authority ADEK and the British Schools Overseas Inspectorate.

Factors That Will Limit The Effectiveness of Your PD

- An approach that is sporadic and does not have students' academic outcomes at its core.
- Lack of motivation, individuality of practice and a link back to overall classroom practice.
- The wrong PD at the wrong time in a school start-up's lifecycle.
- PD that is not followed up or embedded in teachers' practices.
- A 'one-size fits all' model that demotivates, fails to challenge and lacks a contextual fit to the school and its needs.

Professional Advice On PD

Professional development can be a great divider in international schools, as teachers jostle for places on courses and the career development and pay progression benefits they bring. I strongly advise that when you begin considering the professional development that you will offer to your teachers, you do so partly in line with their experience and qualifications. 'Underpinning any form of professional development your school intends to carry out', notes Chris, 'Is a thorough analysis of your teaching and learning performance'.

A great deal of online PD can be done by teachers before they arrive at your school as part of your orientation process. Certainly, they must have a fundamentally secure idea of 1) the curriculum they will be teaching; 2) the context they will be teaching it in; and 3) the resources/environment in which they will be teaching it.

Successful Professional Development In A Start-up

- Use high-quality and effective PD to improve overall teaching quality and improve outcomes.
- Underpin it with careful research that relates to your context, students and staff.
- Teachers understand and demonstrate why they believe it adds value to your academic outcomes.
- Teachers involved in it become interdependent, aware of best practices and equally aware of ineffective ones and myths.
- It is enjoyable and teachers benefit from it, and this directly and positively influences the students they teach.
- HR keeps a full, accurate and up-to-date list of all training undertaken by staff.
- HR engages teachers in regular conversation about the effectiveness of PD, and how it has/hasn't helped teachers to do their job more successfully.

Professor Rob Coe from The Education Endowment Foundation (EEF) suggests 4 mechanisms can be built around to implement effective PD.[14] They are:

1. Build Knowledge.
2. Motivate staff.
3. Develop teaching techniques.
4. Embed practice.

---

[14] Maximising professional development. A balanced approach to Professional Development. Professor Rob Coe.

Build Your Calendar

A major concern for international schools around the world – and families who recognise professional, planned procedures – is the school's calendar and its constant changes. Such parents are likely to openly criticise your school for not being well organised if you make amendments after its release – particularly as many parents will have made international travel arrangements themselves for their entire family.

Great School Calendars	Poor School Calendars
• Are designed to meet the needs of the students they serve. • Include all key term dates, specify 'domestic and international' holidays, observances etc. • Are sustainable by choice, design and practice. • Include all internal and external assessment timeframes. • Include teacher collaboration, PD, teacher meets and parental consultations. • Value PE, Drama and The Arts. • Include the start/finish dates for clubs and Co-Curricular Activities (CCAs). • Include all holidays/public holidays and important cultural, and/or religious observances. • Include report deadlines and data entry requirements – no hidden surprises! • Dedicate time for parental coffee mornings. • Include key dates for staff intentions.	• Are 'teacher centric' and designed from the teaching/not learning perspective. • Miss valuable opportunities to develop your PLCs from the start of your school opening. • Are void of curriculum activities leading staff to think it is the norm. • Add extra-curricular activities ad-hoc • Miss out key holidays and requirements for staff to make up certain public holidays. • Move data entry for reports forward, damaging staff morale and commitment in the process. • Leave parents till last. • Leave staff guessing when it is they should decide when they stay or leave.

> *Key Tip*
> Avoid the temptation to repeatedly change your calendar!

Design Your Timetable

Challenge
Timetables are historically designed to benefit the teachers who deliver them – NOT students who receive them.

Solution
Design your timetable with learning and the students who follow them as *the* centrepiece.

Barriers To Implementing Your Timetable

- Access to timetabling software. Software from the U.K/USA may not be available or be licensed for your international context.
- Local expectations. You may have to negotiate with local expectations about the organisation of the school day. For example, in China some work with a belief that Maths has priority and should be favourably timetabled.
- Extra-curricular provision. 'International' curriculum contexts can reflect a holistic approach, which gives time and space to sports and the arts. Some contexts may not share this value which could lead to a 'squeeze' on extra-curricular time.
- Teacher resources. You may share teachers with another part of a larger school. To get the right teachers in front of classes you might rely on part-time teachers. Local restrictions may impact the flexibility of staff. Be pragmatic in your timetabling.

Professional Advice On Designing A Timetable
It is perhaps a sad state of affairs that the timetable format my parents, I and my son had, varied very little in terms of time and overall structure. Despite huge changes in work practices, sleep and eating habits, schools do tend to start (and finish) in a predictable manner. When it comes to the timetable, few school institutions create as much anticipation as they do demoralisation. Most teachers – no matter how experienced – take a momentary glance to note what they are teaching and when, before the inevitable comparison with colleagues. To understand the timetable is to know you will never please all of your staff all of the time.

The Golden Rules Of Timetabling

- The timetable is there to serve the students who receive it, not the interests of a few staff who might benefit from its design.
- Impartiality is key. Let the software take the blame, not the individual who produced it.
- Support your school's priorities – not individual or departmental ones.
- Start early and hand it to your teachers in plenty of time.

Remember: when it comes to timetabling, DO NOT make promises that you simply cannot keep. Be prepared to listen to objective criticism that is clearly based on improving learning.

Creating Policies and Procedures

Policies
Your school's policies and procedures should represent the school's mission and overall culture you are trying to embed. They should also be used as a highly valuable tool to demonstrate what staff can expect from you – not just what you expect from them. Every policy and its corresponding procedures needs to fit your school's needs. At a former international school where I worked, most of its policies had been duplicated from the UK founding school it was twinned with. All were written for a British teacher audience and not contextualized to China. As a result, many were worthless. If, as principal, you give the impression to your staff that your policies are an irrelevance, you will be taking a serious compliance risk in how the school operates.

Creating new international school policies from scratch takes a considerable amount of time. You may choose to find examples that are similar in your Mission, Core Values and operating procedures and refine them to yours. Make sure that the most essential policies from which you plan to build your school's culture are ready, robust and in place from the time you begin your recruitment process. Your policies may well be your 'mission infrastructure'.[15] Before opening, your policies and procedures should be continually reviewed and refined.

Every policy cannot be critical; some simply have to be more important than others. Communicate the non-negotiables, and in doing so avoid placing your school, its staff and students at risk. Do not assume that your staff are aware of them, understand them or have all interpreted the same message form them – they won't. All policies must be:

- Clearly written.
- Shared with all staff electronically/physically and appropriately communicated.
- A receipt of understanding needs to be received by you, the Principal/CEO

---

[15] R. Lake, A. Winger, and J. Petty. (2002). The New Schools Handbook: Strategic Advice for Successful School Start-Up in Partnership with School District Officials, Staff and Community Members.

Your Key Founding Policies – In Order of Implementation

- *Keeping Children Safe In Your International School.* Safeguarding Policy including Child Protection and Anti-Bullying.
- *Professional Expectations & Working Practices.* How you conduct yourself, interact and model your behaviours inevitably becomes your school culture.
- *Admissions and Marketing Policy.* Clear, widely understood and easy to expedite, the faster you'll sell your school places and get to breakeven and beyond.
- *Safer Recruitment Practices.*
- *Diversity, Equity & Inclusion.* How will your school show fidelity here? Elaborate policies often revert to default mechanisms that breed inequality. You may face severe pressure to academically stream your students, and with little evidence it will develop your school's overall culture. Such policies may also go against the belief systems of curriculums such as the IB.
- *Curriculum Policy.* How will teachers plan, deliver and assess? What are the expectations and resources used/not used? Cultural observances, and what can/cannot be taught – particularly important in China and the Middle East – are significant.
- *Learning.* How your students are expected to learn.
- *Teaching.* The way teaching is to be carried out.
- *Assessment.* What assessment looks like: how teachers design and implement effective assessments and what they do with the results of it.
- *Behaviour Management.* Before teachers arrive and begin teaching, they need to be aware of, understand, and be prepared to be questioned on the school's behaviour policy.
- *Reporting Policy.* Reports designed and prepared; How reports are written/shared, when and the process.
- *Electronic Devices,* Social Media Policy and Communication with Parents. An increasingly important policy in our international schools, yet often overlooked, with some teachers communicating directly (and privately) with individual parents without the school's knowledge.
- *Trips/Educational Visits Protocol.* A risk assessment for all off-site visits and, wherever possible, a prior site visit as an established form of good practice.
- *School Nurse's routines.* Policies to treat: asthma, allergies and diabetes. Standardised letters to parents for head injuries, accidents,

termly health reports, lice/hand foot and mouth disease, and food choices (in local language and English).
- *Boarding policy and procedures.* Including staff ratios, lights-out times, and food/drinks permitted.

Barriers to Creating Successful Policies

- Cultural Irrelevance. Policies are mirrored and taken from international partner schools and thus have limited contextual scope and applicability.
- Poor implementation. Launching a policy and then not monitoring or reviewing its overall effectiveness/performance.
- Inconsistency. Failing to hold staff, students and wider stakeholders accountable to the standards that you set and articulate.

Remember

Upon any inspection and accreditation visit, you will be expected to provide evidence of your policies in relation to safeguarding and child protection. General Data Protection Regulation (GDPR) around the world can vary substantially and your staff may need specific training on the collection, storage and access to the data your school holds.

We can't highlight every policy that will be important to you, but here, we highlight two, given our collective experiences in international education, that will be critical in relation to how your school operates – we begin with keeping children safe.

Keeping Children Safe

When I began working in Malaysia in 2015, it quickly became apparent to me that international variations in how we keep children safe exist. Travelling through the Malaysian jungle in a pick-up truck with children standing in the rear left me full of fear.

Although it still surprises me, there is growing confidence among younger teachers who think it is acceptable to experiment with drugs and communicate their elaborate drug CVs to anyone prepared to listen. Any teacher who experiments with the use of drugs in their position as an international teacher is not fit to work with children – period. Make sure your school policy relays this message and deals swiftly and effectively with those who contravene the law.

Note – Cannabis Is Now Legal In Thailand

Many schools are now waking up to the fact that cannabis is now legal in Thailand for personal use. Tourism Thailand, a public body, publishes a list of criteria any international school principal/CEO needs to be aware of.[16] They are:

- Individuals under 20 years old, pregnant women and breastfeeding women are not eligible to use cannabis except under the supervision of health professionals.
- Possession of extract containing more than 0.2 THC and synthetic THC requires permission.
- Cannabis-contained dishes are available in authorized restaurants.
- Approved cannabis health products are accessible through specific channels.
- Smoking cannabis in public spaces, including schools and shopping malls is illegal.

In Thailand, your policy on cannabis will need to be explicitly clear to staff, many of whom may arrive with the assumption that they are legally within their right to use it in the privacy of their own homes.

Procedures For Reporting Staff Absences

One of the policies you will need to pay particularly close attention to in your founding year – particularly if you want to create the right culture and climate – is your approach to staff absence. Your staff will have experienced a wide number of professional (and perhaps unprofessional) practices. Some will not let anyone know until the final possible moment they are absent; some will try their hardest to contact you – the principal; and others will know the procedures inside out and will be determined to make the most of the 10 or 12 days of paid absence they may be granted. Therefore:

- Make sure that you communicate your policy and procedures around the reporting of absence continuously, not just at the start of the year.
- Have staff sign off on them to demonstrate receipt/that they have read it.

---

[16] 10 Things Tourists Need To Know About Cannabis In Thailand - Tourism Thailand

Key Questions Around Policies

- Do you have full and practical understanding of your role in keeping children safe, and all aspects of Child Protection?
- Do your policies protect the wellbeing of your staff and improve the probability of effective staff retention?
- What will your policy be on publishing your examination and assessment results in your founding year(s)?
- What school/academic data will you/won't you publish?
- How secure are your potential systems for identifying, supporting, and communicating individual educational needs that your students may have?
- Do you have a clear and practical understanding of the cultural expectations and limitations that may be at work in this sensitive area?

When Drafting Your Founding School Policies

- *Use your why.* Explain what the policy is, why it is needed, what it intends to do, and how it will support your school and its overall aims.
- *Refer back to the school's vision* to support the aims of the policy and the school culture you are trying to develop.
- *Focus on learning.* Use future curriculum/accreditation organisations as support.
- *Involve wider stakeholders.* Have regular parental engagement sessions to articulate your curriculum aims, processes and approaches to dealing with behaviour. Be explicit about your school's complaints procedure and its channels to parents.
- *Establish an evidence base.* Involve professionals and organisations centred on academic excellence in their design.
- *Contextualise your policies.* What worked in Dubai is unlikely to fully work in Japan or China.
- *Use 'intentional language'.* Set out explicit actions that support how words convey meaning.
- *Monitor and review* the performance of your policies – give individuals responsibility for doing so.
- *Insert dates* for updates.
- *Allow time to gather feedback* and suggestions around how policies might be further improved. Ask questions about their design, scope and how they might be implemented in your context.

'In Azerbaijan, I always found it incredibly challenging to establish policies and make them stick, as rules can often exist as a shade of grey, rather than black and white. This made it hard to develop momentum in school improvement and changing the educational approaches to a more modern pedagogy'. Principal - Azerbaijan

Accreditations, Authorisations and Memberships

WHAT ARE ACCREDITATIONS?

Accreditations are systems of school review that verify to all stakeholders – including future customers – that the operational systems, and the policies and practices that underpin them in your school, are aligned with the school's mission, philosophy and vision of how to achieve them. They represent the values, culture and ethos behind the particular type of school you will become. Here, we separate accreditations into accreditation organisations (such as the Independent Schools Inspectorate – ISI for British international schools) and membership organisations (such as the Council of International Schools – CIS). First and foremost, you need to ensure that your owners or board members know and are distinctly able to articulate the difference between the two models. This will save a lot of time and emotional trauma when your owner asks, 'Why aren't we accredited with the IB?' or 'How long before we get accredited'? Talk your owners through this process – diligently. Each accreditation and membership has contrasting purposes and criteria to meet, as well as varying amounts of time needed to become accredited with them. The goal should not be about getting them as fast as you can, but instead delivering a school climate and culture that shows your intentions and practice in both achieving and sustaining the high standards, processes and policies that underpin your vision for the school. The opportunities and challenges they present to you and your school will also differ. Here we explain further.

Accreditation of British International Schools
The Independent Schools Inspectorate (ISI) has approval from the UK Department for Education to inspect British Schools Overseas (BSO). It provides an across-the-board inspection process for all British schools overseas, with reports published with the full authority and oversight of the British government.[17] The following organisations amongst others can carry out inspections of British international schools overseas.

---

[17] British schools overseas: how to get accredited

- Independent Schools Inspectorate*[18]
- Penta International*[19]
- Cambridge Education*[20]
- Educational Development Trust [21]

Curriculum-based International School Accreditations such as the IB, Cambridge and Edexcel exist to provide a level of quality assurance in the curriculum, its underlying core values and how it is assessed. The IB PYP accreditation process should start in the first year if possible and takes about 3 years to do thoroughly before you offer it. IB DP has to be started before you open/or before you start doing it. Cambridge and Edexcel- again, before you start offering them.

Accreditation of American International Schools

There are a number of organisations who work with schools in the Americas and worldwide, particularly if one is offering traditional American curricula or AP's. Some of these bodies are only able to work with Not-For-Profit schools or those that have charitable status. As with everything in the world of education, this is changing all the time so checking each organisation's particular scope is, of course, necessary.

- Cognia, formerly AdvanceED and before that, the Southern Association of Colleges and Schools (SACS)[22]
- Middle States Association of Colleges and Schools (MSACS, but usually known as MSA)[23]
- Western Association of Schools and Colleges (WASC)[24]
- Southern Association of Colleges and Schools (SACS), also known as AdvandedEd[25]
- New England Association of Schools and Colleges (NEASC)[26]
- North Central Association of Schools and Colleges (NCASC)[27]
- Northwest Association of College and Schools (NACS)[28]

---

[18] Independent Schools Inspectorate (ISI) British schools overseas
[19] Penta International Training, consultancy, school management & inspection
[20] Cambridge Education -- Quality Assurance
[21] Education Development Trust - Accountability and school inspections
[22] Cognia
[23] Middle States Association Commissions on Elementary and Secondary Schools
[24] Western Association of Schools and Colleges
[25] Cognia - Accreditation and Certification
[26] New England Association of Schools and Colleges
[27] Higher Learning Commission
[28] Northwest Commission on Colleges and Universities

What Are Membership Organisations?

Membership accreditations are essentially an award of quality assurance that can be displayed as part of your school marketing campaign to show that your school has reached an externally prescribed set of recognised standards in that particular aspect. They are primarily for peer review, quality assurance, maintaining standards, support and training for staff, and networking for heads. Accreditations elevate your school in an international marketing context. To gain accreditation status, for example, schools first pay a membership fee and in most cases a 'registration fee'. After becoming accredited, there is an ongoing annual recurring fee. As Greg Parry, CEO of Global Services In Education (GSE) notes: 'There are many organisations that offer this with varying levels of credibility, but they will all measure the school's operational performance against a clear set of criteria and standards'. Anyone wanting to go down the CIS route, for example, needs to be 'devoted to its mission and vision for students, focus on the quality of teaching and student learning, and constantly seek improvement', he adds. Memberships such as COBIS/CIS/FOBISIA etc. can usually be started as affiliate memberships in the first year of a school start-up; charges are normally dependent on the number of students. The cycle of school evaluation generally varies between three and five years. Member organisations include:

- Council of British International Schools (COBIS)
- Council of International Schools (CIS)
- Federation of British International Schools in Asia (FOBISIA)
- Accreditation services for International colleges (ASIC)
- New England Association of Schools and Colleges (NEASC)
- Western Association of Schools and Colleges (WASC)

Why Are They Valuable to a Start-up?
Membership accreditations, both academic and non-academic, add an enormous amount of value to your school. They provide opportunities for formally recognised professional staff qualifications, annual seminars and online webinars, student competitions, links to professional associations, and sporting competitions in your host country and overseas. The FOBISIA sports tournaments at Under 11/13/15 provide some of the most memorable and highly marketable opportunities your school can get.

> **Key Note**
>
> As Gráinne states, 'As principal/CEO you need to be aware of the different types of accreditations, their application systems and the time you are likely to need in obtaining them'. Do not underestimate the number of hours, meetings and follow-ups that they will consume. 'Accreditations are not superficial and will eventually be supported in the way that you have successfully managed to set up your school leadership structures, with clear, purposeful and accountable distributed leadership. You simply cannot do it all by yourself', she says.

These Might Stop You From Becoming Accredited

- A lack of understanding among the owners as to what the accreditation pathways look like and how they can be of benefit to the school.
- Paying lip service to any recommendations or findings in your self-assessment.
- Delays in key appointments, including Head of EYFS, Head of Primary/Secondary, Premises Officer, HR and Exams Officers.
- Mismanagement of the exam process, including the setting, collection and storage of exam papers.
- Financial pressures to reduce operational costs in your founding years.
- Company/ownership processes that do not fit the educational, financial or regulatory parameters of the accreditation's framework.

Professional Advice On The Accreditation Process

Accreditations are a reliable way to give your school a clearer presence and identity in a crowded education marketplace. They often help overcome the frequent isolation of independent, private international schools that might not have a place in the local education ecosystem. They aid student recruitment and can support staff recruitment, too – particularly if you allow your staff to become part of the accreditation process of other schools. As such, they are one of the best professional development experiences you will be giving, so think carefully about how you may incorporate this into your leadership development and training system. Bring this up at the interview stage, if you intend to use it as a core leadership development strategy.

Behind any accreditation – as well as in the process of meeting the required standards – sits your school's overall integrity. To adopt an idiom, accreditation is how your school can 'wear its heart on its sleeve': it shows who you are and what you stand for. Accreditations can be strategically deployed to set a new direction to meet your school vision, or to 'amplify' the impact of an aspect of the vision both within the school and wider community. Each accreditation process requires significant personal leadership, from your staff, from students and from within the wider learning community and parents.

Accreditations are also an opportunity to build your team, both within and between the diverse academic and administrative departments of the school. They can be a way of injecting energy and necessity into an area of school effectiveness that needs extra emphasis or urgency to take it to the next level. It can also represent an opportunity to re-prioritise educational values such as creativity, critical thinking and communication skills if such criteria are required to gain the qualification. Use an accreditation to focus minds on embedding improvements in the long-term culture of your school, so that they become more sustainable in the process. In some countries an annual renewal process for accreditations may be necessary, so do your due diligence.

Making The Right Decisions About Accreditations & Memberships

- Examine your context carefully and where your overall school priorities lie.
- Examine the school's budget and where the accreditation might fit in.
- Look at other schools in the local area.
- How will you analyse your school performance data and who/what will you benchmark it against?
- Who will be responsible for monitoring and evaluating the quality of planning, teaching, learning and assessment?
- How often will you review the quality and impact of the curriculum? Who will carry this out and how will you communicate the findings and act upon them?
- Oversee the performance management and appraisal of your staff. Do you have a system in place?
- How often will you review your school policies, and in which order of priority?
- Will you use pre-existing teacher, parent and student satisfaction/wellbeing surveys or design your own?
- Who will deliver accountability of your own senior leadership and the governance of the school?

Section Four: review questions

- How is your curriculum aligned with the Mission, Aims and Values of the school?
- If you're aspiring to an international leadership post how would you align your vision and values with the school's to create your best possible learning environment?
- What is the function of the curriculum in your current school? Is it driven by marketing? Or by teacher supply? Is it delivering sustainable short and long-term learning for ALL learners in your school and community?
- How effectively does Professional Development support curriculum delivery?
- How authentically do you ensure that effectively meeting the needs of learners is the ultimate justification for every part of your PD provision?
- How well do you measure the impact of Professional Development on standards of learning and teaching?
- Are you taking maximum advantage of the benefits that thorough Assessment for Learning practices bring?
- Can every learner reliably identify 'gaps' in knowledge, skills and understanding measures by good formative assessment practice?
- Do all teachers routinely give diagnostic feedback on academic progress in terms that students can understand and work towards?

PART FIVE
MARKETING, COMMUNICATIONS AND ADMISSIONS: BUILDING A COMMUNITY

**PART FIVE – MARKETING, COMMUNICATIONS AND
ADMISSIONS: BUILDING A COMMUNITY**   224

Branding   227
    Your Personal Brand   227
    Branding Your School – A Style Guide Checklist   229

Marketing Your School   233

Admissions   238

Build Your Community   242
    Working With Stakeholders   242

Chapter Review   245

This section takes a deep dive into how you market your school. We start with branding – how to achieve the right brand for your school and its geographical context, including identifying the particular parent groups you are targeting. We explore how to market your school to different cultures, parents and target markets. In addition, we then explore the admissions process, before ending with how to build a community and how to work with your stakeholders.

Key learning outcomes include:

- Acknowledging personal branding, and its growing importance for you, as the lead public face of your international school.
- Awareness of the most commonly used marketing strategies in international schools.
- Understanding the key steps in the admissions and onboarding process for new students.

Branding

Your Personal Brand

As principal, you are the face of the school. Many international school parents choose a school based on the leader, their educational background and reputation, in addition to that of the school. It is often a decision based on trust and integrity of the overall brand and how you represent it. Being a brand in your own right is therefore incredibly important. Know how to develop your personal brand and avoid the traps that can drain your time and energy when doing so. Anne Dickinson, former Head of Admissions and Marketing at Jerudong International School, Brunei (JIS) says of her role, 'My job was to market the principal and to market the school. Schools such as Rugby School in Thailand and Marlborough College in Malaysia have an enormous advantage in terms of the history of the school and reputation that can support their overall brand', she adds.

Barry Cooper, Principal, The Global College - Madrid, says, 'As principal, my personal brand allows me to share what I do and to attract students to the college, and at the same time tell them who we are and what we are all about'.

Professional Advice On Personal Branding
The quickest, most effective and easy way to develop your personal brand is on LinkedIn. As a principal, you are in a tremendously advantageous position, as teachers, leaders and those looking to join your school will all seek to add you as a connection. Although other media platforms are available, LinkedIn has by far the greatest professional reach and engagement across the international education sector. Get the most out of LinkedIn by writing a weekly or fortnightly newsletter that is visible to your followers. You can schedule this and use periods of quiet to upload 2 or 3 and then sequence them to go live at particular times of the week.

There are some common mistakes to avoid when developing a personal brand.

- Do not mix your political or religious views with your educational brand.
- Where possible, comment positively on others' posts and good practice – become known for your generosity towards others. Opt

- for writing a short comment – this has far greater value and meaning than 'liking'.
- Your personal brand and school brand need to be in alignment.

How To Brand Yourself as Principal/CEO

- Articulate the school mission and philosophy and repeatedly share them with the wider public.
- Understand the cultural expectations of a school leader in the country in which you are working and work with this framework.
- Work closely with your marketing department to clearly define the role for you as principal, your public image and important events that you should attend.
- Develop professional networks and identify a mentor who can support you to further your voice and reach.
- Identify a select number of events that you can attend in support of your brand and that of the school.
- Research and identify the culture and etiquette of the country in which you are working and dress professionally with this in mind.
- Focus on 'inclusive' practices that develop choice, balance and overall quality.
- Model the expectations you hold for all staff and clearly define them during orientation.

KEY TIP

If you are interested in being a guest on the Leading Your International School Podcast, or in writing a Principal's Blog, then do contact us – a great personal branding opportunity!

Branding Your School – A Style Guide Checklist

Identify Your Brand Mission.

- What are you trying to achieve?
- How is your school different from others in the same location? It is important for every member of the marketing and admissions (and wider school teams) to not only identify the school's mission but also to practise the mission of your brand and work towards living it out.
- What is your brand trying to say and how is it said? Effective brands are audience-focused and have powerful narratives behind them, yet adapt to the ever-diverse needs of the customer.

Understand Your Historical Context. If your school is fortunate in having an esteemed history, such as the Marlborough College (Malaysia), then work hard to exploit that brand to its maximum value. It is important for your marketing department, therefore, to know as much as they possibly can about the brand, its history, academic achievements, successful former alumni and the outstanding rates of university applications it has previously secured. This may involve a trip overseas to visit the partner campus, meet and discuss with staff how they have successfully branded the school and any adjustments or cultural nuances that you will need to make it work in your context. If you are a completely new school, then study the historical narrative and brand of other schools. Use their experiences and journey to help guide yours.

Study Your Audience. Take the time to learn as much as you can about your target audience. Profile them (positively); begin to think and act like them. As you build powerful professional relationships with parents, some may want to contribute to this. What languages do they speak? Where do they shop, eat, or travel on holiday? What social media platforms do they tend to use and when? What activities do they take part in when they are not working? Knowing this information will help your brand to stand out and align with others whose vision and values may match your own. How your marketing department communicates your brand is highly important.

Your Brand Vision. The vision you hold for your (school) brand is your 'mission in action'. How will your marketing department and staff live, breathe, and articulate the school's brand in everything that they do?

Consider setting out a brand-style guidebook with actions that support the school's overall mission when it comes to marketing. Make sure the marketing department itself is branded, and it is not a sterile room with whitewashed walls!

Form Concrete Values. Every brand needs to know what it stands for and your educational pitch is no different. Ask yourself what your school values are. Do you value quality education and the rigour that supports it? Or perhaps you value the classroom and learner as an ever-changing dynamic that places far greater emphasis on the learner. One such school forging a route along this path is the Garden International School (GIS) Malaysia, where student agency plays a leading role in the thought processes and design of educational experiences that are driven to a great degree by the students themselves. Form concrete values that can be clearly articulated and understood in the range of languages used by your target groups.

Physical / Digital Branding. With concrete values, you will be able to begin the design and generate the design brief of what you want your physical and digital brands to be. When generating a design brief, go back to your audience and sample products and services that are targeted at your audience. Study your international competitors fastidiously to identify all that you like and equally and, perhaps more importantly, don't like. Colour, tone, choice and size of text will all be important and where they will appear on your school's documents and resources. As Gráinne says 'Remember that colours may hold national significance, so research, research, research!

Adopt Your Brand Logo. Who and what are behind some of the most successful brand logos? What made them visually appealing and how did the appeal of the brand lead them to stick in the minds of generations to come? Again, go back to your mission and ask yourself, 'Does the logo we have represent who we are and what we are aspiring to do and become?' With the growing importance of a sustainable and inclusive school culture, many are attempting to make their brand and logo more people-oriented.

If Your Brand Could Speak – What Would It Say? I want you to pause for a moment and ask yourself: How does your brand talk to you? How does it sound? Does it communicate with ease, grace and a professional manner that draws people in and purveys knowledge, confidence and inclusivity to its audience? What does your brand say in the languages and cultures of your target market? Be careful that your brand does not end up over-generalising or repeating overused academic buzzwords that go out of fashion as quickly as they come in. Some marketing is becoming irreverent and intentionally funny in an appeal to connect with the audience and send the message that 'we don't take ourselves too seriously, in the important age of wellbeing'. However - be careful how playful your messages become. What balance of information, light-heartedness and inclusivity do you want to promote? Make sure that when people write about your school, they get the brand and tone 'spot on'. There is nothing worse than reading reviews about yourself and coming away thinking 'That's not us'. As Chris says, 'I would advise that you should study not only competitors in the national market but also learn something of the history and cultural values attached to education locally'. He adds 'This is critically important in the case of new markets because you may find a lack of awareness or even an hostility towards international education.

Video And Audio. International schools are beginning to realise the power and potential of online video content. Some are exploiting this extremely well; others are playing catch-up. A lot of video content is 'curated' and artificially designed. I am sure we have all seen the videos online of incredible tricks that draw the audience in. The greatest content is often raw, natural and regularly unplanned. Video montages of a school under construction, with well-matched music and audio, are a valuable marketing tool. Interviews with parents about why they chose your school are also useful. Make sure that the voices(s) behind your school fit in with the product you are trying to sell. Clear, articulate pronunciation doesn't have to come from native speakers, but people must understand what is being communicated. To go forward, sometimes it pays to look back. For two outstanding video advertisements search online for the 'Face' advertisement from British Airways in 1989 (designed by Saatchi and Saatchi) and the Guinness dominoes advert of 2007 (by ad agency AMV BBDO). The latter reputedly costing Guinness in the region of $20 million dollars. Both are masterpieces.

CASE STUDY – CHARTERHOUSE SCHOOL, LAGOS, NIGERIA

As the first British Independent School to come to Nigeria, the Charterhouse School is working hard to establish its narrative in people's minds. Indeed, its Founding Principal, John Todd notes, 'Most people are perfectly trustworthy and perfectly normal, but when you say, oh, we're bringing a British brand, a lot of people have come into the office to say, "we wanted to be sure", "we're not convinced" … or "why would someone spend this much money in Nigeria?" And you know we're delighted that you are". But there's another level of disbelief. If your school is breaking similar ground, like Charterhouse, you may need to invest a tremendous amount of time simply telling people you are the genuine article and not an imitation.

Marketing Your School

The notion of a 'marketing campaign' is misleading. It suggests a short-term event with a defined start and end. If you want to retain parents, think instead of an ongoing marketing presence in your chosen media that builds 'brand loyalty'. When you think you've found the most productive media platform for your school, bear in mind that, for parents/customers, the platform is full of 'siren voices', offering them alternatives. If your school is not 'present', these alternatives can become more attractive. Update the content of your channels with high-quality new stories which will keep parents satisfied that they have made the right choice and act as a disincentive to look elsewhere.

Challenge

As a start-up school, you will rely heavily on external marketing before opening your school. It is, however, internal marketing that holds the long-term key.

Solution

Ensure that your marketing strategy moves from external to internal marketing in a timely and coherent manner.

What Research Tells Us

Charlie Peng, Principal at Whartonn School, Chengdu, suggests that the best form of marketing for an international school is Internal Marketing, which includes, 'The whole team – the teaching team and non-teaching team – providing services to students. Most importantly the holistic services to students'. As a result, says Charlie, 'When I interview, I'm looking for a real educator, not just a teacher. Of course, in the end people will look at results. But this will build up the reputation of this school. As a start-up, we had to depend on the external marketing'. External Marketing, on the other hand, concerns your brand awareness, notes Charlie, 'The more people know your brand; the more people have the chance to find you'.

Options Available

The 'demo' lesson has become the staple go-to marketing strategy for international schools and one I've taken part in dozens of times in my international school career. They are an excellent driver of footfall to your campus. Unfortunately, most demo classes can only take place from the second year, when there are sufficient teachers with the requisite skills to carry them out. Consider carefully your first senior leadership appointments. If they can deliver quality demo classes before opening it can help you get a head start. Gráinne notes 'Allowing parents and visitors to the school to see the resources you will be using with the students at various stages is also very effective. Reading books, published schemes, small equipment and larger resources and clear information about their use, their efficacy and their intent is a concrete way of sharing practice with parents when one does not yet have the children in the school.

School Website

Your school website should be the hub of traffic that acts as a growing historical narrative about your school, its brand and the journey you have taken. Increasingly, the power of video means that, upon landing on your website, people should immediately see high-quality shots and action images of the school and students, once your school is open. Good websites increase engagement and deliver an experience that can ultimately lead to a potential sale, or create an environment in which the customer is pleased to visit repeatedly. We have studied hundreds of international school websites over the years. In absolutely no particular order and with no affinity to the schools and people who run them, here are some school websites that we recommend you look at to help guide your thoughts and design process.

- British School – Muscat (BSM)
- The International School of Paris (ISP)
- Beech Hall School Riyadh
- Tanglin Trust School Singapore[1]

Use this checklist to guide the design and function of your future school website:

- Your school brand is easily reflected.
- Writing is effective, clearly presented, and easy to read.
- It is easy to navigate and access the information that you want to present.
- It can feature important emergency notices on the homepage that can increase the effectiveness of your communication strategy.

---

[1] https://britishschoolmuscat.com; https://www.isparis.edu; https://www.beechhallschoolriyadh.com/; https://www.tts.edu.sg.

- The server is tried and tested in your location, and will not suffer from intermittent connection issues or poor download speeds.
- The customer should ideally be no more than 3 clicks away from the information they require.

Remember to pilot and test your website with a select few of your leadership team, governor(s) and a parent or two – if you are fortunate enough to have set up your PTA before the school's official opening. Allow plenty of time for website designs and edits, especially if your designers are working in different time zones.

Barriers To An Effective Marketing Strategy

- Marketing staff that have great local expertise and experience, but have never worked in, or represented an international brand.
- A lack of guidance, development and training with your school's marketing team, leading to a lack of clearly defined strategy.
- Issues of translation that differ between the intended message and the one that is delivered.
- Poor website landing pages or social media platforms that fail to engage the end user and generate further enquiries.
- Keywords are too vague or too popular, or your target market is not aware of them.
- An over-reliance upon online marketing.
- Your website is not actively curated so that material becomes out of date.
- Your website is not culturally sensitive to the legal and cultural norms of the host country.

Professional Advice On Marketing

A retired international school principal recently told me, 'As a Founding Principal, the biggest job you have is marketing'. Great marketing is essentially about the belief in who you are and what you do. I have witnessed both outstanding marketing in a new school start-up and mediocre marketing in another, which lacked professional autonomy and waited for guidance from the school's principal in every aspect of its role.

There is a misguided belief (particularly amongst a new breed of marketing professionals) that nearly all marketing is online. It isn't. Much of the marketing for a new school can be done by joining professional associations; developing links with potential accreditation partners; lectures, webinars and community presentations on your school and its guiding philosophy; and any links you may have to universities. Pay close attention to how you represent what is included in your school curriculum. As a former member of staff at Malvern College School in Chengdu told me. 'You're not going to go surfing in Chengdu!' Be careful of how you choose to develop your brand and the strategy behind its enhancement. Parents are much savvier nowadays and will quickly realise what does and doesn't take place at your school.

Marketing teams consisting of local staff present unique challenges to the overall understanding and awareness of your school's mission and vision and how they will be achieved through your core values. Spend considerable time onboarding and orientating marketing staff with your school's history, and the way they interact with parents. Make sure they understand the general underlying message that you want them to get across. Even the simple act of translation needs to be carefully considered, as staff may feel reluctant to translate your speech verbatim, meaning crucial marketing details may get left out of your pitch.

Good marketing takes an inordinate amount of time. The simplest act of just talking to people about your new school can help to spread the message of who you are and what you are trying to achieve. As a former Founding Principal at the Wycombe Abbey schools group states, 'Know what your market wants and respond to it rapidly'. Gathering the longer-term intentions of your parents and their needs should be done as early as practically possible.

The Power Of Your Story
Identifying appropriate marketing drivers is important – particularly for a private school. Highly successful marketing campaigns include:

- Search Engine Optimisation (SEO) tools to build your online presence.
- Billboard (train/bus stop) marketing, radio marketing, expat magazines, upmarket paediatricians and children's services, all chambers of commerce, and all consulates/embassies.
- Presentations and speeches to any local groups – not just to promote school specifically, but to speak on topics important to the community, such as 'How to choose the right school for your child', 'What do educational acronyms mean?', 'What does IB mean?', 'What is enquiry based learning?', 'How do university admissions work?', etc.
- Blogging tools. Allowing others to see your journey as you navigate your path towards the school's opening.
- Coaching your marketing department and future teachers on the importance of internal marketing.

- Develop a consistent small number of hashtags that are used regularly and help to leave a digital footprint of what you do and when.
- Personalise your product. Consider paying staff to actively engage in social media branding, and use your students to share success and achievement.
- Try to speak to at least 100 people about your new school. Include current and retired principals and the local Chamber of Commerce. Each time you speak to someone get a recommendation of who to approach next.

Admissions

Challenge
How you align your admissions and enrolment strategies with your school's mission will have an enormous influence on the type of school you become. Tensions may arise as you begin to learn how much, or how little, control you have in a private school context over admissions supply and demand drivers. The context of your school will likely have a significant influence on admissions, particularly if the school is in a highly competitive market.

Solution
Use a values- and principles-led approach to admissions as far as you can. The objective is the closest possible match between what your school can offer and the needs of individual students. Minimise undesirable student turnover and maximise student compatibility with your learning culture and overall school ethos.

Hurdles That You May Face In Your Admissions Process

- Significant disagreement between you as School Leader and others involved in the Admissions Process.
- A misalignment between the admissions department and the financial pressures/budgeting process or school governance board growth strategies.
- Pressure to admit a student who you consider to be inappropriate to the school. You will have to manage the ethics of such a situation.

'There is a danger in focusing on two-dimension financial projections that don't take into effect the incremental and contextual human data that admissions departments receive daily. True alignment between admissions and finance is at once a necessary inquiry-based and iterative process', notes Courtney Knight, Advancement and Engagement Director of the International School of Paris.

Professional Advice On Admissions
Here, Chris shares his thoughts. 'In a privatised, market-led and commercial education sector, recruiting and retaining students can be an existential struggle for the school, let alone filling classrooms with students

who match what your school can offer. Messages given out by owners are likely to be highly significant. These may reflect an elitism with which you feel uncomfortable, but that your employers have interpreted as the only way to reach financially viable thresholds. Over time – and with persistence and good communication – you may be able to move to a more inclusive admissions strategy if this is your vision. I was very lucky to work with a school owner who shared my vision that during admissions we should be looking for student potential, rather than simple attainment'.

'One process that has been very effective in getting the right mix of students in my school is personal involvement in the interview process by both myself and the school owner. In this, his focus is on the family, their values, their parenting and their aspirations. This leaves me to focus on the learning skills, the attitudes to learning and the wider personality of the student. We then compare notes before making a decision. If yours is a start-up, you may well find that you are talking to parents who are first-time customers of private international education. It is vital from the start that they can make informed decisions about what is best for their child based on the reality of study in your school, not based on personal interpretations of what they may desire or perceive. I have been very fortunate in that the school owner is quite prepared to say 'no' to families where we identify a mismatch'.

As part of the Admissions process, testing has a role, but I do not make it a determining factor. We try to make use of the tests in English and Maths to make formative assessments and match the student with the best starting level in the school. You will probably find that students come to you from a wide range of previous educational experiences and curricula, so a test score will reflect this rather than their true potential. An interview where you can measure the student's logic and thinking skills is much more effective, not to mention getting a clear idea of how they manage a discussion in English if they are a bilingual or multilingual learner. As Courtney Knight says, 'The information that you are provided with may or may not be 100% reliable or even applicable, depending on the individual situations students may be transitioning from, such as curriculum, location, prior inclusive or selective school environment, or impact of online learning/COVID, to name a few. Only your school can determine the validity of the different admissions components, including the recommendations, tests, or interviews based on your local context'.

The probationary period is an essential filter. Some private international schools are residential whereas domestic education is typically day school. The student and the parents must have first-hand experience of living on campus, away from home, before signing on the dotted line. Furthermore, you can correlate the admission test scores with real data about learning and achievement from inside the classroom. Give every potential trialist a 'buddy' from the class so that you can gauge how well she or he makes relationships with other students since this is likely to be a critical factor in later retention'.

Key questions in the admission process you'll need clarity on are:

What are the overall aims of the owner(s)?

- What are the expectations of the 1st year intake? How does this compare with any 3, 5 or even 10-year financial models?
- Evaluating the sensitivity of your growth inputs, both demand and supply-driven. For example, could academic scholarships bring in some high-performing students, increase diversity, and round out higher level classes in the first instance?
- Will the academic standard change over time, if so, how?
- Will you become more selective as demand for places increases?
- If you are taking in students with varying educational needs, do you have the structure and professional capacity to support them?

'As a new school, people are appraising your trust'. Vice-Principal, China

Your Admissions Journey

- **Enquiry.** The speed and individualized nature of the response is vital. 'I have parents who have said the reason they selected our school over others, was that they were impressed with the speed of response', notes Anne Dickinson.
- **Standard Responses.** Your admissions team will need to be aware of the school's position on every potential enquiry. This will also need to be individualised. Slightly delayed responses to enquiries can be an effective tool which means your parents may assume the response was individually generated rather than automatic.
- **Timescale.** When are you going to follow up the enquiry? The faster pace of international schools means that this should never (where possible) be more than three days. The time you take to follow up on your leads will be crucial in your ability to sell school places.
- **Personal Connection.** Depending on the volume of applications that you receive, you will need to decide who you can meet. Will you (as principal) make a commitment to meeting every individual parental applicant, or if you are unavailable, who else will it be?

Your team's alignment with the school's mission and philosophy is paramount.

Effective Management Of Your Admissions Process

- Clarity of information about the school, both online and in-school documentation. Any ambiguities will lead to inappropriate enquiries.
- The communication skills of the Admissions Team are essential. They are your filter, allowing you to reliably attract potentially suitable students while effectively deterring inappropriate enquiries.
- A written application procedure is superior to an oral word-of-mouth process because you can collect better background information.
- The admissions interview is critical and should be carried out by you or a senior leader who can effectively but politely deter inappropriate applications.
- Use Admissions Tests as formative assessments to yield useful information – not just about levels but learning skills and cognitive and linguistic ability.
- Where possible, the Admissions procedure should include a probationary period during which both the school and the prospective student and her/his family can make a 'no fault' decision to decline the place.
- Where the student or family withdraws the application, ensure an 'exit interview' is conducted to identify the reasons for withdrawal. This might reveal an important weakness in provision. Equally, it might prevent a dissatisfied customer from attacking the school's reputation publicly.

Remember

No matter how well your admissions may have been planned, your staff will need to be flexible and, at times, wear many hats. The type of school you are creating will determine much of the overall process itself. For a start-up Principal, the initial interviews should be done personally – not only is it something that appeals to parents, but it is the best way to train staff.

Build Your Community

First and foremost, you've got to be very clear about what you are. You need a very clear vision and as Nick Magnus, Founding Head of Dulwich College (Singapore), points out, it's important to say and be what you are, 'This is what [Dulwich] looks like in Singapore, in Suzhou ... this is what type of school we will be'. He continues,

> The biggest mistake that new schools make is that they try and be all things to all people. If you try and be all things to all people, you end up being pretty average at everything. Do not deviate from who you are. This is a massive leap of faith that parents are taking, to entrust you with their children. In China we did untold presentations to parents; in Singapore, we used focus groups. I had some parents who came back 3 or even 4 times; some agreed with where we were going and some disagreed. Some even disagreed yet joined further down the line. We had the friends of Dulwich and set up the Parent Teacher Association (PTA) before the school opened, so months before the school opened, we were organising social events and getting parents together. We made every effort to keep the momentum going. It was never a fact of people signing up and then seeing them eighteen months later. We created a sense of identity and belonging long before the school opened. The parents became advocates for us.

WORKING WITH STAKEHOLDERS

One of the things about working with stakeholders, notes Barry Cooper – Principal, The Global College Madrid, is 'Being able to see the school through the eyes of the stakeholders ... trying to make sure the elements of the stakeholders' ambitions are reflected in the day-to-day operations of the school, while at the same time ensuring the stakeholders understand the limitations of your context. He adds, 'The principal is the person who connects staff with parents and students and stakeholders, with the result being fantastic outcomes for the students. It is about constant communication and reflection. You will need to distribute relationships with other stakeholders to others, the more you involve the community the greater the end result'.

As an international school, you will have to manage the diverse needs of your stakeholders and their desires to sometimes become over-involved in the day-to-day operational management of the school. It is likely that a substantial number of people, the goods and services that they offer, will be clamouring for your time and custom. Stakeholders, when acknowledged as a force for good, increase accountability, ask effective questions, and also help promote and market your school at no cost.

Who Are Your Stakeholders?

- Owners/Company
- Head/Leadership Team
- Human Resource Team
- Builders/contractors
- Marketing & Admissions
- Parents/Customers
- Pupils/product
- Staff
- Landlords (if the building is leased); the Construction company
- Licensing Bodies/Legal permissions to operate
- Governing Body/Board (if any)
- Partners
- Professional services (education)
- Curriculum organisations
- Recruitment consultants
- Professional services
- Transport providers
- Sustainability advisors
- Grounds staff
- Contracts for food, guards, cleaners etc
- Immigration companies
- CCA providers
- CPD providers
- Accreditation authorities
- Memberships and Subscriptions Services
- Medical services
- Contractors/service providers
- Charities and service agencies
- Partner Schools
- Social Workers and Psychological Services
- Faith / religious organisations
- Voluntary organisations
- Resource suppliers

Parent Stakeholders

Are your parents aware of their responsibilities as stakeholders? Ensure they understand the need to:

- Respect all staff.
- Guide their child to treat others fairly and with respect.
- Guide their child in adhering to the school's Code of Conduct and other guidelines.
- Communicate views and concerns through appropriate channels.
- Be available for Parent-Teacher conferences and other consultations.[2]

The Stakeholder PLC

The idea of professionally managing and socialising your stakeholders in a founding school may not immediately seem a priority, but introducing them to each other in a clear, coordinated and progressive manner will enable your school start-up to be the essence of a team. Consider running regular stakeholder professional learning sessions where stakeholders share their experience and professional capital for the benefit of the school. Consider grouping them carefully across traditional hierarchical lines to foster inclusivity and diversity of thought. Provide first-hand real-life connections from your stakeholders that present learning opportunities to your students.

Effectively managing your stakeholders is important. Having someone whose direct role is to manage the most important stakeholders and keep them informed and up-to-date is a good strategy. To do that consider:

- Stakeholder mapping – who, what, where and when you communicate with them.
- Priorities. Stakeholders involved in the planning, design and construction of the school are likely to be of far higher initial value than organisations involved in the review and evaluation of the school's curriculum.
- Tools for collaboration – What communication and information-sharing tools will you use with each?
- How Does Culture Affect Your Stakeholders? The communication method you adopt with Singaporean and Chinese parents may be significantly different from the one you use in Indonesia. In the USA, you are likely to have a far greater number of stakeholders than in Norway, given the growing deregulation of public education, and the wealth of school services, including counselling and therapy to address alcohol and substance abuse rates.

---

[2] *Courtesy of the Singapore Ministry of Education* (MOE)

Chapter Review

To support your professional learning, we advise that you now take the time to reflect on the following questions:

- How are you developing your personal professional branding? How will you become the lead public face of your international school?
- What do you consider to be the most effective marketing strategies in international schools? How are you applying those strategies in your international context?
- What do you consider to be the key routines in the admissions and onboarding process for new students? How do you apply these in your international context?
- What are your top three takeaways from this chapter? Draw up a brief professional action plan detailing how you will implement these ideas in your start-up.

Summary

With this book we have endeavoured to provide the skeleton of your school plan, including all aspects that must be considered, explored and decided upon running up to the successful opening of an international school. In addition, we have aimed to support the wide range of school licenses, types and formations that are routinely found in the world of international schools.

Founding a school, particularly in the international world is a considerable risk. As many have found, that risk is not just financial, but involves people's careers, their trust, their aspirations, the lives of children and their families, and ultimately a school's reputation. We want those of you who are considering opening international schools to understand the magnitude of what you are entering into and ensure that you have a clear plan – both strategic and operational.

There are, of course, aspects of the process that will be chronological, but much of the process will be happening around you at the same time! This can feel overwhelming, messy and never-ending. At times like this, it is vital that you keep the endpoint in mind. There will be many, many months (if one has a long lead-in) where the joy of working with students, staff and parents will not be able to be sustained as you do not yet have children, their parents or even many colleagues with whom to discuss and ponder things. These sorts of times are particularly difficult for charismatic passionate Principals who in the main, are people people! Being a people person is so very challenging when you do not have those fabulous, vibrant, amusing, perplexing, joyous daily interactions with the people you serve and about whom you feel so strongly. Alternatively, some Founding Principals may find themselves with almost no lead in time, for whatever reason, and will be constantly fighting against the clock and against deadlines that must be achieved. Principals in that position feel they have no time to talk to or discuss anything with anyone. It all rests on their shoulders – a frightening and worrying position to find oneself in.

Remembering and envisioning the purpose of your position – that is, getting the school up and running and open on that first day – can carry you through the most challenging and dumbfounding of experiences. Keep it at the forefront of your mind. With a guide like this to help and instruct you, you WILL get to that finish line! You will greet those staff as they get off those flights and settle into their new homes. You will see enthusiasm, expertise and potential in them as they come on board to help prepare the school for opening. That first day of welcoming children and their parents will happen and those parents will cherish the trust you have built with them, knowing their daughters and sons will be known, recognised, supported, nurtured and developed academically, socially and emotionally in the best possible way in your school.

Just recently I was reading a piece about international school start-ups and a single word was used consistently in that piece: Legacy. This is your legacy. This school will live on, serving children and families long after you have moved on. This school could be the best professional experience your team members have ever had, using what they have learned, seen and experienced to enrich, inform or create other superb schools around the world. The children you and your team serve will go on to change the world. What greater legacy could there be?

Use this book to guide you both strategically and practically. Use it also as a working document – keep notes on the chronology of your particular project and how each development or problem might be approached if you were given the chance to undertake something similar, again. Each school and each project is unique – we want this book to support you and your needs.

Last but not least, we want to send you our sincere good wishes for great and sustainable success. Getting an international school up and running is a tremendous achievement. Please let us know how you get on, and going forward, how we might be able to help you to settle the school, grow the school and thrive. GOOD LUCK!

Gráinne O'Reilly. 2023

To connect with André, Chris or Gráinne about your plans for starting a school, email:

andre@leadingyourinternationalschool.com

chris@leadingyourinternationalschool.com

grainne@leadingyourinternationalschool.com

Glossary

ABSA – Australian Boarding Schools Association

BSO – British Schools Overseas

BSME – British Schools in the Middle East

BYOD – Bring Your Own Device

CEO – Chief Executive Officer

CFO – Chief Financial Officer

CIS – Council of International Schools

CISTA - Council of International Schools of the Americas

COBIS – Council of British International Schools

COO – Chief operating Officer

CP – Child Protection

DaO Directors and Officers (insurance)

DEIJ – Diversity, Equity, Inclusion, Justice

ECEO – Educational Chief Executive Officer

EiM – Education in Motion

ESG - Environmental, social, and corporate governance

EU – European Union

EYFS – Early Years Foundation Stage

FOBISSIA – Federation of British International Schools in Asia

GSE – Global Services in Education

HEAD – Holistic Evidence and Design

HR – Human Resources

KSAOs – Knowledge, Skills, Abilities & Other Characteristics

IB – International Baccalaureate

IMS – Information Management System

IPC – International Primary Curriculum

ISC – International Schools Consultancy

KDHA – Knowledge of Human Development Authority

KPIs – Key Performance Indicators

MIS – Management Information System

NPQH – National Professional Qualification for Headship

NDA – Non-Disclosure Agreement

PD – Professional Development

PM – Project Management

PTA – Parent Teachers Association

SEO – Search Engine Optimization

SDGs – Sustainable Development Goals

SLT – Senior Leadership Team

SOPs – Standard Operating Procedures

UAE – United Arab Emirates

UN – United Nations

UNESCO – United Nations Educational, Scientific & Cultural Organization

www.ingramcontent.com/pod-product-compliance
Lightning Source LLC
Chambersburg PA
CBHW071227170426
43191CB00032B/1070